A JOURNAL
OF JOURNEYS

BY Dick Dunn

Edited by Mark Wilson
Cover design by Edward Wong, Vertex Design
Book design by Edward Wong, Vertex Design
Proof-reading by Kaleena Sessions and Chris Yost
Printed by CreateSpace
First Printing: November 2014
ISBN-978-0-9938983-0-3

Contents

Acknowledgments

I am most thankful to Norm Klenman for the encouragement he has given me over the years to consolidate and publish my diverse reports;

to Mark Wilson, my editor, for the sterling effort in correcting my most egregious errors of fact and grammar;

to Edward Wong of Vertex Design for formatting my maps and photos and designing the cover;

to Kaleena Sessions for her proof reading, and keen eye in picking up typos;

likewise to Chris Yost for identifying new typos and errors of fact;

and to my many companions on the adventures and treks, including Jet Johnson, Larry Dekker, Bob Hyndman, Ed Wight, Gary Anderson, Steve Mackey, Roger Sylvestre, and, last but not least, to my wife Danielle Dunn, also known as Dany.

Sincerely,
Dick Dunn

Foreword by Norman Klenman

Somewhere deep in our souls lies the almost inexplicable desire invoked by human curiosity – that mysterious demanding force which drives the adventurous among us to outface the pain of primitive travel, the danger of weather and unknown inconvenience, even of connivance and treachery, simply to witness and apprehend the odd, the strange, the compelling world of known and unknown places.

Anyone who knows Dick Dunn must surely have needed no more than a glance at his own career of adventure and travel, his air force and civilian flying services, to know he would be the exact choice to face the new career of travel author. And do it at the cost of his own time and treasure.

Because those many readers who know the work of great traveller journals in our time sense the community of spirit they all share. Lewis and Clark revealed their spirit in 1804 on their epic journey from St. Louis to the Pacific. Saint-Exupéry sought his routes in the skies, and gave us the incomparable Wind, Sand and Stars in 1939.

I particularly enjoyed the magic of Nansen's Farthest North, and Heyerdahl's Kon-Tiki.

All of these great adventures (the library lists of over a hundred of the world's best travel and exploration volumes) have this in common: man's insatiable curiosity.

And that is Dick Dunn's motive force, and the great openings in our souls he gratifies. His fresh and personal summations of trips to Hadrian's wall, for example, to Burma, Jordan and Patagonia, even when we have some brief knowledge of them, turn his uncluttered new gaze into easy, cursive prose that relights our own interest and salves the ever-present curiosity.

There are as well the unexpected, which is a central quality of Dick's book: how he reveals the story of the F-86 crash on Grouse Mountain, a calamity I recall from living in Vancouver in those days.

I revelled in his personal notes of his trip to Timbuktu with his guide Tim. And who could not delight in his sharp view and recall of the Chilkoot Trail?

In summary a reader must surely commend "A Journal of Journeys" for its verve, sensitivity, informality and sheer enjoyment of curiosity and wonderment, elements often lost in our time. But brought back with charm and clarity by a new and welcome author in the great literary tradition of travel authorship.

Many will wish to have had the good fortune to do some of these, perhaps all of these trips with Dick Dunn. In delivering to us the Journal of Journeys, he has gifted us with that pleasure in the next best way.

Norman Klenman
Surrey, BC
October, 2014

Introduction

Fulfilling my boyhood ambition, I graduated as a jet fighter pilot with the Royal Canadian Air Force at age 20, serving in Germany and France at the height of the Cold War. I then continued my flying career as a pilot for Air Canada, with temporary assignments to Air Jamaica, Royal Air Maroc, and Polynesian Airlines.

Within is a selection of my travel reports spanning a good part of the globe over the last decade and a half, mostly after my retirement from aviation.

To protect the privacy of the individuals concerned, I have generally omitted people's full names. The exceptions have given their permission, have a historical footprint, or are deceased.

Spelling has been a challenge as Canadian spelling is a blend of British and U.S. forms. I have generally followed the spelling style used in Canadian newspapers as codified by The Canadian Press (e.g. British form for "colour, centre" versus U.S. "color, center," U.S. "program, skeptic" versus British "programme, sceptic"). The exception is proper names such as Pearl Harbor.

Another complication is that the Canadian Government handbook differs from the Canadian Press: archaeology versus archeology. I chose archaeology.

Similarly, place names often have alternative spelling, as in Ghadames – Gadames, Libya; Aksum – Axum, Ethiopia; or Ulan Bator – Ulaanbaatar, Mongolia. I generally chose the one that pops up on Google Maps. Likewise Inca versus Inka. I like Inka.

Maps are original creations using Google Terrain on an iMac.

Each report was written shortly after the visit. The reader is cautioned that circumstances of politics, economics, weather, etc., are all subject to change. A prime example is our visit to Libya, which we found friendly and safe. At this writing, in October 2014, that is no longer the case.

The chapters are in chronological order of my visit, except for the final chapter, which is a work in progress due to recent additions to the "Logbook."

A Glossary defines some acronyms and obscure words.

Below is a link to my website where colour photographs are available for viewing.

Enjoy the journey.

Dick Dunn
Vancouver, BC
October 2014

www.dickdunn.ca

Chapter 1
Inka Trail

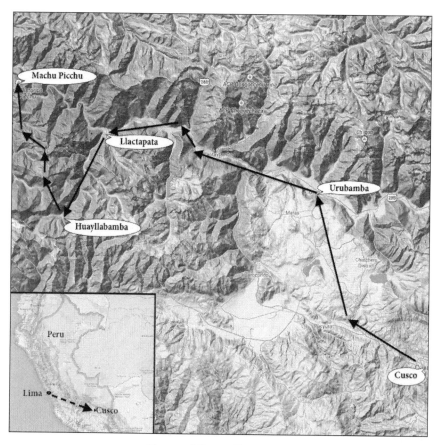

Peru – November 1996

Lima

An uneventful flight brought "Jet" Johnson and myself to Lima, Peru, to meet Larry Dekker and his son Eric at the airport. We enjoyed two days at Larry and Charmaine's luxurious apartment overlooking the city's premier golf course. An executive with a major oil company, Larry had excellent connections and a thorough knowledge of the country. Despite the recent truce with the Shining Path, the Communist guerrilla faction, a tour of Lima revealed that not all is well in this impoverished country. Gun-toting squads in pickup trucks hurtled about the city.

We then met the balance of our hiking party: Annelies, Frans, his daughter Frances, and friend Liesje, all from Holland; and from Canada, Eric's girlfriend Paula. Larry's wife Charmaine had declined to join us on the hike, as she is averse to steep cliffs.

Cusco

An oversold flight resulted in some stress at the airport, but Larry succeeded in getting our party of ten aboard the short flight to Cusco. Lodged at a hotel that was formerly part of a monastery, we spent two days acclimatizing to the 3,800-metre altitude as we toured the city and the "Sacred Valley." Of particular interest were the massive trapezoidal walls of gargantuan, irregularly shaped stones tightly bound without mortar.

On day three, after a quick coffee, we departed the Hotel Monasterio by private bus as the cock crowed. The normal procedure for hikers on the Inka Trail is to board the early morning train to Kilometre 88, but in our case, because of the "Day of the Living" holiday, we planned to pick up our porters by bus, thence to Kilometre 76 to start the trek. We stopped at Urubamba for a nondescript greasy breakfast and a two-hour delay while our guide Fredy attempted to round up the recalcitrant porters. Of the ten porters and cook, nine were still drunk or, at best, severely hung-over from the holiday festivities. The tenth was a lad of 14, pressed into surrogate duty by his uncle.

Hiking the Inka Trail

After bouncing along the rough road to Kilometre 76, we disembarked, distributed our loads, and crossed the bridge over the Urubamba River. Briefed by the guide to expect a "level" hike, we started at 2,800 metres amid exclamations of "This is level!" The trail was good but in places quite narrow, half a metre wide, with a sheer drop of 150 metres to the river below. No place for Charmaine. Along the path we chanced upon a hut serving cold beer for a modest price of two sols, or about one dollar. Obviously, the law of supply and demand had not reached the lady proprietor.

We reached a cliff overlooking the junction of the Cusichaca (Happy) River with a grand view of the terraced ruins of Llactapata, including the circular temple on the opposite bank. Hiram Bingham discovered this site in 1913. Just upstream is a very narrow gorge with what appears to be fortifications. On closer scrutiny, the left side of the valley, undercut by the river, had apparently experienced a massive land slump, and dropped a volcanic dike from 200 metres above. We descended to the valley at 2,600 metres, spreading out as we began climbing again, moving southwestward with the river on our right, through a wet forest enlivened by pesky mosquitoes. Knowing that Jet, following closely behind lacked bug repellent, I left a container on the trail for him. Emerging from the forest, I crossed the raging Cusichaca over a small wooden bridge.

As I climbed on, darkness approached, with lightning, thunder and soon heavy rain. Shortly I came to the village of Huayllabamba (Grassy Plain) at 3,000 metres after about 14 km travelled this first day. Because of our late departure, we found the better camping sites already occupied, and found not a grassy plain but a mud-plastered enclosure behind the village store. The advance porters had just assembled our two-man mountain tents, so I dove into the nearest and stripped off to dry and change clothes. About an hour later, the rain stopped just as the laggard porters stumbled in with our packs, Jet arriving shortly afterward to share the tent.

The store sold beer for 3.5 sols and 1.5-litre bottles of water for 5 sols. My feet were in good shape as on my last flight to Hong Kong

I had bought eight pairs of 100% silk stockings and distributed these to the men. No socks for the ladies as they were too large, the socks that is.

We all joined in at the mess tent for a fine dinner of noodle soup, chicken, and rice, accompanied by four of the sixteen bottles of white wine which Larry had burdened the porters. Looking across to the campground of a German group where a vigorous campfire blazed, Larry insisted that as a "first-class" group, we should have a fire as well. Ultimately, our guide Fredy found three sticks of wood and ignited a small fire to brighten our dinner. Thence to bed for a fitful sleep.

We were awakened by Fredy at 5 a.m.. After a good breakfast of coffee, fried egg, porridge, bread, and jam, Fredy briefed us and urged everyone to pack and get on the trail. Stretching and loosening up, I was the last to depart, climbing through the village and turning northwest along the left bank of the Llullucha River. A stooped farmer tilled his cornfield with a hand hoe, not unlike that of his ancestors of 1,000 years earlier. I passed Annelies and Frances, then Jet, and climbed on through a series of steep switchbacks alongside a jungle stream. Breaking out into a small glade, I met the lead hikers resting, including Larry, who without shame had hired (for 10 sols) a young girl to carry his daypack!

Trekking through an alpine meadow on the relentless climb to Dead Woman's Pass, we spread out like a squadron of B-17s returning from Germany. Just before the pass, "Pizarro" Eric came bounding down and offered to take my pack. I declined the offer and continued the remaining 50 metres to the pass at 4,200 metres, where Eric, Paula, and Larry were celebrating the apogee with handshakes all around.

Since I was the eldest, I declared myself "Inka Dick" and offered West Coast salmon jerky to all. Although clouds obscured the far side of the pass, the sky soon cleared to reveal a majestic vista of the trail to the valley below, and beyond it the ascent to the ruins of Runquraqay and the second pass. As the guidebook noted: "views that no pen or camera can ever adequately record."

We did not tarry, for a chilling wind arose. Larry and company departed as I stopped to change my socks. A short way down the trail, I stopped to enjoy the spectacular view and the serenity of the vacant trail. My thoughts turned to my late friend Ross Mayberry, as is the custom whenever I am in the highlands, or hear the plaintive sounds of Andean music. It was in La Paz, Bolivia, at a similar elevation, that I learned of his untimely death five years previous.

Thence down the trail again, with frequent change of weather and temperature. Still afflicted by a chest cold, I was glad to have heeded Fredy's suggestion to buy a scarf in Cusco. It helped cut the cold wind on my chest.

Descending moderately steep stone stairs of 3 metres breadth, I arrived at the valley bottom after a 12-kilometre day. Entering a large campsite at elevation 3,400 metres, I saluted the flags flying over the permanent buildings. Our well-sited green and purple tents overlooked the valley from a perch above buildings hosting wash facilities and flush toilets.

Downing shots of pisco, we chatted with others hiking the trail, including Piper and Madeline, stalwart lasses from London. About 4 p.m. the balance of our party arrived, including the porters. Thence to the creek with Larry for a wash and shower under a flex hose, the water bracing but quite refreshing. A good dinner followed, curry soup and spaghetti. Mindful of the load burdening the porters, we drank the rest of the wine. Thence to bed.

Arising at 5:30 to a light breakfast of cheese, bread, and cocoa. I packed my gear and set off at 6:30. We climbed to the ruins of Runquraqay (meaning egg-shaped, or round) at 3,700 metres and continued past two small lakes to the second pass at 3,850 metres. After photos, we descended to Sayacmarca at 3,500 metres. Passing five ritual baths, we rested and were briefed by Fredy. A green tree snake, very visible and somewhat out of place against the black soil of a dry well, reminded us of local slithery hazards. Down through the "orchid" jungle and near an algae lake, we joined the original

Inka Trail of very fine stonework, including a 20-metre tunnel. A climb to the third pass at 3,560 metres presented a wonderful view of the Urubamba River far below.

The group assembled for a photo overlooking Phuyupatmarca (Cloud-Level Town), then descended on very steep steps to the lower terrace for a lunch of soup and tuna. From here we had an excellent view of the back face of Machu Picchu (Old Peak), and the distant Sun Gate barely visible with binoculars. The descent on very steep steps included a spiral staircase on a cliff face above a 10-metre tunnel.

Overlooking a youth hostel about 500 metres below, we diverted from the rock-paved Inka Trail to a dirt path. Fortunately, the weather was fine; otherwise, this trail would have been extremely slippery and hazardous. Arriving at the 2,700-metre youth hostel at 5 p.m. with knees aching from the downhill pound, I very much appreciated the cold beer available at 4.5 sols.

The outside campers experienced thunder, lightning and heavy rain throughout the night, but in the hostel it was warm and dry. Up at 5:30 for coffee, we descended to the ruins of Huinay Huayna (orchid), discovered in 1941. From the upper circular "temple," we passed a fine series of ritual baths to the dwellings below. Fredy gave a good explanation, including a demonstration of securing and locking the inner gate of the ruling-class compound.

We hiked back to the hostel for a hearty breakfast of cocoa, pancakes, and fried egg. Departing at 8, we soon encountered a perilous cliff trail, including a wood bridge over a chasm. The influence of the upper Amazon became apparent, with temperature and humidity increasing as we climbed ladder-like steps to an Inka fortress. A further short climb brought us to the Sun Gate at 2,800 metres and a spectacular view of the ruins of Machu Picchu. Luck was with us, for clouds rolled in shortly afterward and completely obscured the ancient site. Descending in the mist, we passed a party of workmen repairing the trail.

Machu Picchu (Old Peak)

On my first visit to Machu Picchu many years before, I had taken the tourist train to the valley below and ascended by bus along the switchback road. We had enjoyed only a brief visit before we had to return to the train on the day trip from Cusco. We now booked into the rustic hotel at Machu Picchu, giving us ample time to explore this unique and spectacular complex.

After I checked into my room overlooking the plaza and Huayna Picchu, Larry assembled us for a group photo with guide and porters. He thanked the porters, handed over their tip, and presented Eric's packsack to the young lad, eliciting a great smile from the lad and a scowl from Eric.

At 3 p.m. we set off for the ruins following a local guide, who gave a very comprehensive and informative tour including:

- the "Southern Cross," a polished shaped stone pointing to the constellation of the same name;
- the "map," an amazingly accurate outline of South America;
- an "echo" stone, essentially a miniature rock replicating the surrounding hills;
- the Intiwatana sundial, or "hitching post of the sun," a carved rock pillar whose four corners are oriented to the four cardinal points, used to predict the solstices;
- down to the "Guinea Pig," or "Sacred Stone," a large slab on a raised platform, interpreted as the outline of a guinea pig, or alternatively as a portrayal of the mountain behind;
- thence to the "Mortuary," a carved rock with staircase, allegedly used for mummification;
- to the "Temple of the Condor," a natural rock formation skilfully shaped into the outspread wings of a condor in flight;
- crawling down recently discovered steps to the lower cave, illuminated only at the summer solstice;
- through the "virgins' quarters."

Thence back to the hotel for beer and a fine dinner of sea bass.

Huayna Picchu (New Peak)

I arose at 6 to find no running water in this so-called five-star hotel. With the restaurant closed, there was neither breakfast nor coffee. The poor substitute was hot water, Eric's dried apricots, and a cookie, as we set off with our small party of Jet, Larry, Eric, Paula, and me.

After registration at the control gate to Huayna Picchu, a series of climbs and small descents led to the pinnacle. Steep steps, several with ropes and one with a wood handrail. Just when we thought nothing could possibly be steeper, we faced a near-vertical wall. Nearing the top, we lost contact with Jet and thought he might have fallen off into the jungle. At a fork, we followed the right-hand route and came upon a very narrow and low tunnel requiring removal of our packs. Emerging from the tunnel we found Jet. He had taken the left route and been first to the summit. We all joined at the peak for a breathtaking view of cloud-swathed ruins and the Urubamba River below. Pictures all around as we perched on the high rocks. Again, not a good place for Charmaine!

I noticed that what appeared to be a seat was also an echo stone of Machu Picchu, the Sun Gate and the bowl enclosing the ruins below. A spine behind the rock seemed to be aligned due south to Machu Picchu.

We cautiously descended a precarious pyramidal face on the left trail. At 2,550 metres we diverted to the Moon Temple at the back of Huayna Picchu. It was a long descent. Forewarned by our guide, we continued despite speculation that we might have passed the site. We found the cave at 2,300 metres and within it the Moon Temple, reputedly the finest carved stone of the complex. Overhead was a structure with trapezoidal walls, one of them formed by natural rock. A long and tiring grind followed as we climbed through the jungle to rejoin the main trail at 2,500 metres, then down and back to the hotel.

I picked up my laundry and hopped on the bus for a twisting ride on the switchback road down to the Urubamba. A young boy soliciting tips raced ahead on the direct route, meeting us at every switchback. At the village of Aguas Calientes, an expanding service centre for Machu Picchu, while the others had lunch, I hiked up the hill to the hot springs for refreshing plunges alternating between cold and hot water. Changing into my freshly washed clothes, I returned for lunch. At the train station I bought the inevitable T-shirt and boarded the rearmost car to a reserved seat.

The train moved slowly up the valley of the Urubamba on narrow-gauge rails. Caution: do not stick your head out. The next rock face might cut it off. We passed our starting point at Kilometre 76 and disembarked at Urubamba for the bus to Cusco, and to the Hotel Monasterio for a final group dinner. Early in the morning, it was up and away for the flight to Lima.

A porter on the trail

The "egg" structure

"Without shame"

Overlooking Machu Picchu from Huayna Picchu

Chapter 2
Mine Ahoy!

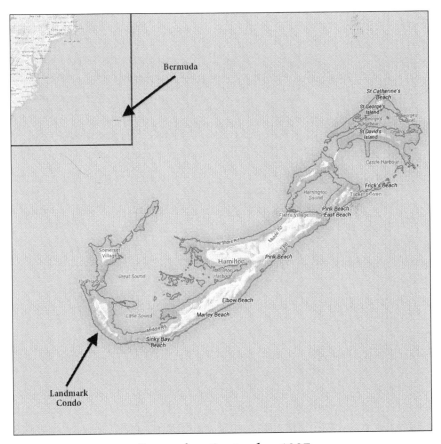

Bermuda – September 1997

Bermuda

When Air Canada in their imponderable wisdom replaced the B-747-400 with the Airbus 340 on the Orient routes, I had a choice of converting to the Airbus or remaining on the B-747 on routes out of Toronto. I gave the plastic airplane a pass and transferred to Toronto. Rather than living in that self-appointed World Class City, we decided to live in Bermuda. Our rented Landmark Estate condo fronted the ocean at Southampton, facing the setting sun.

Snorkel discovery

Early in September 1997, Dany flew to Paris for a short visit with her twin sister, and I departed to Toronto for a week of scheduled flights. In our absence, Hurricane Erika passed to the east of Bermuda. Its winds generated immense waves that moved a lot of sand, in the process depleting the beach at our private swimming cove.

On my low-tide snorkel swim following our return, I encountered a partially exposed curved object in a sand-depleted area. Danielle being nearby, I asked her what she thought it might be. In her inimitable French accent she replied, "It's a b-b-bommb!" and hastened to the other end of the reef. Thinking it might be an old cannonball from one of the nearby forts, I telephoned the Maritime Museum to see if they had any interest in such an artifact. The director was away on a diving trip. So I rummaged through my landlord's storage closet and found a heavy air tank, which I thought I could use as a weight to hold me on the bottom. Predictably, once in the water the tank proved neutrally buoyant and useless as a weight. When I released it, the action of the waves bobbed it up and down onto the object, which responded with a resounding clang of metal on metal. Oops!

Another blunder was using Danielle's garden spade to dig around the object in an attempt to confirm its apparent spherical shape. After partial excavation I estimated its diameter at about 60 cm. A charming feature of Bermuda is the ubiquitous pinkish tint of the sand. To my consternation, the sand I dug up was not pink, but black. In a round hole on the object I saw what appeared to be barnacles, which on closer inspection looked more like corroded wires. Feeling some anxiety at my foolishness, I moved the tank well away from my "cannonball" and moved myself ashore to telephone the police marine detachment.

The EOD

Corporal Ian MacMillan of Glasgow, a member of the Explosive Ordnance Disposal Unit (EOD), arrived and, being a professional, refrained from touching the object. Ian requested confidentiality to avoid public curiosity, and while we quaffed a beer, he described the standard EOD procedure: excavate, take pictures, and send them to London for positive identification before taking any action. Since it was Friday afternoon, London was shut down for the weekend and his team decided to wait until Monday. On Monday morning a four-man detachment arrived: two divers with full scuba gear and, as in the movies, two men ashore sheltering behind a large rock. A neighbour whose condo overlooked the site had to evacuate. I strode into the water with Ian and Sergeant Mark Bothelo, who showed his Bermuda heritage by remarking of the 80-degree water, "This is cold!" Once again sand covered the object, but with flipper power I was able to remove enough sand to expose it. As I expected, Ian did not use metal spades in his excavation.

At that point I had to dash off to Toronto and thence to Paris. On my return Mark told me the object had not been positively identified but was definitely an anti-shipping mine, probably from World War I. Between 20 and 100 kilograms of high explosive could be in place, but on the other hand it might have been converted to some other use, for instance as a mooring buoy. As swords to plowshares, mines to buoys. Unfortunately there was no quick way of determining the contents from the outside; hammers and acetylene torches were not recommended. The experts in London suggested blowing it up, but since our condo and associated water tank were close to the cliff overlooking the site, Mark sensibly declined to detonate the mine in situ.

While I was away flying, Dany reported, the police boat had arrived to lift my "cannonball." However, the sea was very rough and they had to abandon the project. The sand they excavated with their suction dredge washed right back in and eventually covered the object. It lies buried to this day. At the EOD Christmas party to which we were invited, Mark expressed "our thanks to Captain Dunn for keeping us in business."

Divers enter the water

Chapter 3
The Great Wall

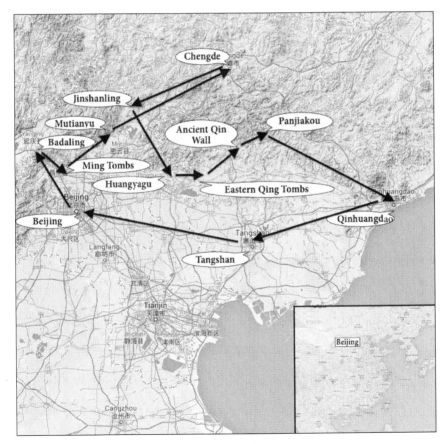

China – September 1998

Beijing

Arriving late September in Beijing, locale of our 1985 honeymoon, Dany and I joined our friends Jet Johnson and Larry and Charmaine Dekker, later meeting the balance of the Great Wall hiking group: Shirley, Sully, Chuck, and Patty, all from California, and hike leaders Tony and Mister Li.

Tourist Wall

Driving north to the Great Wall at Badaling, we stopped first at an interesting museum, featuring scale models depicting the wall's construction and military themes, and a "circle vision" theatre screening aerial shots and battle reenactments. Badaling means something like "hub," and was a focal point for communications. It is now the site where the world's visiting dignitaries pose for the requisite photo op.

We climbed the wall to the east, passing hordes of tourists, both Chinese and foreign. I climbed to the highest tower and, looking back, saw the cable car built sometime after our first visit in 1985. Dany could not pass up the opportunity to be photographed in the costume of Empress, while I played warrior, hitting four of five arrows on the 1/3-metre target below. "Take that you miserable Mongols."

Ming Tombs

I awoke early and walked the broad street as China National Day began, a scene reminiscent of George Orwell's "1984." Loudspeakers blared strident music accompanied by speeches, presumably exhorting the workers to greater efforts.

We departed for the Ming tombs complex, entering the Yongle Emperor's tomb (circa 1424), where a self-locking device had failed to operate as planned. The colossal doors were left ajar, enabling relatively easy entry for latter-day archaeologists.

Twenty-five metres deep, it is a rather plain tomb of three chambers, one each for the emperor and his two wives. After an archaeological excavation in 1958, and despite communist control, the caskets were left lying around, to be subsequently "liberated" by the locals for furniture. Near the thrones lay large vases, once containing oil to provide eternal light. The flames, of course, extinguished as the oxygen depleted.

Another Tourist Wall

An hour's drive brought us to Mutianyu Great Wall, another of the restored sections well-trod by tourists, many ascending by chair lift. We climbed the footpath to join the wall about 500 feet above, where again Dany was happy to have her photo taken in Empress garb.

As we walked through the ornately roofed guard post, we found Charmaine perched just below extremely steep steps, having decided "enough is enough." Of heights, that is. Dany remained with Charmaine while I climbed to the end of the restored section, finding Patty and Chuck photographing the deteriorated wall beyond.

Dany and Charmaine descended by chair, while Jet, Larry, and I boarded small wheeled carts for a slide descent. What might have been an exciting ride became a ponderous one as the fat man in front of Larry braked excessively, forcing us to slow also. Jet, knowing of the language gulf, continuously harangued, "Hey fatty, speed it up."

Chengde Summer Palace

As we vacated our rooms of diverse size, Charmaine asked of Tony: "In the future, could you ensure that the larger rooms are allotted to the couples." This gave Jet a new quip: "That's okay, as being the only single person, I will happily take any old broom closet."

We boarded the bus and took self-appointed seats, agreeable for us in front, less appreciated by those in the rear. However, this arrangement gave Jet a golden opportunity to retell his vintage stories to a newly found captive audience. Soon there was a ceaseless din of jokes from Jet and movie stories from Patty and Chuck.

Winding high above a fertile river valley, we eventually came to the resort city of Chengde, mercifully spared the ravages of the Cultural Revolution. After checking into the venerable International

Diplomatic Hotel, we drove to the Emperor's Summer Palace, a large park surrounded by a mini–Great Wall enclosing structures of diverse architectural styles from various parts of the Empire.

Crossing the river we hiked to the "Emperor's Thumb," otherwise known as the "Stone Rod," or by me as "Dik Rok." According to legend, touching this 38-metre monolith assures a life of 130 years. Great views abounded as we crossed the basal platform, ignoring the pressing crowd and the sheer drop on either side. No place for Charmaine.

Returning to town we climbed to the replica of the Dalai Lama's temple-fortress of Tibet. During World War II, Japanese troops stripped the gold sheathing from its lower roof, but the golden pinnacle still blazed brightly in the sun. It provided a majestic backdrop for Dany, again in costume, this time surrounded by children eager to be photographed with the Empress.

Hiking Jinshanling Ridge

To Jinshanling Great Wall, where Tony hired a woman to guide three of us on the longer hike. It was a perfect day for hiking and the view of the wall snaking over hills and valleys was exhilarating. We stopped for rest and a group picture against a backdrop of the wall above, after which we diverged. The lower trail exited along a decayed wall and Charmaine again had a look of terror as she negotiated the slippery slope.

As the main group descended, Chuck, Larry, and I climbed onward, tower after tower. Where the wall had eroded, exposed granite reinforcement at the crenels and guardhouse portals revealed the strength of the construction techniques.

Our guide departed as we rounded the last turn, but not before attempting to sell us miscellaneous trinkets and souvenirs. Descending, we glimpsed a large suspension bridge crossing the valley, and a long lake. We paid a modest toll to cross the bridge, climbing to the opposite wall. Beer in hand, we descended to greet the others who had traversed through villages and farms. Refreshed with rice and beer, we drove east through fertile lowlands to the Garrison at Huangyaguan.

The Garrison at Huangyaguan

Arriving late at our hotel, we found our spartan rooms within the Great Wall Garrison. At daybreak I climbed to overlook a parade square, discovering that the vintage garrison is in current use by the People's Liberation Army. Raw recruits drilled and marched beneath the historic garrison walls.

We hiked along the original Great Wall of pre-Ming configuration, i.e. with a firing rampart facing outward only as opposed to the double ramparts of later construction. Climbing beyond a precipitous metal staircase, Larry and I inspected a derelict signal tower. Abutting it was a shaky ladder that I climbed to peek inside. Higher up, erosion showed that the core of the wall was essentially the rock of the ridge. We looked out over a col and the derelict wall progressing to the far hill; then reluctantly turned around, disappointed that we could not continue.

Departing on a switchback road, we came to a colossal statue of the infamous General Wu. It was Wu who, after repelling several attacks, opened the gates to the Manchurians to help him retrieve his concubine from rebels in Beijing. His treachery culminated in the establishment of the Manchu Dynasty. A two-hour drive brought us to the industrial city of Zunhua and a first-class hotel.

Eastern Qing Tombs

On another sightseeing break, we leisurely strolled through the imposing marble gate and along the "sacred way" of the Eastern Qing Tomb complex. The four-kilometre marble path illustrated the adage "nothing new under the sun," for as with our modern aircraft runways, the footpath was crowned and fitted with grooves on either side. This feature permitted the water to drain, ensuring that the Emperor did not slip, lest a courtier or two lose their heads.

Passing statues of animals, warriors, and scholars, we crossed the moat on a marble bridge and entered the tomb of the Emperor Qianlong, ruler for some 60 years until abdicating in 1795. His ornate tomb was secured with great marble doors, immensely strong but, alas, unable to withstand the 1928 dynamite attack of a local warlord intent on stealing the goodies within.

Thence to the contrasting stark tomb of the Dowager Empress Cixi, the 80-year old bat responsible for monstrous cruelty throughout the empire that only ended with her death in 1908.

Ancient Qin Wall

Arriving at Luowenyu by rough road, we began climbing through a walnut grove to an original wall of Emperor Qin, circa 220 BC. Danielle, attired in high fashion and flat running shoes, had some difficulty gaining a foothold on the slippery ground. Atop the ridge we hiked along the crumbling wall, acquiring thorns and brambles that only Dany's silk apparel seemed to repel.

We paused to watch a stooped villager, having gathered what appeared to be only weeds, shoulder his heavy burden as he descended near the ancient wall. Crossing the stream and road, I walked through narrow streets, and upon making the universal sign for drink was directed to the village store. I bought four large beers for the equivalent of US $1, much to the amusement of the locals, conceivably entertaining their first foreign visitor. Beer on high, we congratulated Sully and Shirley for their persistence on difficult terrain.

The "Water" Wall

From the enormous dam at Panjiakou we boarded a motorboat for a 45-minute journey on the 100-km-long reservoir. Arriving at a small village, we started to climb an ancient Ming wall. Asked how far we should go, Mister Li suggested climbing to the "white spot" on the wall above. As we approached, the "spot" proved to be a goat, slowly prancing up the mountain, giving us ample justification to continue climbing. However, it soon became evident that the trail was impassable, and we turned and descended. Haze and smoke obscured an otherwise spectacular view of the mountain wall gently submerging into the reservoir, guard towers protruding as island sentinels.

With my camera out of film, I missed a potentially amusing photo of the kneeling Jet, self-proclaimed environmentalist, pummelling a large bit of the wall into a smaller bit for a souvenir.

Mountains, Coast and Yalu Sea

Arriving at the port city of Qinhuangdao, we checked into an excellent modern hotel. It was doubtlessly owned by the People's Liberation Army, for it contained the full range of amenities including a massage parlour and bar girls. A short drive brought us to a dry riverbed fortified with huge portals and gates; the adjoining walls rose precipitously from both sides of the valley.

During a brief diversion to a theme park, Jet, predictably losing interest in history, continuously scanned the sky with my Zeiss binoculars for the MiG-19s flying from a nearby air base. As we were ready to leave, we stumbled upon a derelict MiG-15, providing a suitable photo opportunity for two ex-fighter pilots.

From our final pinnacle, we absorbed an expansive view of the wall in transition from mountainous terrain to coastal plain. Descending, we hiked along the coastal wall, the only level section of our hike. Some 10-12 metres high, the wall was in an advanced state of ruination. Much of its outer cladding has been purloined for local construction, exposing the earthen core.

A five-kilometre drive to the Yalu Sea brought us to the Wall's origin at the Dragon's Head. We assembled for a group picture dressed in our China Great Wall T-shirts.

Return to Beijing

The return was a ride of some terror, the intrinsic rule being BIG has the right of way, typically in the form of ubiquitous blue trucks. We drove through Tangshan City, site of the devastating 1976 earthquake. I was surprised at its closeness to Beijing, for I had thought that the death toll of upwards of 200,000 people was partly a result of the city's isolation.

To Tiananmen Square, site of the massacre, now peaceful and thronged with sightseers, the military presence limited to the Guard of Honour and a lone soldier on a bicycle chastising the many kite vendors.

Strolling through the entrance to the Forbidden City beneath the giant portrait of Mao, I could not help notice the contrast with our first visit in 1985. Then the square was a sea of blue and brown, Mao suits and army uniforms. Now all colours of the rainbow reign.

Exiting the palace by the rear gate, Dany bought a "Xian warrior" for 50 yuan, only to find another vendor selling it at 20 yuan, illustrating the profit potential of our newfound capitalist friends.

Ancient Qin Wall

Jinshanling Ridge

Happy Hikers at the Wall End

Chapter 4

Burma Bound

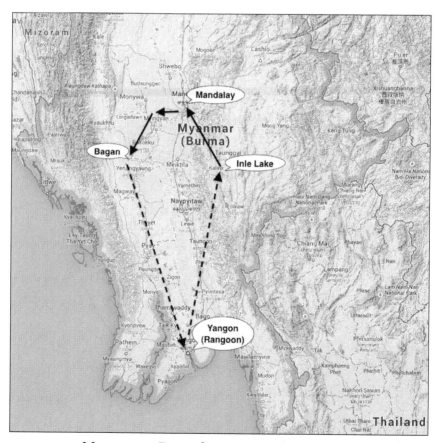

Myanmar – December 1999 to January 2000

arize yourself with the fees for your journey by visiting our <u>airline</u>

airline operating the first flight for each direction of your

opportunity to help reduce the effects of climate change and

avel through the <u>purchase of carbon offsets</u>.

<u>Get Adobe Reader®</u>

Yangon

Arriving in Rangoon, now called Yangon, in Burma, now known as Myanmar, we met with Sally, manager of the renowned Strand Hotel dating from 1896. An unusual and vicious cold front blanketed Southeast Asia, resulting in many deaths. Sally told us that our next destination, Inle Lake, altitude 900 metres, would be very cold, and kindly lent Danielle a couple of sweaters.

A visit to Myanmar was controversial because of its repressive military government. One school of thought held that the country should be boycotted. Another was that tourists should visit to help its people in their struggle for a livelihood. We subscribed to the latter view and found people warm, friendly, and appreciative of the opportunity to improve their lot.

Inle Lake

Arriving at Inle Lake on Christmas Eve, we were surprised to find our hotel bedecked with festive decorations including a large Christmas tree. We learned later that the proprietor, a Chinese Christian, had a hand in many enterprises of the village.

As darkness fell, villagers gathered at the hotel for a traditional ceremony of launching paper balloons. The balloons are about a metre high, with small baskets of twigs strung below. Ideally, when the twigs are lit, the hot air filling the balloons would cause them to rise and slowly drift over the village. However, the extreme cold made the temperature differential so great that the balloons shot up like rockets and were quickly lost from view. A fitful sleep followed, sweaters and blankets piled on in our attempt to keep warm in the unheated room.

Next morning we boarded a 12-metre outboard canoe and motored to the floating islands. The local folk construct islands of reeds and grow their vegetables on the soil created from the decaying vegetation. Houses, stores, and workshops are on stilts, including the blacksmith's shop where a young lad trod on a leather bellows to power the forge. The blacksmith's shop fabricates all tools, and implements required for the water-bound village.

Motoring to a lakeside monastery, we passed a fisherman with fine diaphanous conical nets. He powered the rudder-oar with one leg as he stood precariously on a plank extending from the extreme stern of the canoe.

Mandalay

"On the road to Mandalay," but we saw no flyin' fishes play, for we came by road to this city of nearly a million inhabitants. Situated on the banks of the Irrawaddy River in central Burma, it was once the capital of a powerful empire continuously at war with neighbouring Siam. By the time the highly militaristic dynasty clashed with the British in present-day northeast India, it had built the largest empire in mainland Southeast Asia. Three wars over the following six decades ended with Burma a British colony. World War II battles destroyed the imposing palace and most pre-colonial edifices.

Our guide drove us to diverse factories and workshops, for the city is now a thriving local manufacturing centre. At the first workshop, massive blocks of white marble were being transformed into giant Buddhas. As the statues were intended for the Chinese market, the facial features were distinctly Chinese. At another shop, workers pieced together sheets of bronze cast by the ancient lost-wax technique. At a gold-foil factory, sweating men hammered a small bit of gold into a sizable sheet, then cut it into smaller bits that they again pummelled repeatedly until the sheets were only a few molecules thick. The thin strips of gold are sold for offerings at Buddhist shrines.

Mandalay Hill, blanketed with pagodas, stupas, and monasteries, towers 240 metres above the plain. Fortified by the Japanese during WWII, it was the scene of fierce fighting when a Gurkha battalion stormed it in March 1945. A plaque commemorates the battle at the summit, where we enjoyed a grand view of the city and surrounding plain as the sun set low.

Bagan

In early morning we boarded a riverboat for a day-long journey down the Irrawaddy, stopping often to disembark and embark passengers at villages along the muddy banks. We docked late in the afternoon at Bagan, land of thousands of stupas. A stupa is a mound-like or semi-hemispherical structure containing Budddist relics. Some are closed, while others have an interior space that can be entered. Of the 10,000 stupas, temples, pagodas, and monasteries built here at the height of the empire, 2,200 stupas survive, filling the vast plain along the Irrawaddy. Stupas run amok, you might say.

Visitors to the stupas need to remove their shoes, something I'm not too keen about in this dusty land, but that is the rule. Another rule, No Pointing, was directed at the Brits, who would point their umbrellas or canes at diverse religious artifacts. The locals considered this to be rude.

Tourism is the major economic activity, with lacquerware manufacture providing employment. Another is larceny; when a few young folk attempted to sell Dany a "ruby" for $100, I whipped out my 10-power loop and quickly determined the stone to be a fake.

Touring Yangon

On returning to Yangon we checked into the five-Star Sedona Hotel. A city tour brought us to the magnificent Shwedagon Pagoda, burning bright with its dome of gold. The great Buddhist shrine was looted and then fortified by British troops in the 1824 war and in 1852, and later restored. About 5,000 diamonds and 2,000 rubies sheath the crown 99 metres above. The pinnacle holds a 76-carat diamond! Since I could see no armed guards about, my thoughts mischievously wandered to Rudyard Kipling: "Ow the loot! Bloomin loot! That's the thing to make the boys git up an' shoot!"

Meanwhile, back at our hotel, workers had transformed the swimming pool into a dance floor for the gala Millennium dinner-dance. Military officers had commandeered several large tables, cutting into the expected profit somewhat. At midnight fireworks ushered in the new millennium, though it seemed we were under attack by errant projectiles. Shortly afterward, a berserk cook smashed windows, chased the assistant manager, and stabbed him on the dance floor. The military officers scooted for the exits and guests scurried for the hotel elevator. The gala over, we returned to our room to watch millennium fireworks around the globe.

Bagan - a sea of Temples

Millennium Gala

Chapter 5
Alaska Cruise

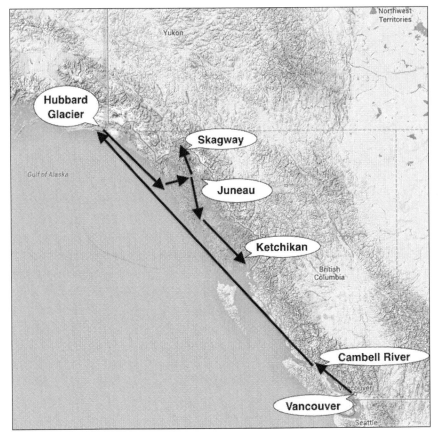

Canada & USA – August 2000

Cruise to Alaska prelude - Sabre Pilots' Reunion

In early August 2000, about 630 ex–Sabre pilots and significant others assembled for a three-day reunion at Harrison Hot Springs near Vancouver. In keeping with tradition, Dale Horley, Ron Stewart and I hosted the "Lion's Den" for the 60 members of 427 Squadron in attendance. Our large 427 banner again dominated the affair, first draped over the Den's top-floor balcony and later as centrepiece of the closing formal dinner.

Former Commanding Officer "Doc" Payne appeared, and just as mysteriously disappeared before I could learn the full details of his amazing saga. He told of ditching near Helgoland in 1945, and of his capture 12 days later. Apparently, there is a grave in Sweden with his name on it!

Saturday we bused to the Abbotsford Air Show, viewing the flying display in comfort from the Sabre chalet. Considering the military budget cutbacks of the preceding years, it was an impressive show. An expected F-86 Sabre failed to appear, having slid off a runway somewhere in Alberta. All agreed that the reunion was a great success, with the relative isolation of Harrison enhancing the ambiance.

Cruise to Alaska

Sunday, we drove to Vancouver and boarded the Vision of the Seas for a one-week cruise to Alaska. I'm not much of a sailor, generally finding that if the sea is calm I get bored and if it is rough I get seasick. However, this voyage was delightful. The sheltered Inside Passage afforded spectacular views, generally calm seas, and interesting historic ports. A lively party atmosphere continued with the 330 ex–fighter pilots and company aboard. We found our modest stateroom on the second level well-designed, with adequate storage space.

Slipping out of our berth at Ballantyne Pier, we soon had a grand view of Vancouver receding under a clear sunny sky. Entering the dining salon for the second sitting, we were soon shuffling for position; for various parties had changed their assigned seats. Evidently after the first night, passengers are confined to their respective tables for the entire cruise. This custom is primarily for the benefit of the waiters, who hope to garner large tips at voyage end.

Tuesday afternoon we arrived at the Hubbard Glacier, the largest tidewater glacier face in North America. Captain Lief Bang, of Viking heritage, proved his skill as he gingerly eased the ship through the ice field to within 800 metres of the glacier face. Great chunks of ice calved, crashing noisily into the sea. We later learned that we had shared the greatest display of calving ever observed by Captain Bang.

Skagway

Thence to Skagway, gateway to the Yukon gold rush of 1897-98. Disembarking early, Dany and I boarded the narrow-gauge railway. On tracks cut into granite cliffs and flung over deep gorges, we climbed to the summit at White Pass. An engineering marvel built in little more than two years, the White Pass & Yukon Railway is now a UNESCO heritage site. Returning to Skagway, we toured the historic lawless town, renowned for the scams of the infamous Soapy Smith. Among the excellent films and displays at the Ranger station was a 3D relief map, based not on the American but on the 1898 Canadian survey.

Next a brief visit to Haines, a short distance down the Lynn Canal. An unexceptional port, its original function was as a garrison for the Fort Seward military force during the Alaska Boundary Dispute at the turn of the century. Skagway, hemmed in by mountains, was too crowded for a military base. During the 1840's Oregon Boundary Dispute, the slogan "Fifty-four forty or fight," expressed the American temper of the time. That perspective again prevailed at Skagway. At the 1903 U.S.-British tribunal to resolve the issue, Perfidious Albion sided with the Americans and northern British Columbia remains isolated from the sea.

Juneau

We cruised overnight to Juneau, the state capital. Hemmed in by steep terrain, the town has no road access to the rest of Alaska. A visit to the State Museum gave a good summary of Alaskan history, save for the aforementioned boundary dispute, described as having "faded from American recollection." Dale and I then joined several Sabre pilots at the renowned Red Dog Saloon, while Dany set off on a shopping spree, for Christmas ornaments of all things!

Ketchikan

Thence to Ketchikan, where ashore we marvelled at the spectacle of king salmon leaping over rapids to reach the gravel bar above, to spawn, to die; their great white carcasses soon drifting downstream. Departing Ketchikan, the ship slowed to pick up "Mighty Whitey" Hinton and wife, who had literally missed the boat. The captain eased into the narrow channel of the Misty Fjords, a spectacular natural setting of sheer cliffs rising 1,000 metres above us. At the head of the fjord, we wagered on whether the captain would pivot the ship or reverse it. He pivoted, with about 75 metres to spare off the bow. Homeward bound, we passed through feeding waters of humpback whales and sighted about 60, breaching, tail-slapping or spouting their breath.

Cruising Return

The captain had invited us to the bridge, and as we approached Vancouver Island we witnessed the hazardous transfer of pilot from tender to ship. Pilot, navigator, and captain then discussed the timing of our passage through Seymour Narrows, site of the former Ripple Rock obstruction. The world's largest non-nuclear explosion pulverized the rock in 1958

Tidal flows here can run up to 18 knots, and each pilot determines the maximum flow acceptable for a given ship's passage, varying from 3 to 5 knots. Our pilot, described by the captain as "our Canadian cowboy," ordered two engines shut down, and the ship slowed to reach the narrows coincident with a tidal flow of 5 knots.

On Sunday morning the ship docked in Vancouver to the praise of all. Murray Neilson, who had logged 15 cruises, acclaimed our Sabre pilots' cruise as his finest.

Russ Bennet, Dick & King salmon

The Horleys & Dunns at Hubbard Glacier

White Pass & Yukon train

Chapter 6
A Mad Irish Hike

Ireland – July 2001

Escape and Evasion

I had planned to hike Hadrian's Wall early in July, but that area of England was closed because of an outbreak of foot and mouth disease. Instead I popped over to Dublin and joined up with the Wayfarers, a local hiking club that I had found on the Internet. Outfitted with the requisite gear, I made my way to the assembly point, meeting a few of the genial members and setting off with them by car to the Military Road for an "easy" walk in the Wicklow Mountains.

The Irish are mad! I recalled the Escape and Evasion exercise for which I volunteered shortly after arriving in Germany as a fledgling fighter pilot with the Royal Canadian Air Force, almost 40 years before. Another Canadian pilot, Tony Smith, and I teamed up with a Special Air Service captain in London. After a short briefing, we took a train to York, boarded lorries and were dumped on the Yorkshire moors. Our objective was to trek to the safe house on the east coast, evading capture by troops and police practising their skills.

Skirting a sleeping village, we found ourselves mired in terrible walking ground: rows of clumped sod separated by deep soggy ruts, their span being just beyond that of a comfortable step. In my air force flying boots, the smooth soles designed for rudder manipulation and not bog walking, I found myself slipping frequently into the muck.

At dawn we bivouacked individually in waist-high heather, concealed from the searching helicopters, and at nightfall continued our trek across the moor. About 3 a.m., climbing a steep hill, Tony fell flat on his face, his teeth saved by the soft gorse. "Go on, leave me," he mumbled, replicating dialogue from a grade B war movie. We dragged him to a shallow depression on the windswept hill, where we huddled for the remainder of the night. It was mid-February. I have never been so cold. The precipitation cycled through rain, sleet, and snow and back to rain.

Wicklow Hike

But back to the Wicklow Mountains. The Wayfarers climbed a rough track, then traversed along a barbed-wire fence to the summit. Foregoing any thought of a trail, we set out across the uplands, the ground resembling the aforementioned Yorkshire bog.

Mad I say, for whereas I crossed the Yorkshire moors to avoid capture and the certainty of a none-too-gentle interrogation, these folks trekked across this hellground for sport! From my Canadian bush experience I had thought peat bogs were confined to depressions. Here the bog covered the slopes, sponging up and retaining the recent rain.

Irish flies need not take second billing to Canadian flies. About the size of hornets, swarming about incessantly, they were bothersome and persistent, seemingly following us on our multiple ascents and descents. Fortunately they were not particularly voracious, perhaps preferring the blood of the nearby sheep.

From our penultimate summit, we followed the sodden banks of a sluggish stream. I found myself crawling on hands and knees beneath piercing pine branches in an attempt to detour around the adjacent water and muck.

Through most of the hike my flimsy boots remained dry, but eventually my right foot plunged into an unseen hole of muck. Expecting an easy return on the road below, we found our descent blocked by an impenetrable pine forest. Turning about, we climbed again through a tract of thorns and scrub, finally descending along a rock-strewn ditch to the forestry road below.

I had signed on for a four-hour hike but somehow had inadvertently joined the six-hour group. My knobby knees took a beating on the descent, for it was seven hours from the ascent when I limped into the Glenmalure Pub for a refreshing Irish beer.

Wicklow "Mountains"

Military Barracks at Glenmalure

Chapter 7
Soaring with Eagles

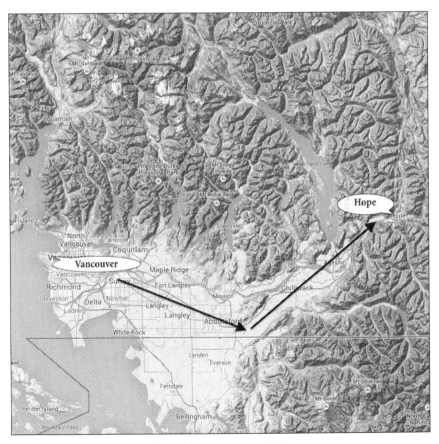

Canada – August 2001

Flight Training

Hope is where it was. The gliding that is. Shortly after I retired from Air Canada, I joined five other retired airline pilots for an intensive beginner course with the Vancouver Soaring Association.

With three instructors, five gliders, and two tow planes flown by retired airline pilots Bill Green and Bob Ayotte, the daily routine was reminiscent of my youthful flying in the Royal Canadian Air Force. On the three parallel runways, tow planes and gliders launched, landed, repositioned, and re-launched in a continuous aerial ballet.

"Lightning" Bob Hyndman, who normally has two speeds, "slow" and "stop," briefly jogged two or three steps while assisting in launching a glider.

As well as basic circuits and landings, we practised stalls and spins on higher tows to 3,000 feet. For a spin recovery, the prescribed concluding action is to "ease out of the dive." As I eased out of my first spin at 70 degrees nose down, my instructor Dave Baker took control and demonstrated his own recovery technique, which is to yank the plane out of the dive using most of the available 5.5 g's.

As I strapped on my parachute preparing for a spin session, my elderly partner Jack Humphries asked, "Why are you laughing?" I replied, "Because here I am, 60 years old, doing what I did at 17 and loving every bit of it." The brisk course schedule left little time for the soaring part, but on my penultimate flight I dropped the tow line at 1,000 feet and worked my way to 4,700 feet in somewhat more than an hour. A very satisfying soaring session.

Mindful of the 20-knot winds, Joe Gegenbauer, our Chief Flying Instructor, instructed me to keep my circuits tight and high. On my check flight, I carved in to final approach with a 60-degree-bank turn. At debriefing, Joe said it was a well-coordinated turn but suggested I take off a little bank to avoid scaring bystanders on the ground.

Mishap

Hope, B.C., is at the juncture of four valleys, and the funnelling effect of the surrounding mountains generates some interesting air movements. Joe repeatedly warned: "If the air goes up, it must also come down." As Ed Wight prepared for his last solo flight, his instructor Marty Vanstone remarked, "No surprises please." At 6 foot 3, "Too-Tall" Ed was renowned for his self-confidence, sometimes misplaced.

Shortly afterward, Bill Green landed his tow plane and announced that a glider was down beside the highway. I hopped in my car and drove to an overpass where Joe snapped pictures of Ed reclining against the glider, feet up, no doubt pondering his good fortune at finding a level piece of ground. The lift that had been prevalent over the nearby knoll had dissipated and afternoon cooling had replaced it with a rapid sink, leaving Ed without enough altitude to make the field. A salutary experience.

After recovering the undamaged glider, we repaired to a nearby pub for a dinner courtesy of Ed, thereby ending a very enjoyable course.

Hope from the Air

Launching

Aircraft down

Chapter 8
The Maltese Falcon – Not

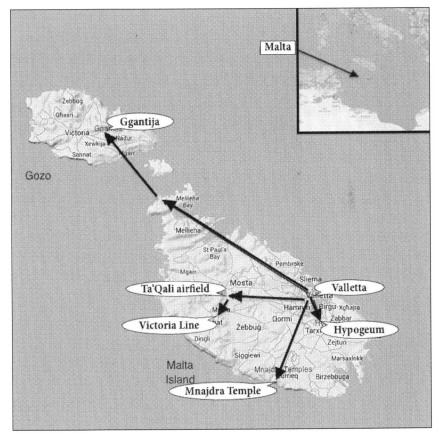

Malta – October 2002

Malta

First impression of Malta? In a word, brown, or more precisely a light yellowish brown, the colour of the locally quarried soft limestone that is the common building stone. Structures are vaguely reminiscent of Moorish architecture. Rare is a splash of colour to grace the overhanging balconies. Generally an arid landscape, with a dearth of trees, and but feeble crops where irrigated.

The sea, however, is blue, crystal-clear, and at 25 degrees Celsius very tempting. Since the Mediterranean lacks true coral reefs, it is not as interesting for a snorkel swim as the waters of my beloved Bermuda.

At the crossroads of the Mediterranean, Malta is replete with historical remnants, from the Stone Age through Phoenicians, Greeks, Carthaginians, Romans, Vandals, Crusaders, Knights of St. John, Turks, Napoleon and the British. Wary of cultural overdose, I restricted myself to World War II sites and Neolithic ruins.

First was Ta'Qali airfield, or rather what remains of it, the postwar Nissan huts now faced with the ubiquitous yellow limestone and occupied by various crafts and shops. From here and from the other four airfields, Spitfires and Hurricanes challenged the onslaught of intensive Nazi and Italian bombing from May 1940 through November 1942. About a quarter of the fighter pilots were Canadians, including ace Buzz Beurling, Lyte Gervais, and Bob Middlemiss, the latter two commanders of my 427 Squadron in postwar Germany. An erstwhile hangar now houses a fine Aviation Museum manned by friendly volunteers. The restoration of a Hurricane recently wrenched from the seabed is almost complete.

My solo visit coincided with the International Air Show and ceremonies marking the 60th anniversary of the awarding of the George Cross to the people of Malta. The outstanding air show featured many NATO fighters, including two German MiG-29s and an ancient Canberra contemporaneous with my air force service. Unfortunately, a promised Royal Air Force Spitfire failed to arrive because of inclement weather over Europe, but the Red Arrows compensated by closing the show with an impressive aerial ballet.

On the second day of the air show, I looked out over Valletta from a derelict fortification at the northern harbour. Binoculars in hand, I reclined against a fractured concrete gun platform as jet fighters, afterburners booming, performed vertical manoeuvres over the distant airfield. A serene sunny afternoon. It was easy to imagine Nazi Stukas on similar vertical attacks some 60 years past.

A noteworthy attraction of Valletta is the Lascaris War Rooms. When not toiling on construction of the monumental fortress overhead, the slaves of the Knights of Malta were confined to dungeons deep within the rock. The British renovated the dungeons for their headquarters during World War II, believing the complex to be impregnable to bombs. From the navy control centre, the Royal Navy planned the Swordfish attack on the Italian fleet at Taranto. Adjacent rooms portray the gun and air-defence control centres, and finally the "Husky" room, where Generals Eisenhower and Montgomery and Air Marshall Tedder monitored the invasion of Sicily.

Neolithic Structures
Bound for Neolithic ruins, I trekked along the Victoria Line, a mini–Great Wall. In the latter part of the 19th century the British dug an immense ditch, 10 metres deep and 7 metres wide, along the foot of a natural escarpment. The building and manning of the line avoided costly fortification of the many western beaches and bays where hostile forces might invade. The ramparts mounted antiaircraft batteries during WWII. Spent shotgun casings littered the ground along the length of the line, evidence of the self-proclaimed right of Maltese "sportsmen" to blast every living bird from the sky. Hence my title "The Maltese Falcon – Not"; for hunters shot the last pair of Maltese falcons in 1982.

My hike brought me to the oldest foundations on Malta, the Skorba huts, dated about 4,500 BC, and to the nearby Ta'Hagrat temple, normally closed to casual visitors. Luckily I chanced upon a government archaeologist conducting a private tour, which he allowed me to join. Among the features he pointed out, still visible after 5,000 years, were traces of red ochre, now interpreted by archaeologists as representative of blood.

The well-preserved temple at Hagar Qim, overlooking the southwest coast, provides impressive proof of the ancient builders' skill. Massive square-cut blocks flank a trilithon entrance that opens into elliptical chambers, formerly covered with corbel roofs. Raised altars within are decorated with pit marks and spiral carvings, the latter similar to those at younger Neolithic structures such as New Grange in Ireland.

Generally the temples face southeast to southwest, but the nearby Mnajdra Temple aligns precisely eastward, with sunrise at the equinox illuminating the interior altars. Arriving about noon on the autumnal equinox, I found the site thankfully devoid of the "new-age drug-crazed hippies" who supposedly congregate at the spring equinox.

Gozo

A short ferry journey from the northwest port brought me to the smaller island of Gozo, where I hiked to the colossal Ggantija temples. On a plateau overlooking a fertile valley, two adjacent temples stand within a common perimeter composed of massive stones weighing up to 55 tonnes each. Dating from about 3,600 BC, Ggantija is reputedly the world's oldest structure. A large section is surrounded by scaffolding to prevent its threatened collapse.

Hypogeum

Back on Malta, the highlight of my visit was a downer, the Hypogeum. Mindful of damage from excessive humidity, this UNESCO-protected site admits only 50 visitors per day, and I needed to reserve a week in advance. A "downer" because, after a video presentation, one descends into a unique Neolithic temple and burial shrine. Carved from solid limestone with deer-antler drills and stone mallets, the three levels of caverns are remarkable for their smooth walls replicating aboveground structures, including trilithon entrances, and corbel ceilings.

The grotesque Fat Lady sculptures and the exquisite hand-sized Sleeping Lady, now in the Valletta Archaeology Museum, once reposed here. The Oracle Room features an opening that, when spoken into, reduces the pitch and booms the amplified sound through the complex. The Hypogeum was constructed about 3,600

BC as a sanctuary; its later use as a necropolis is attested to by the bones of 7,000 bodies found within. The site remained in use until about 2,500 BC, when the Neolithic culture suddenly disappeared. Curiously, archaeologists have found neither lamps nor evidence of torches. The source of light for its construction is a mystery to this day.

Despite the drab landscape, Malta is a rewarding destination. The Maltese language is related to Arabic, but most inhabitants speak English. They are both friendly and helpful.

Hypogeum

Victoria Line

Neolithic Ruins - 3500 years BC

Chapter 9

Good Morning, Vietnam

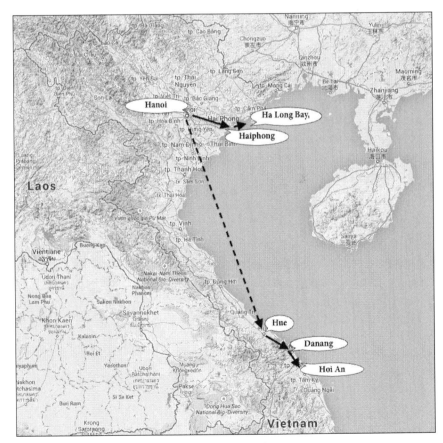

Vietnam – January - February 2003

Hanoi

Although arriving in darkness, we soon learned that Hanoi, in contrast to the skyscrapers of Hong Kong we had just left, consists primarily of low buildings. Many dated from the French colonial period, the French legacy being Dany's motivation to visit Vietnam. With CNN and BBC among the channels available at our hotel, the elegant Hilton Opera, it became clear that Vietnam is a communist country in transition. Uniformed officials were rare, and we met with no obstructions to our travels.

Our afternoon tour took us past the "Hanoi Hilton," the infamous former prisoner-of-war camp. Only a small section still stands; the greater part was demolished for a high-rise building. Displays at the military museum illustrated Vietnam's long history of repelling foreign invaders, from an 11th century attempted Mongol invasion through to the French and, as they call it, the American war. A large illuminated relief model of Dien Bien Phu incorporates an audiovisual diorama of the French defeat. In the courtyard stands a great heap of aircraft fragments, remnants of aircraft shot down during the French era and through to the last days of American bombing. The exhibition left little doubt of the folly of confronting the Viet Cong in their own backyard.

While I toured the military museum, Dany visited the Fine Arts Museum. To her disappointment, she found it exhibiting mostly war paintings. Thence to the Ho Chi Minh mausoleum and his modest stilted house set in parkland around the former French governor-general's residence. That residence is now the Presidential Palace, a handsome colonial building in yellow, the colour of prosperity. After a visit to the university, founded in 1070 AD, our guide dropped us at the ancient quarter, where he hired two push-cycles to convey us through the narrow streets. Cars, cycles, handcarts, bicycles, scooters, and motorcycles jostled for right-of-way in a seemingly chaotic manner, but somehow we manage to progress though the congested streets. The cacophony of honking horns was loud and persistent; the air thick with exhaust fumes, forcing the ladies slinging baskets from shoulder poles to swaddle their faces with masks. With Tet, the Lunar New Year, approaching, there was a continuous traffic of peach-blossom and kumquat trees carried on any of the aforementioned conveyances. The conical kumquat tree with its bright yellow fruit conveys a message of prosperity, while the peach-blossom trees will eventually be adorned with gifts of money.

I was surprised to learn that the Vietnamese use the western Latin alphabet. A Jesuit missionary introduced Latin phonetics in the 16th century, and in 1945 the communist government made its use compulsory, resulting in a general loss of Chinese calligraphy skills but, presumably, in the acceleration of scientific and industrial expertise. Curiously, the Vietnamese language, like ancient Greek, lacks a distinct word for blue. To differentiate green from blue, they say "xanh like rice" (green) or "xanh like the sky."

There are no coins to weigh down the pocket, only great wads of banknotes, the largest being 100,000 dong, equivalent in value to about ten dollars. A hundred dollars makes one a millionaire! The strings of zeros make it quite confusing to determine the note needed for payment. Goods and services are priced, at least for foreigners, in U.S. dollars, as are credit card purchases.

Haiphong

Departing Hanoi, we crossed the Red River on a new bridge, adjacent to the bridge that had attracted the concerted attention of American bombers during the war. Driving is typical of third-world countries: big has the right-of-way and the centre dividing line is purely for decoration. The road was lined by dwellings with a uniform frontage of four metres. Those with the means could build as high as they wanted, but structural constraints imposed a maximum of five stories. The ground floor was invariably used for commerce. Some of the buildings were quite stately, with upper balconies, cupolas, and towers.

The uniformly flat lowland of small rice paddies was tilled by ancient techniques: the father plowing behind a buffalo, a pair of girls swinging a bucket to raise water, and the mother stooping to plant rice stalks, with the omnipresent conical sun hat covering all. Raised above the plain were tombs containing the family ancestors, their presence purportedly bringing luck and good harvest. Intermittent landfill-raised sites enclosed giant factories, including a Ford assembly plant.

Arriving at the riverbank at Haiphong, the port through which Russian ships supplied the North, we crossed by one of the numerous shuttle ferries. A stream of scooters and bikes burdened with a variety of farm products: fruits, vegetables, live chickens and pigs. came aboard. The ferries departed when full, rear ramps laden with late boarders hanging unprotected over the muddy water.

The flatlands behind, we ascended low hills to a small village overlooking Ha Long Bay, its port crowded with diverse tourist boats. In the morning we boarded our private 15-metre boat, manoeuvred around the many vessels and steered to sheer limestone hills in the distance. Disembarking at the island of Cat Bo, we climbed to a recently discovered cavern, now a major tourist attraction. Colourfully illuminated, the stalactites hanging from the 30-metre ceiling presented a breathtaking sight. This magnificent setting is generally crowded with tourists; we were fortunate to share it with but a single boatload of Japanese.

Re-boarding our craft, we cruised leisurely among the 3,000 islands of this UNESCO World Heritage site. As we passed a small community of fisherfolk, a boat came alongside with a fresh catch, which we later enjoyed at a delicious lunch prepared by our crew. The mist-enshrouded islands loomed magisterial and silent as we headed to port. Our drive to Hanoi by way of the northern road brought us past many coal mines and cement quarries, reinforcing the need for UNESCO protection of the islands.

Hanoi Again

An obligatory attraction of Hanoi is the Water Puppet Theatre. Operators behind screens at the back of the stage manipulate the puppets using long wooden handles. The wooden puppets, unique to northern Vietnam, portray farmers, animals, and spirits. The action takes place in a shallow pond, giving the impression that the puppets are walking on water, the murky water hiding the mechanism beneath.

Afterwards, strolling among the crowds while enjoying various Tet concerts, I practised the recommended technique to avoid being struck by the motor scooters jamming the streets: walk slowly, don't stop, and don't run. Surprisingly, it worked!

On our morning drive to the airport, I recalled Macbeth: "... until great Birnam Wood ... shall come," for the streets were again a veritable moving forest of kumquat and peach-blossom trees carried aloft on scooters and bikes.

Hue

A one-hour flight brought us to the ancient capital of Hue and our hotel, on the banks of the Perfume River; extravagantly decorated in the Chinese motif of red, black, and gold. Intense fighting during the Tet offensive of 1968 destroyed many buildings within the Imperial Palace. Restoration of the sprawling complex is largely complete. Following a New Year's Eve folk concert, fireworks burst over the cantilever bridge spanning the river. The illumination of the seven spans cycled through, mirroring the colours of the fireworks exploding above.

Next morning, a short boat journey brought us to the impressive Thien Mu Pagoda, home of the monk who journeyed to Saigon to immolate himself in the early years of the war. Later, strolling amid the serene gardens and lakes of the Summer Palace of Tu Duc, one became aware of the darker side of this 19th-century emperor, and of the general capriciousness of the powerful. Although the enclosure hosts his mausoleum, his remains lie with his treasure elsewhere, the burial site kept secret by the beheading of the 200 servants involved in the burial.

Hoi An

In a private car we drove along the coastal plain and ascended a switchback road to Sea Cloud Pass, where mountains meet the sea. Recent and ancient fortifications stand a silent vigil, marking this geographical boundary between North and South Vietnam. Continuing our drive through Danang, we arrived at Hoi An, an ancient river port and another UNESCO site. The port was foremost from the 15th through the 18th century, losing its predominance when the river silted up. Grand houses of Chinese and European traders line the streets, interspersed with ramshackle tin-roofed huts and a filthy market. The many silk shops were well-patronized by Dany in her quest for more treasures of the Orient.

Our sightseeing at an end, we had time to ponder our journey as we relaxed on the surf-tossed beach at the upscale Victoria Resort. The vast majority of Vietnamese folk, in common with all Southeast Asians, are kind, friendly, hard-working, and intensely focused on improving their life. Foregoing a visit to Saigon, now Ho Chi Minh City, we flew to Thailand for a week of R&R.

Haiphong Bay

Wandering trees

American aircraft bits

Chapter 10
Hiking the Chilkoot Trail

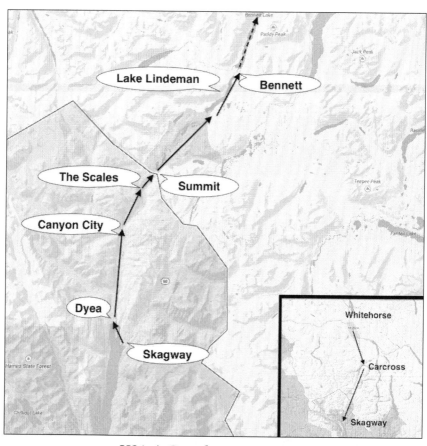

USA & Canada – August 2003

Whitehorse to Skagway

Our group of four assembled at Vancouver airport intending to follow in the footsteps of the 1897-98 Klondikers by hiking the 53-kilometre Chilkoot Trail. The four were myself, retired Air Canada pilot Ed (Too-Tall) Wight, his son Scott, and Larry Dekker, retired geologist and longtime companion on expeditions as diverse as the Inka Trail, the Great Wall of China and the highlands of Papua New Guinea.

It was a bright sunny day as we departed for Whitehorse. Generally, when the weather is fine in Vancouver it is the opposite in the north. Sure enough, we arrived in Whitehorse to light rain and cloudy skies. After briefly examining a Yukon River stern-wheeler, we boarded a bus to Fraser, B.C., from which the narrow-gauge White Pass & Yukon railway would take us over the pass and down to Skagway, Alaska. As the Voice of America News put it:

> In 1994 the White Pass & Yukon line was named one of the world's Historic Civil Engineering Landmarks. It may not sound like an especially prestigious award, but it put this tiny railroad in some pretty illustrious company. The Panama Canal, the Eiffel Tower and the Statue of Liberty are all to be found among the award's 29 recipients. The climb to the White Pass rises 900 meters in just 32 kilometres, making it one of the steepest rail inclines in the world.

Standing on the platform between cars, we had an unobstructed view of the tortuous route through hairpin turns and along sheer cliffs. Passing what was the world's tallest iron railway trestle at the time it was built, 1898-1900, we could only marvel at the audacity of the engineers and workers who conceived and completed the railway in just over two years. The trestle was later abandoned for an alternative route tunnelled through a rocky crag.

A glimpse of a bear below the tracks, then fragments of the original White Pass Trail emerged, including a section along the infamous Dead Horse Gulch. More than 3,000 horses met their demise here at the hands of inexperienced drovers. Coasting past the Skagway rail yards, littered with venerable steam locomotives, we cleared U.S. Customs and walked to the Trail Center for the requisite briefing.

Hiking the Chilkoot

After a fitful sleep, frequently interrupted by the hostel snoring competition, a taxi-van brought us to the Dyea trailhead. Unlike Skagway, which is a time warp retaining many original buildings, Dyea is a flat wasteland with little evidence of the gold rush tumult. At the tidal flat where tons of supplies were landed, eagles now nested and fed on spawning salmon. Donning rain gear, we began our soggy slog through the coastal rain forest, otherwise known as the wet coast jungle. Vast stands of prickly Devil's Club bordered the high bank of the steep trail. The trail then descended to the valley floor, with but a gentle incline for the remainder of our 19-km first day.

While the others pressed on, I crossed the river by a cable bridge to Canyon City, where the more affluent gold seekers would have their goods lifted by an aerial tramway for 7 $^1/_2$ cents a pound. Artifacts strewn about included a massive boiler, which once provided power for the windlass.

A park ranger descending the trail had advised that Sheep Camp where we intended to camp was flooded, muddy, and crowded. Heeding her recommendation, we halted at Pleasant Camp, where, with Scott chopping the wood, Ed soon had a fire blazing in the cookhouse stove. Other hikers trudged on by, giving us exclusive use of the camp and simplifying the drying of our water-soaked gear. Preparing my simple dinner of oriental noodles and salmon jerky, I looked on in disbelief as Ed and Scott piled into a huge dinner of canned ham, potatoes, black bread, etc. No bland dehydrated fare for the Wight lads! In keeping with park regulations, we then slung our food and cooking fuel from 10-metre lines on the bear poles nearby. Apparently the bears will chomp into any carbohydrates, including cooking fuel. In my spacious but heavy tent, Larry slept soundly aloft on his floating bed of air and I slept fitfully on my rudimentary sleeping pad.

Morning brought a marked improvement in the weather, with the others departing before I had packed my tent and gear. I shortly arrived at Sheep Camp, where bedraggled hikers lurched from their mud-splattered tents. Passing a group of Europeans, their metal climbing poles clicking uselessly against the hard granite, I cleared the forest to join our group resting on rocks overlooking the valley and the hanging blue glacier. Sixty-five Klondikers died at nearby Sheep Camp in a series of avalanches in April 1898. Snow slides are an ongoing hazard until mid-July.

Climbing under clear skies and a warming sun, nearing the Canadian border, we reached the site of The Scales, the weigh station for the mandatory one ton of food and supplies per Klondiker. The Canadian government feared mass starvation, since local provisions were unavailable. Although the scales are long gone, the many artifacts strewn about attest to the huge quantity of goods hauled over the pass by 30,000 Klondikers. Ahead lay the infamous Golden Stairs, once carved in ice but now exposed as enormous blocks of black rock on a 35-degree slope. While we had but one climb, the tenacious pioneers made up to 40 ascents each, repeatedly sliding down the snow-covered slope to gather another load. Some Klondikers would hire local Tlingit Indians to carry their goods at one cent a pound. Occasional disputes could escalate the rate to a dollar. The then-discarded goods are now rusting away alongside relics of the aerial tramway.

Climbing what the guidebook calls a "route, not a trail," we carefully ascended along orange marker poles. I soon relearned the importance of having proper gear. As I heaved myself over a massive rock, a shoulder strap of my vintage pack broke loose, shifting my 20-kg load and setting me off balance, fortunately to no harmful effect. The steep talus slope concealed water beneath, and mosquitoes, hitherto absent, made their annoying appearance as we approached the border.

The Summit

The border is at the summit of Chilkoot Pass. Larry and I rejoined Ed and Scott at the Canadian Ranger hut, site of the Royal North West Mounted Police post where the Mounties collected customs duty and registered the gold seekers. After our modest lunch, a family of ptarmigan led us on our careful descent over massive rocks. As we passed Stone Crib, the anchor of the aerial tramway cable, an elderly couple leaning on long wooden staves snapped our picture.

The climate changed dramatically to arid alpine. A profusion of purple flowers dominated the landscape. Skirting Crater Lake, where the Klondikers transferred their loads to sledge or boat, we climbed the ridge to Happy Camp, three kilometres downstream from the lake. A chilly but refreshing dip in Moose Creek ended my 10 hours on the trail.

Day three began with a climb to the ridge overlooking Long Lake. Cascading falls tumbled crystal-clear into its waters, glacier-topped mountains reflected in perfect symmetry on its still surface. Descending to rapids at Deep Lake, I met Jamie, a ranger on his way to help the elderly couple. The rusting skeleton of an iron-framed boat lay abandoned where the Klondikers had portaged their loads around the deep chasm ahead. In the boreal forest beyond, our footing deteriorated, exposed roots intermingling with half-round rocks.

After a pleasant lunch alongside a log cabin on Lake Lindeman, I studied the small cemetery on the esker above, where faded planks marked a dozen boulder-covered graves. Heeding the ranger's advice, I hastened on to secure two of the few desirable campsites at Bare Loon Lake. My anticipated refreshing swim was very brief, for a disagreeable cloud of loose sediment rose from the shallow bottom. After Scott's communal dinner, I relaxed and enjoyed the serene view from the helipad above the camp.

Water Egress

Since I expected only a short hike, I lingered to watch the sun rise over the nearby mountains before setting out on the root-snarled path to Bennett, terminus of the trail. Unexpectedly, I found myself plowing through deep sand deposited by the grinding of antediluvian glaciers. Briefly greeting our group brewing soup on the ridge overlooking the trail end, I descended past the stately church to meet Jack Regan, whom I had hired for our egress to Carcross via Lake Bennett. Grabbing beer from his cooler, I returned to the ridge and loudly asked the assembled hikers, "What trail is this?" At the collective reply "The Chilkoot," I distributed bottles of Chilkoot beer to the thirsty hikers.

Sharing the beer was the aforementioned elderly couple, ferried by the ranger along nine kilometres of Lake Lindeman. Ed fibbed that we had carried the beer the length of the trail, to which the 76-year-old exclaimed, "You are all crazy." Jason, a lad of 82 kg hired as their sherpa, soon told his harrowing tale of multiple climbs on the Golden Stairs, the last with an 36-kg load! He received a well-deserved Chilkoot beer.

As other hikers awaited the train, we boarded Jack's boat for the two-hour cruise to Carcross, thence to Whitehorse for a fine meal of Arctic char. All agreed that despite some excellent photo opportunities, no camera could capture the ambience of our historical hiking experience, that quintessence reserved for the mind's eye alone.

The Scales

Larry on the Golden Stairs

Jason the Sherpa

Chapter 11

Hadrian's Wall

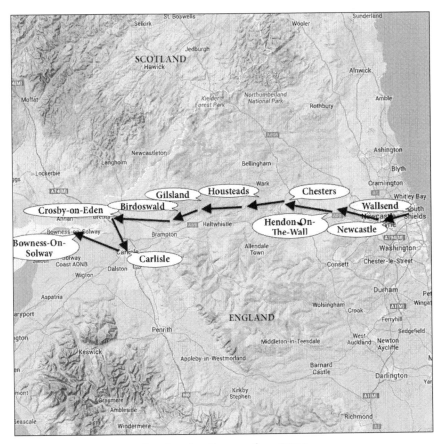

England – September 2003

Newcastle

In 122 AD, Emperor Hadrian ordered construction of a wall to inhibit the proto-"Braveheart" Scots (aka barbarians) from ravaging the northern frontier of Roman Britain. In 2001 AD, a foot-and-mouth epidemic thwarted my planned hike along Hadrian's Wall.

Not long afterward, Natural England, a U.K. government department, inaugurated a new National Trail, the 135-kilometre Hadrian's Wall Path. Officially opened in May 2003, the path is a magnet for challenge and charity walkers.

Arriving in Newcastle a few months later, I visited the tourist office for the accommodation guide and map and met my friend "Bypass Bob" Hyndman at the train station. Bob had suffered a heart attack a few years previously, and following surgery his doctor had prescribed a glass of red wine per day and a regime of regular walking. We intended to overdo both prescriptions.

The city of 260,000 has an efficient underground railway that swiftly conveyed us to Wallsend, the eastern terminus of the Roman wall and our starting point. Little of the wall remains here, the bulk of the stone having been quarried over the centuries for local buildings. A 6-metre-high reconstruction of the wall overlooks a 10-metre long by 2-metre wide excavated foundation. Since the line of the wall crosses the city, the Wall Path diverges from it to pass through industrial areas along the north bank of the River Tyne. It was a long trudge on hard tarmac, the one visual delight being the unique Gateway Millennium Bridge. Massive hydraulic rams rotate the whole structure upwards, forming a parabolic arch for ships to pass under. It's like a closed eye slowly opening. The local nickname is The Blinking Eye.

Dining at a pub, we discussed our program. "How many rain days did you schedule?" Bob asked.

"What are rain days? Don't you have rain gear?"

"Yes, but I don't enjoy walking in the wet."

I thought to myself: "As coal is to Newcastle, rain is to walking."

Village of Wall

Our second day began at Heddon-on-the-Wall, where, again, visible remains of the wall are sparse; the Roman wall is buried under the military road built between Carlisle and Newcastle in the 1700s. The path alternates from one side of the road to the other along newly acquired rights-of-way. The most visible remnants are the defensive ditch to the north and the Vallum, a boundary ditch on the south side that defined the Roman military zone. Twenty-eight kilometres of trudging brought us to the village of Wall and our lodging at The Hadrian Hotel.

Whin Sill Escarpment - The visible wall

Next morning we crossed the River North Tyne and entered Chesters Roman Fort, the garrison for the largest cavalry legion on the wall. The name is somewhat redundant for the word "Chester" is from the Latin for "military camp." Hence the profusion of "chesters" in the names of English towns such as Manchester, Winchester and Westchester. Fine ruins of the communal bath lie just outside the military enclosure, as do footings of the bridge on the far bank. A small museum displays artifacts found in the region, including those of John Clayton, a local lawyer who in the 1800s bought nearby farms to halt the quarrying of stone from the wall.

The hitherto level ground began to rise as we walked, here finding long stretches of wall extant. A succession of steep crags overlooked sheer cliffs to the north, eliminating the need for the defensive ditch. A steep climb followed by a steep descent ended at Housesteads Fort, where the Roman commandant's grand residence incorporated hypocaust-heated floors and walls. Clearly, life was good at the top.

Bob had gone ahead. As I exited the fort, the rain began and I hastened to don my gear. But as Newfies say, "There it was: gone." My gear had slipped off my straps somewhere along the path, poetic justice, no doubt. Not wanting to be soaked, I opened my emergency foil blanket and wrapped it around my shoulders. Thus attired, I entered our lodging at the Once Brewed pub to jibes of "Ah, the Spaceman has arrived." Later I learned, to my surprise and relief, that a young couple had picked up my gear 10 kilometres back and lugged it to the pub. At the nearby Twice Brewed Inn, as a party of charity walkers enlivened the evening in exotic Roman costume, I gratefully hosted a meal for my newfound friends, Angela and Conrad.

While Bob set out hiking the wall, I detoured to Vindolanda Fort, an ongoing archaeological dig where an anaerobic environment has preserved fragile organic artifacts in near-perfect condition. Recently discovered card-sized writing tablets are now regarded as the most precious artifacts of British history. The tablets tell the tale of everyday life on the frontier, evidence that a soldier's life has changed little over the centuries.

> "I have sent (?) you ... pairs of socks from Sattua, two pairs of sandals and two pairs of underpants, .. Greet ... ndes, Elpis, Iu ... enus, Tetricus and all your messmates with whom I pray that you live in the greatest good fortune."

The best-preserved remnants of the wall and its associated forts, milecastles and turrets lie in the sector from Vindolanda to Greenhead, for the steep terrain along the crags and gaps inhibited quarrying. I paid a short visit to the Roman Army Museum before ending the day's hike at Gilsland with a typically bland English country meal.

As Bob waited for the morning rains to end, I donned my recovered rain gear and set off, shortly arriving at Willowford and the massive remains of an abutment of the Roman bridge over the River Irthing. Crossing the stream on a nearby footbridge and climbing the high bank to Birdoswald Fort, I eschewed the museum and pressed on, leaving the last of the visible wall behind. Shortly after departing the hamlet of Walton, I diverged from the wall to Crosby-on-Eden, where I awaited Bob at the pub.

The West Coast

Our sixth day of hiking started on a soft path along a meander of the River Eden to Carlisle, where we parted, Bob entraining for Manchester, I trudging the city streets past Carlisle Castle to continue hiking along the Eden. Expecting a long road walk on this last stretch, I was pleasantly surprised to find a dike running along the river with a soft path atop. Feet beat, I entered the pub at Bowness-On-Solway, greeting Angela, Conrad, and other hikers of the day.

Contemplating the journey over a pint, I realized that the indiscriminate destruction of the wall is but one chapter of the story. Despite Imperial Rome's enormous economic and military power, the Roman legacy had completely dissipated within a few generations of the Legions' departure.

The defenceless Romanized Britons were easy prey to Scots and invading Saxons. Edifices tumbled, the law withered, coinage disappeared, and barter became the norm for 200 years. So complete was the obliteration of the Roman social fabric that in the eighth century the Venerable Bede attributed the construction of the wall to the ancient Scots! A cautionary tale.

Wallend

Spaceman on the wall

Bob Hyndman at Carlisle

Chapter 12

Indiana Dick and the Lost Ark of the Covenant

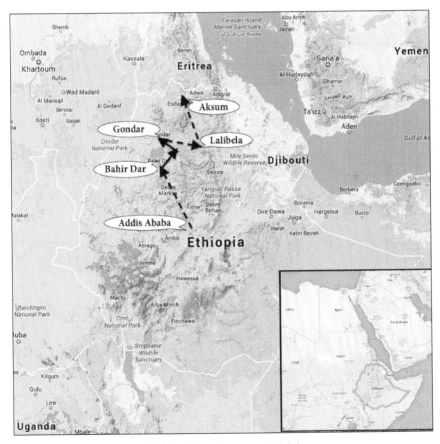

Ethiopia – January 2004

Egypt

Murky water lapped the freeboard as our felucca, white sails set, tacked across the Nile to Elephantine Island, just below the Aswan Dam. Despite the cool water beneath, there was no respite from the bright blazing sun and the scorching wind from out the Sahara. Disembarking, Danielle and I set out for the Aga Kahn's tomb, passing a nascent archaeological dig. It was the fall of 1981, and the diggers later reported a Jewish temple buried on the Egyptian island.

This unearthing became a focus for Graham Hancock's book "The Sign and the Seal," which postulated that Jewish protesters carried the Lost Ark of the Covenant through Egypt to Elephantine Island, and thence up the Blue Nile to the highlands of Ethiopia. A sizeable community of black Jews, or "Falasha," living in Ethiopia until recently and observing obsolete rites of early Judaism, lent credence to the hypothesis. To this day the Ethiopians claim that the Ark is within their borders. Every Ethiopian Orthodox church has a cloaked room, the Holy of Holies, containing replicas of the Ark of the Covenant and the tablets of the Ten Commandments, or Tabot. At the festival of Timkat during the orthodox Epiphany, each church parades its Tabot.

Addis Ababa

And so it came to pass that some 22 years on I joined my friend "Jet" Johnson in Rome, whence we flew to Addis Ababa in our quest for the Lost Ark. Not unlike Indiana Jones, but without the whip. Arriving without benefit of air or hotel reservations, we planned to wing it. An ill-advised program, for we arrived just before Timkat, the busiest festival of the year. Acclimatizing in Addis for a day, we examined the 3.5-million-year-old skeleton of Lucy, found nearby in the Great Rift Valley, cradle of humankind.

A fruitless morning followed at the modernistic steel-and-glass air terminal, as we waited patiently for a flight with our full-fare but wait-listed tickets. We chanced upon three affable Indiana Brits, Tim, Justin, and Bob, who were on the same quest but in a worse predicament, as they had only space-available tickets. With all flights booked over Timkat, they invited us to join them and drive the 1,100 km to the historic city of Aksum.

We settled into a nearby hotel, where I attempted to mitigate my jet lag with an afternoon nap. It was soon interrupted by Tim suggesting I inspect the proposed vehicle. Impatient at waiting for the elevator, I turned to walk down the stairs. Unbeknownst to me, there was a thin wall of glass in front of the stairs. It promptly shattered, inflicting a nasty gash on my right hand and other, superficial wounds to arms and legs. Binding the gash with toilet paper, I commandeered the vehicle, driving to a nearby hospital where competent medical staff applied ten sutures, making me whole again. Not an auspicious start to our quest!

Lake Tana

Nauseous from the antibiotic, and maybe suffering a little shock, I declined the offer to join the drive. The following day Jet and I boarded the last of four flights to Bahir Dar on Lake Tana. Oral history avows that the Ark was first ensconced on an island in this great lake, headwaters of the Blue Nile. A short boat journey brought us to a circular monastery where a friendly, wizened monk displayed the treasures of the small museum, including ornate silver crosses, crowns, and ancient illustrated manuscripts. The real trove, of gold and diamonds, was safely out of view, guarded by a deacon armed with a Kalashnikov submachine gun. Returning past a papyrus boat paddled by a man and wife taking their load of charcoal to market, we entered the swampy bay from which issued the Blue Nile, source of 85% of the flow of the lower Nile.

A 30-kilometre drive brought us to Blue Nile Falls, the Tis Isat or Smoking Water. Disregard Doctor Who and his fictional time machine, just fly Ethiopian Airlines to the hinterland and journey back to biblical times. As we hiked to the Portuguese Bridge spanning the chasm below the falls, we joined barefoot villagers returning from a market, goods balanced on their heads, driving cattle and donkeys with the ubiquitous wooden staff, their way of life unchanged in 2,000 years. The panorama of the falls from an elevated viewpoint was a mere vestige of our expectations, partly because it was the dry season but mainly because a recently built power-plant spillway diverts 75% of the flow.

Gondar

The following morning we set out by hired minibus on the Chinese-funded road to Gondar, 17th-century city of castles and Ethiopia's capital for 250 years. In the time-honoured tradition of buying third-world UN votes, the Chinese had financed reconstruction of the road. After five hours of pounding along the bone-jarring dirt and rock track, a few mercifully completed paved sections snagged my vote.

The location of our hotel at Gondar, directly over the plaza where the Timkat procession would pass, compensated for its shabby decor and amenities. We walked up the hill to Debre Berhan Selassie (Light of the Trinity) Church, surrounded by fortified walls and towers at the summit. Ethiopian churches are normally circular, but here an unusual rectangular structure overlay the circular foundations of an earlier church destroyed during a war with the Muslims. Allegedly built to house the Ark, the rectangular shape replicates the form of a Jewish temple. Among the bright frescoes completely covering the interior, the much-photographed ceiling depicts a Host of Angels, all with downcast expressions, contrasting with those of the locals who despite their abject poverty invariably exhibited broad smiles.

On the eve of Timkat, the colourful procession passed our balcony accompanied by a cacophony of drums, cymbals, and horns. After shooting a few photos from on high, I rushed down and sprinted ahead of the slow-moving procession, camera in hand ready to capture the elusive Tabot. Inexplicably, an official armed with a stout stave grabbed me by the arm and pulled me past the flanking soldiers into the midst of the procession, just behind the dancing nuns and immediately in front of the colourful umbrellas covering the Tabots. Unsure what to do, I danced along a bit and then turned to photograph the cloaked Tabots from an unbelievably close range. Exiting the procession, I moved ahead to the enclosure where the procession was to end at the Emperor's pool. Army guards barred entry to the enclosure, but they soon admitted foreigners, and eventually some religiously attired locals. I positioned myself beside a tree, 10 metres from the narrow gateway, and soon the procession swept by, assembling in front of a bridge leading to a small castle in the middle of the pool. With the entire enclosure now teeming with patrons, I clambered astride a stone wall, gaining an unobstructed view of the procession carrying the Tabots and ornate crosses across the bridge to the castle. There they would repose over the scum-covered water until the dawn baptism ritual.

The tide of humanity funnelled back through the gate, where a soldier equipped with a small stick and a big stick was ready to whack anyone who got out of line. As the seething mass carried me along, I felt a hand on my pocket. I yelled "Hey," whereupon the small stick came down and the soldier hauled the youngster away.

Forgoing the dawn baptism ceremony, we stopped at the pool on the way to the airport, instructing our taxi driver to remain where we had parked. We made our way through the throngs to the castle gate, finding it impossible to enter as the congregation came streaming out. A tourist informed us that in contrast to the mass bathing in the Ganges, only 30 at most had dared the fetid waters. With a flourish, the procession exited and continued up the hill. We returned to our taxi and, "there it was, gone."

Without passports, tickets, money or possessions, our quest looked doomed. We hopelessly envisioned the unknown taxi driver living a life of luxury at our expense. But as the crowd slowly dispersed, Jet espied a yellow taxi far off beside the stadium, whither we hastened. We soon learned that the police had compelled the driver to move farther from the procession. Much relieved, we continued to the airport.

Lalibela

Our aircraft landed on a plain at 1,800 metres elevation, whence we drove by minibus to Lalibela at 2,600 metres. Midway along the ascent, our progress was halted by a Timkat procession moving up the mountain. Making the best of the opportunity, we left the minibus and ran ahead in an attempt to photograph the Tabot, again shielded under colourful umbrellas.

Lalibela, sometimes called the eighth wonder of the world, is little known outside Ethiopia. The village is renowned for its monolithic churches hewn out of solid rock, described as granite in the guidebook but actually hard basalt and volcanic tuff. Amazing architectural detail adorns facades and interiors. It is important to hire a local guide to lead one through the many passages and tunnels which connect the churches. They are in two great clusters, save the cross-shaped St. George's church, which stands apart in its own deep pit. In one of the dimly lit churches, I surreptitiously photographed a shroud-covered "Ark" behind its curtain.

The following day we interrupted our viewing of the second array of churches to watch the last of the Timkat processions, that of St. Michael's Day. The colourful procession slowly advanced up the hill to the plaza above the rock-hewn churches.

Aksum

Descending to the airport next morning we picked up a hitchhiker, an Ethiopian living in Scotland who was stranded after an early morning visit to a hilltop monastery. Our newfound friend, George, was to prove invaluable in our quest after we landed at Aksum, capital of a once-mighty empire. Here lie the ruins of a palace, allegedly that of the Queen of Sheba, with an oral-historical link to the Ark. A recently discovered stela inscribed in three languages, one of them Greek, confirms conversion to Christianity in the early fourth century. Ancient royal tombs nearby are surrounded by gigantic stelae including the largest obelisk in the world, 500 tonnes of hard granite, now in pieces after a toppling in the distant past.

Continuing past the largest church in Ethiopia, the new St. Mary of Zion, built by Haile Selassie, we entered the old St. Mary's. There the keepers unveiled huge frescoes, one of which particularly pleased George. It was a Black Madonna, depicting Mary and the Christ child as black Ethiopians instead of the customary Caucasoid guise.

Between the two churches stands a small chapel, secure behind a grate of iron bars, where purportedly the Ark is concealed. George, after giving solemn assurances that we would not attempt to take photographs, arranged for us to meet the Guardian of the Ark. The minders gave a signal and the Guardian came forth, resplendent in yellow robe over a black habit, head capped with a purple-blue fez. His visage, a two-pronged beard, jet-black face, brilliant eyes, warm smile, was most worthy of a photograph, but it was not to be. The priest blessed George, touching his forehead and cheeks with his 30 cm solid gold cross, its centre embellished with rubies and sapphires. After questioning George, and presumably receiving the correct answer, the Priest blessed Jet and me, and moved back to his garden.

We strolled over to examine one of the guardhouses flanking the chapel. Jet snapped a photo of the guard with his Kalashnikov. George and I returned to the garden to question the Guardian, when suddenly he disappeared into the chapel and the minders forced us up against the grate, much to the consternation of George in view of their nearby Kalashnikovs.

Next day we went back to the site. After viewing an 800-year-old illustrated manuscript in the new church, we returned to see the Guardian. He came out to meet us and explained the previous day's discord. When Jet photographed the guard, his flash alarmed the minders who assumed we were trying to take a picture of the Guardian. Given assurances that this was not our intent, he was apologetic and again gave his blessing with his gold cross. Some 60 years of age, he had been Guardian of the Ark for 20 years. With George translating, I attempted to elicit information about the size, shape, and configuration of his charge. As we had been forewarned, he gently turned aside such questions, leaving us in the dark about the Ark. When we were ready to depart, he presented us with ash pellets from the temple's censer. George remarked that this was an exceptional honour, since many believe the ash has curative powers. With my wounded hand still festering, I chose to stick with the antibiotics.

Faced with this passionate and steadfast defence of the Mystery of the Ark, and with due consideration for the firepower of its guards, we reluctantly abandoned our quixotic quest, boarding a flight to Addis Ababa and home.

Blue Nile Falls

St George's Church

Stella at Aksum

Chapter 13
The Desert Mice – the Desert Rats, Not

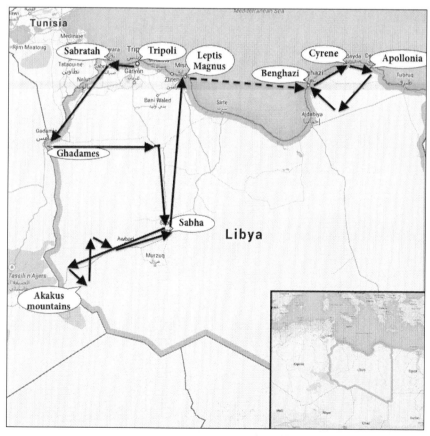

Libya – November 2004

Tripoli

I emerged from Immigration Control at Tripoli airport to be greeted by my friends Gary Anderson and Jet Johnson, our driver Mohammed, and our guide and minder Hafid Wahshy.

Unaccompanied tourist travel has been forbidden in Libya since renegade tourists attempted to smuggle plundered rock paintings out of the country. An "invitation" from a Libyan national is now a requirement for a visa. Hence the meeting with Hafid, whom I had engaged through the Internet. Gary, world traveller extraordinaire, came armed with his latest toys, including a GPS device and a hi-tech digital camera to capture photographs for his annual slide show.

Sabratah

Comfortably ensconced in a Mercedes van, we immediately drove 80 km west to Sabratah, where we were welcomed by the warm smiles of many attractive young ladies lounging in the hotel lobby. "Oh, oh," I thought, "what type of hotel is this?"

Gary raced off in a futile attempt to photograph the nearby ruins in the late afternoon light. We had arrived in Libya in the middle of the holy month of Ramadan, when the Muslim faithful fast and forego water during the daylight hours. Understandably, the custodians were unwilling to permit entrance to the ruins just as their fasting was about to end.

Meanwhile Jet, in his customary manner, approached the two remaining young ladies and silently flipped though his photo album featuring baby seals from his Greenpeace and Sea Shepherd expeditions. He departed to his spartan room unaware that the ladies spoke fluent English, being among a group of thirty Indian nurses and ten doctors billeted in the hotel. The imported medical staff bespoke our future observations that the Colonel was now directing Libya's substantial oil wealth to social needs and infrastructure.

The next morning we entered the ruins of an originally Phoenician port that became Roman after the destruction of Carthage in the third and last Punic War. After the devastation of the expansive city by earthquake in 365 AD, sand covered and preserved the ruins until they were unearthed and rebuilt by Italian archaeologists in the last century. If and when the tourist boom arrives, a magnificent theatre overlooking the sea will undoubtedly become a popular performance venue.

Libya comprises a series of stepped plateaus rising southward from the Mediterranean. We reached the first escarpment after a two-hour drive, encountering the first of many security checkpoints. Hafid presented a copy of our heavily stamped "invitation" to the sombre guard, after which Mohammed resumed our southward journey at 160 km per hour, slowing only for drifting sand and an immense camel herd crossing the road.

Ghadames

Reaching Ghadames in the late afternoon, we settled into a comfortable local house. Ghadames is the junction point of ancient routes from Tunis and Tripoli leading south to equatorial Africa, along which prodigious camel caravans conveyed salt to the sub-Sahara and brought back ivory, gold, and slaves. The tranquil old city, built around a prolific spring, is now a UNESCO heritage site. Modern government-built housing easily persuaded the inhabitants to move from their homes.

Clear water flows in channels to the mosques and communal fountains and thence to gardens, the flow strictly controlled by a unique metering system based on a "water clock." The Guardian of Water fills a bucket from a shallow well, and hangs it on a nearby peg. He ties a knot to a palm tree to alert the landowner who then diverts water from the irrigation ditch to his garden. The water drains from a hole in the bucket and when empty, the procedure is repeated for another landowner to claim is share. Although a modern clock would accomplish the same results, the method has been in use for over 3,000 years and there is no inclination to change it.

Dark, covered alleyways, providing considerable respite from the heat of the midday sun, connect the thick-walled multi-storied dwellings. Women traversed narrow ledges to socialize and market their goods on rooftops reserved for them. A pleasant lunch in a restored house gave an insight into the comfortable life of the more affluent villager.

Near sunset, we boarded a jeep and drove westward to a huge sand mountain. As the driver lighted a small campfire, we climbed a ridge, and espied several pinnacles in the distance. I plunged down the steep slope of the ridge to the basin below, then hiked to the highest of the pinnacles on a curving, scimitar-like second ridge; soon gaining my desert legs and the ability to distinguish treacherous soft, from wind-packed hard sand. Plowing through soft, collapsing sand, I reached the pinnacle to be rewarded by a magnificent sunset.

Back at the campfire, the driver asked Jet to pass him a stick, and with it brushed away ash and sand to reveal a loaf of flat bread that had been baking under the fire. The bread made a delicious accompaniment to mint tea, our now-customary evening drink given the lack of beer in this dry land.

Sabha

Our next destination, the Akakus mountains, lay 500 km to the south, but the lack of a direct road across the intervening 16,000-square-kilometre sand sea compelled a diversion: 400 km east, 400 km south to Sabha, then 400 km southwest. At Sabha, a burgeoning administration centre, we lodged in thatch-roofed huts surrounded by a menagerie of exotic animals and not-so-exotic cocks, which crowed aggressively through the night to the accompaniment of Gary's curses.

Next morning we bade farewell to Mohammed and boarded the venerable Toyota Land Cruiser of Legwy, our local driver. Four hundred kilometres southwest, at the oasis of Al Waynat, Gary brought joy to the sidewalk merchants as he bought assorted Tuareg silver jewellery.

Sahara dunes

Leaving the road, we headed south into the Akakus, an enormous landscape of sand, sand dunes, dry wadis (beds of ephemeral rivers), and rocky crags. Like Moses we wandered, seemingly aimlessly through what is now a desert but at the end of the last ice age was a fertile savannah teaming with wildlife. Ancient inhabitants carved and painted the cliffs with images of their prey and, later, their domestic livestock. The paintings and petroglyphs record climate change spanning 12,000 years, from post-glacial wet to present arid. Legwy, a Tuareg of the desert with intimate knowledge of the region, drove us to the most noteworthy sites. While Hafid served a lunch of olives, dates, and canned tuna, Legwy slept beneath a ledge sheltered from the sun. Though in plain view, he was virtually invisible cloaked in his khaki robe. Little wonder Bin Laden was still at large. About an hour before sunset, we pitched our tents and were soon dining under a brilliant night sky. The complete absence of ambient light revealed so many stars we could hardly distinguish the familiar constellations.

During our four days of wandering Gary kept editing his photographs, and before long had depleted his battery. When he attempted to recharge it through the vehicle's cigarette lighter, he found the lighter inoperable. "We must be in the only vehicle in the entire country without a cigarette lighter, they all smoke," he said in disgust. Fortunately he had a backup conventional camera, which sufficed until he could recharge his one and only battery.

In a scene Hollywood would love, Legwy sped north across the hard plain. Tongues of the nearby sand mountains whipped by at 80 km an hour, an exhilarating experience evoking images of the Long Range Desert Patrol of World War II, or with poetic license, the Desert Rats.

Ahead, north of the main highway to Sabha and a narrow irrigated field, lay a seemingly impassable range of sand mountains. We left the highway and crossed the field. Ascending through a low pass, we were soon racing along valleys, climbing ridges, and plunging down steep slopes, penetrating deep into the sand sea. As is the desert custom, we stopped to offer assistance to a French couple hiking alongside camels laden with their gear. Some 30 km into the dune field, we halted and set our camp as the low sun transformed coarse sand into globules of gold. The sun dipped below the hill, its rays a broad brush painting the clouds yellow, then gold, pink and finally a phosphorescent purple. A swath of black followed and the incandescent Milky Way appeared, bisecting the dome of luminous stars. A speedy vehicle approaching from out the dark interrupted our peaceful interlude. Not interlopers, but Tuareg friends of Legwy who were soon sipping tea, the flickering fire illuminating their turbans and robes in a scene reminiscent of ancient caravans.

Arising before dawn, I hiked to the nearest sand pinnacle, led east by the brilliant conjunction of Venus and Jupiter. As the sun broke the horizon, I conjured a silent sentry guarding the camp below. Soon under way, we paused at the rim of a precipice to photograph a small lake framed by sand and green palms. Down at the lake, as Gary haggled with vendors, I stripped and swam to the centre, finding the water briny but surprisingly cool. When I emerged, Hafid pointed to a depression where an excavated pit provided fresh water for a refreshing rinse.

Resuming our journey to a nearby dry lake, probably drained by extensive irrigation, we found ourselves pushing in unison to free the vehicle from the embrace of soft sand. With the front hubs defective, Hafid abandoned the plan to visit a renowned coloured lake. We returned to Sabha and to Gary's favourite, the motel of the crowing cocks.

Leptis Magnus

Next day Omar, our new driver, speedily traversed the 900 km to the coast. As the desert gave way to extensive olive groves, we reached the ancient metropolis of Leptis Magnus. Rebuilt by the Byzantines after the earthquake of 365 AD and then abandoned, the city was buried in the sands until the early 20th century. Colossal columns of pink granite lay scattered about, hard stone quarried at distant Aswan in Egypt. The metropolis rivalled Rome in splendour, wealth, and decadence, with steam baths, forums, temples, villas, lighthouses, markets, triumphal arches, an amphitheatre seating

20,000, and that most peculiar of Roman institutions, communal toilets. Numerous dwellings with hypocaust-heated floors and walls attested to the luxurious lifestyle of the citizens, not to be confused with that of the slaves who toiled at the furnace.

Cyrene

After a short flight to Benghazi, we were soon strolling about the ruins of Cyrene, perched on an escarpment overlooking the coastal plain. From beneath a cliff issued a prolific stream, which the original Greek settlers channelled to the temple of Apollo. Across the gorge stood a stately villa, occupied by Rommel during World War II. The stream supplied ample water for his Afrika Corps.

Founded about 620 BC, the city eventually matched Athens in splendour, as attested by the temple of Zeus, similar, but somewhat larger than the Parthenon. Descending to the port city of Apollonia, we passed thousands of catacombs hewn into the cliffs and stopped for an eerie lunch in a large crypt converted to a restaurant.

The museum at Apollonia houses an impressive collection of statues and mosaics, including an outstanding Venus discovered but two years ago by the museum guide. Comparing the Roman and Greek mosaics, he convinced us that the early Greek designs were the finest. We climbed a gentle hill to a gargantuan cistern where, torch in hand, I descended as if to the River Styx. At the port, now blocked with silt, lay the remnants of a towering lighthouse, formerly second only to the beacon of ancient Alexandria.

To Tripoli

Antiquities behind, we drove south in search of the Great Man-Made River, at the time the world's largest engineering project. A gigantic pipeline, five metres in diameter, delivers water to the coast from vast aquifers under the Sahara. The project is not without controversy, for mining the water could lower the water table and might spell the end of the desert oases, although Libyan engineers believe the aquifers hold the equivalent of 200 years of the Nile's flow. A fierce dust storm arose, thwarting our quest. Visibility was reduced to 100 metres and then to 5. We slowed to a crawl, then halted when silent spectres, a herd of camels, loomed out of the dust and crossed the road.

Our driver became disoriented, and was ready to turn back when Gary transformed his GPS toy into a useful tool, showing that we were paralleling the main highway. Intercepting a crossroad, we joined the highway and drove northwest to Benghazi arriving at the fish market just before sunset. Bedlam reigned as vendors, buyers, and cooks frantically bartered, for sunset marked the end of Ramadan. Soon the site was almost deserted, leaving us to enjoy our fresh seafood dinner in tranquillity.

The dust storm long delayed our flight to Tripoli, but provided an opportunity to speak with some real Desert Rats, British veterans returning from the Remembrance Day ceremony at Tobruk. After hearing their harrowing tales of warfare in the desert, we felt compelled to change our appellation to Desert Mice.

Approaching Tripoli at 4 a.m., I remarked, "Well at least we'll have a fast ride into town, there'll be no traffic at this hour." How wrong I was. The streets were clogged with cars, the shops open and the walkways teeming with celebrants marking the end of fasting. After a short sleep we walked to the Green Square, site of the balcony favoured by both Mussolini and Gaddafi to address the masses. Here we joined families in posing for photos amid a variety of colourful settings, most notably one with me astride a docile white stallion. All agreed that Libya is interesting, safe, and friendly as we bade farewell to go our separate ways, I to France, Gary to Malta, Jet to Rome and home.

Tuareg Silver

Apollonia Theatre

Sand Sea

Ghadafi Not

Chapter 14
Wales "Madness"

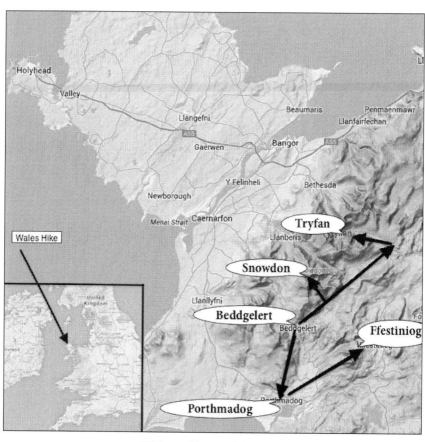

Wales – November 2005

Wayfarers in Wales

Following the London funeral of Group Captain D.H. Burnside, wartime commanding officer of 427 Squadron, I joined 24 Irish hikers in Wales, driving with them to the picturesque village of Beddgelert, at the confluence of two small rivers whose names I can neither spell nor pronounce. The lodging of the Wayfarers hillwalkers comprised five well-furnished houses in an estate only 100 metres from the village centre. I had first hiked with the Wayfarers in Wicklow, Ireland in 2001, as recounted in Chapter 5. Stashing our gear, we hurried to the nearest pub, which to our disappointment had stopped serving food. We quickly moved on to the Saracen pub, arriving barely in time to order a meal.

The weather forecast the next day conveyed the bad news of lashing wind and rain, along with good news of unseasonable warmth, for the strong winds were blowing from the south. Congregating at the base of Tryfan, a steep rocky crag in Snowdon National Park, we began climbing the lower slope on stone steps. During the Great Depression the government hired unemployed miners to laboriously build these as a make-work project.

An asthmatic girl had forgotten her inhalator and decided to turn back. As our leader Keith Mooney dealt with her, we pressed on, inadvertently following a team of elite blue-clad mountaineers. Soon we were up against a narrow slot, faced with a near-vertical ascent. I asked myself, "What is a 65-year-old retired pilot doing here?" Soon our leader regained the front, and we descended to find a somewhat gentler route. The operative word is "somewhat, " for the going was very steep, and the risk of falling rock much present in my thoughts. "Scrambling," they call it. I call it madness. Passing through another narrow steep slot, we eventually reached the summit. There the fierce wind lashed against two gigantic monoliths known as Adam and Eve.

As I descended the far side, an encounter with a slippery rock took me down on my backside, with a slight twist to my knee. That was enough of an excuse for me to abandon the ascent of another crag enshrouded in mist. Leaving the group after lunch, I made a relaxed descent down the cirque, arriving at the Mountain Rescue Station just before the heavy rain. A notice in the hut warned of gusts of 60 to 70 mph at the summit. When the rain-drenched hikers arrived several hours later, a few remarked, "You made the right decision."

Sightseeing

On Sunday I decided to forgo the hike to let my knee recover, and joined the sightseeing group bound for Porthmadog. At that port town we boarded a narrow-gauge steam train for the climb to Ffestiniog. This is reputedly the oldest operating railway company in the world, the track purpose-built to haul slate from the quarries above. I later learned from the driver that the first steam locomotive was in use only from 1863. Before that time, the loaded cars descended by gravity and the empty cars were drawn uphill by horses.

Contrary to our expectation of a music festival, there was nothing happening in Ffestiniog. So we followed Inese Kupla, a lovely Latvian tourist, 1.5 km to the slate quarry and museum. Donning hard hats, we descended by funicular to the deep mine caverns. A recorded commentary related the miners' tasks at each of the 10 chambers. Clearly they had a very tough and austere existence. Candles bought with their own meagre wages dimly illuminated the slate blocks as they toiled 12-hour shifts in the dark, dank caverns.

After touring the museum, we returned by steam train to the port and thence back to Beddgelert. There we learned that the hiking group had returned to the village at 2 p.m., having quit their hike in the face of driving rain and very high winds. As it happened, our sightseeing group had enjoyed fair weather throughout our excursion.

Mount Snowdon

On Monday we drove to the base of Mount Snowdon, highest point in England and Wales. We mustered in three groups. One set off on a circuitous route. The hard hikers climbed a hill known as The Crib, from which they would proceed along a razorback ridge to the top. Moments after they set off, a gust of wind persuaded one of them that discretion was the better part of valour. He returned to join those of us climbing the easy Pyg Track along stone pathways and steps.

As we reached the summit, the brisk wind allowed only a brief moment for the requisite photo op. Of the 10 hard hikers attempting the ridge scramble, only two made it across. The others turned back and followed in our footsteps.

Rather than return to the car park, I decided to walk directly to Beddgelert. At the point where I had planned to turn left, the wind was so overpowering that I decided to keep to the path, crouching low along a narrow ridge to avoid being swept over the cliff. The wind abated as I descended to the road. To avoid a lengthy road walk, I climbed to make my way across fields and pastures, eventually emerging in the centre of the village directly behind the Saracen pub.

Despite the wind and rain, I thoroughly enjoyed the mini-vacation of sightseeing and well-organized hikes.

Climbing a Crag

Steam Train

Scrambling

Chapter 15
Hiking the Baja, from Sea to Sea

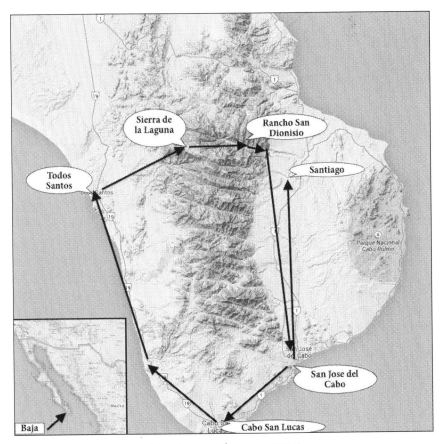

Mexico – February 2006

San Jose del Cabo

Arriving by air at San Jose del Cabo on the southern tip of Mexico's 1,100-kilometre Baja California peninsula, I joined retired airline pilot Ed Wight at Larry Dekker's spectacular oceanside condo. The three of us had hiked the Chilkoot Trail together two and a half years previously.

The next morning Larry drove us north to sites he had recently discovered, of which most tourists and locals were unaware. Our first stop was a massive boulder sitting on the bedrock of a dry riverbed, nearly spherical, 7 metres in diameter. Its western face was covered by prehistoric rudimentary paintings of hands and obscure geometric forms. Raging torrents had tumbled this "erratic" rock from its origin in mountains far to the west, where we planned to hike in the following days. Ancient inhabitants likely regarded it as a sacred site.

Continuing further into the hinterland, we hiked up a rugged stream to a deep pool where we stripped and plunged into clear water. Refreshed, we returned downstream, where Ed and Larry lounged in a shallow pool continuously replenished with hot water springing from granite rocks along a major geological fault.

Last stop before the beer was "Tombstone City," an early Spanish graveyard overlooking the oasis of Santiago, replete with wooden crosses, houses for the dead, and ornate tombs. We half-expected Clint Eastwood to appear on horseback.

That evening we met our other two hiking companions, Jaap Zwaaan, retired mining engineer, and Dave Vanderwerf, semi-retired construction contractor. Despite a chronically painful knee, Dave was keen to take on the challenge.

Todos Santos

After an hour-and-a-half drive west through Cabo San Lucas and thence north on the coastal highway, we stopped for a liquid lunch at Art and Beer. Sipping what must have been the world's largest Caesar cocktail, we marvelled at the many species of birds that flew in and about the cactus garden.

A short drive on a garbage-strewn road ended at Fisherman's Beach. Humpback whales cavorted offshore and 7-metre boats lolled about awaiting a big one. No, not whales, but a big ocean swell. When it came, the boatmen gunned their outboard motors to ride the wave and power their boats high up the sandy beach on the breaking surf.

As the others drove off I dipped my boots in the Pacific, then set out on a 6-km hike to the village of Todos Santos. Our lodging for the night was the delightful Casa Bentley, where thick walls of local stone and expansive trees provided respite from the desert heat. Wineglasses in hand, we listened attentively as the proprietor, Professor Bob Bentley, summarized the geology of the mountains we would be traversing. It is essentially uplifted crystalline granite that had been intruded by younger volcanic rock as the Pacific plate subducted under the North American plate.

Sergio, of Todos Santos Eco Adventures, followed with a briefing on our forthcoming four-day hike into the nature reserve of Sierra de la Laguna. Larry had contracted Sergio to guide us and provide logistic support for the excursion. Afterward we enjoyed a fine dinner at the renowned Hotel California, ending with a cake in honour of Larry's birthday.

The climb to Sierra de la Laguna

Forgoing a boring walk along a dusty road, we drove to altitude 480 metres in the Sierra de la Laguna foothills. Unloading the van, we left our personal gear with Sergio's Louisiana-born wife Bryan and his father Sergio Sr. They remained behind to supervise the loading of the gear and supplies on Pedro's mule train, which was late arriving.

Hefting my daypack burdened with 4½ litres of water and emergency provisions, I set out up the narrow track. We soon spread out, with me in the lead, for on this 1,500-metre ascent each must find his comfortable pace. As we climbed, the lowland scrub and cactus gave way to an amazing variety of vegetation, palms, conifers, and deciduous trees, including my favourite, the broad shady oak.

Not yet acclimatized, I began feeling the heat and my pace eventually slowed. Larry the Flying Dutchman passed me as I rested on large rocks beneath a cooling oak. Sergio had assured us at the evening briefing that we would not encounter any snakes, for they were hibernating. Continuing my climb, I narrowly avoided stepping on a 70-cm red-spotted snake, sans rattler and sluggish. Sergio later informed me that it was a harmless gopher snake.

After a final steep slope the path descended to an open meadow, where Larry awaited. I doffed my boots and cooled off in the shade. Presently Ed arrived, followed by Sergio and his assistant Mauricio, having passed Dave and Jaap some time before. After a long wait, I decided to go back to check on their progress. I found the pair slowly descending to the meadow, exhausted, for they had been without water for the past hour. I had an extra 1½-litre bottle that I gave them to share, and gave Dave one of my walking sticks, which he very much appreciated.

Arriving at our campsite on the far side of another broad meadow, we scrounged about for firewood while waiting for the mule train. Sergio showed us our water supply, a thin trickle filling several slimy pools. He designated the upper, deeper pool for drinking and the lower for washing. Presently the mule train arrived, hoofs clattering through the grungy stream; our drinking water! Cooking table and tents erected, Ed, the Master of Fire, ignited a great blaze. It was to last throughout our three-night campout. Gustavo, a park ranger, visited the camp after dinner and led us to a supply of clean water issuing from a spring in the middle of the meadow.

From sea to sea

At 1,800 metres, under a clear sky, the air cooled during the night to just below freezing. After breakfast we retraced our steps to the first meadow, then hiked along a shaded path to El Picacho, the second-highest peak of the Sierra. Our exertions were rewarded with a spectacular panoramic view of the Pacific to the west and the Sea of Cortez to the east. From sea to sea, so to speak, by seeing!

Descending from the summit, we approached a lesser but far steeper pinnacle. It was walking sticks down and "All hands to the pump," or more succinctly "All hands to the wall," as we grasped the great granite boulders and scrambled to the apex. An 800-metre cliff dropped to the west. After a brief lunch, we descended the precarious terrain, very, very carefully, and returned to camp.

That evening under a brilliant canopy of stars, Sergio gave an illuminating talk on the prominent constellations overhead and elaborated on the mythology conjured by the Greeks.

The waterfall

Continuing down the grungy creek that watered our campsite, we overtook and passed a group of strolling youngsters. Cautioned by Sergio to keep our boots dry, we shuffled over slippery, water-polished boulders. Imperceptibly, the trickle swelled to a full-fledged stream. Three kilometres downstream, a huge angular boulder barred the way. Grasping the sidewall, we slid down a steep incline, landing on coarse gravel near a shallow pool of clear water. Beyond plunged a 9-metre waterfall, which we skirted by scrambling down the canyon wall. Ed was first to strip and dive into the frigid water, possibly winning the world title for briefest swim on record.

I returned to the upper pool and stripped for a bracing dip with shampoo and soap. Presently the youngsters arrived, one youth nearly coming to grief when he slid down the incline fast enough to land with a painful thud. After a leisurely lunch, we carefully ascended the slippery incline to return to camp. Larry, Ed, and Dave left first, followed by Jaap, then me and Sergio some time later. Sergio pressed on to catch up with the group, while I climbed at an unhurried pace along the picturesque stream.

At 2 km from our turnaround I met Dave and Sergio. They asked whether I had seen Jaap. "Not since he climbed out of the canyon." Dave and I decided to wait, in the unlikely event that Jaap had somehow been left behind. After 20 minutes the leader of the youths appeared, and we asked if anyone had seen a gringo. "If it is the one with the cowboy hat, he is ahead." With that positive, but erroneous, information, we continued up to the camp. "Where is Jaap?" Sergio asked on our arrival. Fearing the worst, Mauricio and I returned immediately to the canyon, while Sergio assembled gear and Larry made for the ranger station to initiate rescue procedures. Partway down the valley, Mauricio announced that Jaap was on his way. The only man with a GPS, he had made a 90-degree turn in the canyon and followed another stream for about a kilometre before he realized his mistake and turned about. This non-event was a lesson on the hazards of relying on a GPS without taking due cognizance of map and terrain.

Eastward exit

I arose at 6:30 with the thermometer registering minus 4 Celsius. A brisk shake dislodged chunks of ice from my tent. After a hearty breakfast we packed our gear for mule transport back to Todos Santos and prepared to hike to the Sea of Cortez. Our pickup point was 12 km east as the crow flies. Not being crows, we followed Gustavo, the park ranger, whom Sergio had hired to guide us on a circuitous route along the intervening ridges and valleys.

The well-trod path first took us southeast over relatively gentle terrain, sheltered from the sun by verdant forest. Again we spread out, each hiker finding his comfortable pace for the multiple climbs and descents. At an opening in the forest, Gustavo halted for the group to assemble. Perched above a cliff face, we gazed at the distant sea. Telescopic walking sticks now in hand, we began a steep descent. At the bottom we immediately ascended another ridge, the path but a third of a metre wide.

On the other side of this razorback ridge, the trees thinned as we descended. Four hundred metres below, an oasis of tall palms nestled in a deep valley. Arriving at the stream after three hours of hiking, I shed my boots and laid my socks out to dry while awaiting the others. Presently Sergio arrived with cheese and bread for our paltry lunch.

The path onward, obliterated by floodwaters, was not readily evident amid huge boulders. Fortunately we had a guide who led us safely up and away from an inviting but hazardous route. From a lofty height, Gustavo pointed out the track below, with but one more climb ahead. The narrow path slithered steeply down an eroded granite nose. The last of the oaks gave way to desert cacti and the temperature rose to 30 Celsius under a scorching sun.

As Dave struggled to traverse a dry riverbed obstructed by immense boulders, it became apparent that the steep descents had inflamed his knee, causing intense pain. He endured it without complaint. We reached the main valley and walked along the high bank, sheltered from the sun by the scrub forest. Eight hours after our start we emerged from the bush at Rancho San Dionisio, where the vivacious Bryan dispensed cold Pacifico beer as Ed remarked: "You are the highlight of the trip!"

Larry gave thanks to Sergio for a fabulous experience and adventure.

Big Rock

Pacific Start

Seeing - Sea to Sea

Chapter 16
Pounding Patagonia

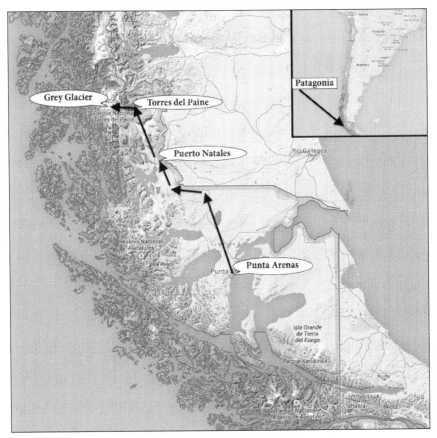

Chile – December 2006

Santiago

A tedious one-and-a-half-hour cattle queue followed my overnight American Airlines flight from Dallas to Santiago, Chile. Contributing to the lengthy delay was the need to pay a US$132 "reciprocity" fee imposed in retaliation for the Canadian government's levy of a visa charge on Chilean nationals.

At about the same distance from the equator as Los Angeles, and with a similar climate, Santiago has a similarly severe smog problem. Unlike Los Angeles, it has a well-developed transit system including four subway lines. The city is remarkably European, although the friendly inhabitants seem somewhat short in stature. After touring the old city, I stopped at the fish market and then crossed a swift-flowing river to the main market, where every conceivable article was for sale.

I walked to the base of Cerro San Cristobal, a large hill surmounted by a statue of the Virgin, and began climbing a well-trod path under the beating sun. A hundred metres above the city, I topped the smog layer and beheld the hitherto hidden snowcapped mountains to the east.

Punta Arenas

Two days later I boarded a Lan Chile flight to Punta Arenas, a port city on the Straits of Magellan and the world's southernmost city of 100,000 or more inhabitants. Amid the contemporary buildings are several luxurious mansions built by sheep and cattle barons at the end of the 19th century. Next day I joined Dave and Eduardo, from Switzerland, and our guide Mauricio, from Andes Mountain Expeditions, for our drive to the north. We passed a live minefield, remnant of a 1970s border dispute and evidence that hiking along the Argentine border could be hazardous.

Torres del Paine

A three-hour journey across the pampas ended at Puerto Natales, a nondescript town caught between the frontier era and the 21st century. The next morning we set off on the three-hour drive to Torres del Paine National Park. En route and in the park, we saw a veritable menagerie of wildlife: ostrich, flamingo, skunk, hawk, giant condor, and a lowland species of llama. A view across a lake presented a picture-postcard view of our objective, the Torres del Paine or Towers of Blue. "Paine" is apparently an aboriginal name for blue, as in glacier blue.

After the ranger's briefing, we crossed a narrow steel bridge and drove to our campsite, where we dropped our packs with Pedro, proprietor of Andes Mountain Expeditions. Outfitted in my venerable army-surplus gear, I was severely outclassed as Dave and Eduardo donned the latest in hi-tech mountaineering equipment and microfibre apparel. Given their relative size and appearance, Mauricio dubbed them Batman and Robin.

We set off slowly up the W circuit, so named for the shape of the track into the valleys. As we began the climb over glacier moraine, I pulled ahead and after a descent to a river stopped to await the group. Resuming the climb, now through beech forest, I reached the boulder-strewn route to the towers, and chanced upon a young couple who had sat opposite me on the flight from Santiago. Scrambling upward amid the giant boulders, I crossed the lip of the terminal moraine, stunned by the view before me: a cirque-bound green lake fed by a hanging glacier over a vertical cliff, surmounted by three vertical spires of pink granite, their peaks feathered by windswept clouds. Lunching on a boulder with binoculars in hand, I spied two climbers on the vertical face of the furthermost spire. Reluctantly leaving this amazing vista, I began the descent, meeting Mauricio, Dave, and Eduardo ascending. Having reached the top in three hours, and mindful of my wobbly knees, I continued down, reaching the camp in about three and a half hours.

Pedro, handed me a cold beer as I admired the large dining and cooking tents he had erected. I remarked, "It surely would be nice to have a shower," whereupon Pedro pointed out the camp facilities beyond a line of trees. What a delightful surprise for a campground, spotless toilets and hot showers! While we hikers sipped fine Chilean wine, Pedro and his cook prepared a sumptuous dinner on the barbecue. Appetite and thirst satiated, I ducked into my tent just as soft rain began to fall.

Last-minute vacancies having materialized at the "refugio," we left our sleeping pads and tents behind as we prepared for the short hike to Refugio Los Cuernos a large cabin with bunk beds, bathrooms, and dining facilities. Batman and Robin loaded their hi-tech packs. My gear went into a green garbage bag for transport by my porter. The track reminded me of the Chilkoot Trail, with footing varying from round rocks to sharp rocks, mud, clay, and tangled roots. This being Patagonia, where four seasons can be experienced in a single day, it was rain gear on, rain gear off, rain gear on again. The lower slopes were ablaze with "firebrush" sprouting brilliant red flowers. A four-hour trek brought us to Refugio Los Cuernos whose common room soon filled with rain-drenched campers. Though Chile is home to some of the world's finest grass-fed beef, the cook managed to transform the meat into something resembling shoe leather.

Daybreak brought improved weather as we hiked to the ranger's hut, where we stowed our packs for the climb to Frenchman's Valley. Initially gentle, the path deteriorated into another boulder field as the wind began to freshen. Ice crashed periodically from the great hanging glacier on the far side of the valley. At an exposed col, I sheltered from near-gale-force winds behind immense boulders as I awaited our group. Presently they arrived, and we carried on climbing through a sheltered forest path, thence upward along an exposed stream until the force of the wind caused a halt. Ahead lay the spectacular Cuernos Diablo, another pink granite intrusion topped with crowns of black basalt, whence the name "Horns of the Devil."

Turning about, we carefully descended the rock field and crossed a suspension bridge over a raging river. The remainder of this day's 25-km hike lay over a gentle earthen path, largely devoid of the aforementioned rocks and roots. The tramping of countless hikers had eroded the path into a trench a third of a metre deep, whence my title Pounding Patagonia.

As we approached another valley, fierce winds whipped the lake below into a frenzy, the low sun creating the rarely seen phenomenon of a horizontal rainbow. A profusion of firebrush framed the spectacular Horns as we approached Refugio Pehoe, modern, spacious, and spotlessly clean. Dinner was a very tasty dish of turkey, accompanied by boxed Chilean wine.

Grey Glacier

Next morning we trekked to Grey Glacier along a meandering path of multiple ascents and descents. Arriving at a lookout blasted by strong winds; we beheld the first calved icebergs. The glacier looked close at hand, but the appearance was very deceptive. It was another two hours hike to Refugio Grey. Although the refugio was rather rudimentary, the staff was very friendly and helpful. Stashing my gear, I hiked to a nearby promontory for a photo of the glacier, but found photography impossible with the rain and wind blasting my lens.

The following day we hiked along a narrow path to overlook the face of the glacier. A reverberating boom sounded the calving of a huge chunk of ice. The deep chasms and crevasses at the glacier front gave renewed and vibrant meaning to the colour known as glacier blue. We boarded a much-delayed ferry by zodiac and motored to about 100 metres from the glacier face. Sipping a pisco sour chilled by glacier ice, I asked a group of Ruskie day-trippers, "What, no vodka?" Savouring scotch whisky, they were quick to inform me that they were not Russian but Ukrainian aircrew, flying a heavy cargo Ilyushin on an Antarctic resupply mission. Naturally, we aviators toasted each other with exuberant rapport as the vessel returned to the other end of the lake. Disembarking by zodiac, we walked for 20 minutes across the pebble beach to our vehicle. Three hours later we arrived at Puerto Natales just after midnight, ending a very fine hiking experience.

Shortly afterward I returned to Santiago, where I planned to meet my friend Jet Johnson for a flight to Easter Island.

Towers of Blue

Aircrew at the Grey Glacier

Chapter 17
Enigmatic Easter Island

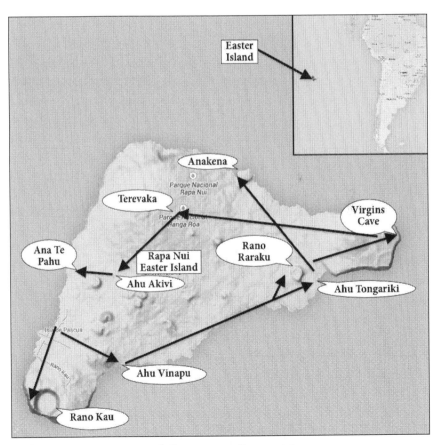

Chile – December 2006

Santiago, Chile

Rocks. Big chiselled rocks. Stones, and piles of stones. Over the years I have beheld a great number of the world's iconic stones, including the pyramids of Egypt and Mesoamerica; the jigsaw walls at Cusco, Peru; the granite obelisks of Aswan, Egypt; the megalithic tombs of Malta and Ireland; the Great Wall of China; the Parthenon; Angkor Wat; and Stonehenge, to name only some. But it remained an abiding ambition of mine to see at first hand the stone statues of the mysterious and enigmatic Easter Island.

Following my Patagonia hike, I joined my friend Jet Johnson in Santiago, where we boarded Lan Chile for a five-hour flight straight west across the Pacific, to what is arguably the most remote habitation on the planet.

Rapa Nui

We arrived late evening during a tropical downpour. It was any port in the storm, and we booked lodging from one of the agents trolling for customers at the airport. Finding the hotel rather dismal, I perused the guidebook next morning and arranged a room at Hotel O'Tai, a short stroll from the harbour and reputed the finest on the island. Notwithstanding, an early stroll proved somewhat hazardous, as what appeared to be a sidewalk was a covered ditch with great gaping holes in the concrete. After settling in, we walked a kilometre to the museum for an informative overview of the history and culture of Rapa Nui, as latter-day Polynesians called the island.

The island is roughly triangular in shape, 30 km at the base and 18 km along the sides, with an extinct volcano at each apex. "Ahu," or raised ceremonial platforms, are common throughout Polynesia, but it is only on Easter Island that gigantic representative statues have been erected, presumably caricatures of ancestral settlers. Colonized by an extended family of Polynesian seafarers around 400 AD, the island soon supported an estimated 10,000 inhabitants, ruled by a strict hierarchy of hereditary elites. Blessed with fertile soil and a benign climate, Rapa Nui yielded food with minimal human effort. The cult of the "moai," enormous stone statues of torso and head, probably began primarily as ancestral veneration, but later evolved as a means of keeping the underclass under control. As they say in the military, "If it moves salute, if it doesn't, paint it." Ultimately, the transport and erection of increasingly large effigies consumed all the trees on the island. The ensuing soil erosion and crop failure resulted in a revolt in 1680. Protesters deliberately toppled most moai during the fierce tribal wars that followed. The population had plummeted to about 4,000 by 1722, when the island was first sighted by Europeans. It was an Easter Sunday, and the Dutch captain gave the island its name.

Also unique in Polynesia are tablets bearing a hieroglyphic script. With no Rosetta Stone available, it is unlikely the script will ever be deciphered. The last elites capable of reading it were carted off by Peruvian slavers in 1870, along with another 2,000 souls.

Moai

A short stroll to the beach brought us our first glimpse of the moai, their sightless gaze taking in the grazing horses so common throughout the island. The coastal moai all face landward, presumably to impart to the clan their "mana," or spiritual power. A short walk past the colourful cemetery brought us back to the small harbour, where we dined on fresh-caught seafood.

We passed the airport in our rented jeep, taking the road along the south coast where derelict ahu and toppled moai lined the shore. The ahu are the slopping stone platforms on which the moai stand. Evidently, the platforms needed at least as much labour to build as the moai they supported. More than 900 moai bestrew the island, including those abandoned during construction or transport. Rounding a small bay near the eastern peak, we came upon a line of fifteen gargantuan moai on the enormous Ahu Tongariki. As I trespassed on the platform, Jet shot a photo of me, midget-like near a ten-metre moai with a seven-tonne stone hat atop its head.

Toppled after the revolt of the working class and later scattered by a powerful tsunami in 1960, the moai were re-erected in 1992 by a Japanese crane manufacturer. Nearby lay a row of stone hats lacking their statues, possibly because the statues were too unstable, or maybe because the restorers were unsure which hat belonged to which moai.

On a hill nearby stood a solitary moai with a plaque commemorating Thor Heyerdahl and his Kon-Tiki expedition. Heyerdahl speculated that South Americans might have reached the island by reed rafts, a theory rejected by most scholars today. However, evidence supporting a South American presence is the exceptional stonework of Ahu Vinapu, which bears astonishing similarities to the stonework of Peru. Unlike stone walls elsewhere on the island, these walls are trapezoidal, a form which provides great stability in earthquake-prone Peru. Although the current population is clearly of Polynesian origin, only 111 inhabitants survived the Peruvian slaver raids. Genetic evidence would not necessarily be decisive in resolving the debate. (*Note 1)

After a hike up the nearby volcanic cone, and a dip in the crystal-clear ocean, we enjoyed a cold beer at the concession stand amid the palms at Anakena.

Exploring

Next morning we drove south to Rano Kau, the nearest volcanic crater, its floor a caldron of freshwater and reeds. Perched on the rim of the caldera, overlooking the sea, is the reconstructed village of Orongo, replete with low, dark, stone houses and mythical beasts carved in basalt. It was from here that the cult of the Birdman became preeminent as a means of dividing scarce resources after the overthrow of the moai elite. Nominees from each clan would descend the shoreline cliff and swim across shark-infested waters to a rocky islet. The first to return with an unbroken bird's egg gained a year's supremacy for his clan.

We drove to the easternmost volcano, where Jet sheltered in the jeep as I hiked a rutted track along the flank in search of the Virgin's Cave. Pale skin being prized, young maidens were ensconced for half a year in a cliffside cave before being presented as mates to the nobility. Soaked thrice by passing showers, I crossed a narrow eucalyptus forest to emerge onto a wasteland of red volcanic soil cut with deep ravines. Scattered about were shards of black obsidian, the volcanic glass used by stone-age peoples as cutting tools.

Holding on tenuously, I peered over the cliff edge but could find no evidence of the cave. I learned later that the opening was well below, with ropes and rappelling gear required for access. Turning about, I hiked to the summit, thence back to the jeep, my mission unfulfilled.

Rejoining Jet, I engaged the four-wheel drive and powered up the muddy track to Terevaka, the northernmost volcano and the island's highest point. Archaeologically indifferent, the summit nevertheless afforded a vista encompassing the entire island. Descending westward, we examined Ahu Akivi, where seven moai stood in a precise north-to-south alignment. Unique among the erect moai, they faced the sea, and the setting sun.

Resuming our descent, we chanced upon Ana Te Pahu, a large lava-tube cave containing extensive interior fortifications. Likely inhabited during the clan wars, it later provided refuge from the Peruvian slavers. We concluded the day with an easy drive to the village for a lobster dinner at the ocean's edge.

The Quarry

Next morning we diverted from the paved southern coastal road along a short dirt track to the mother lode of moai, the quarry at Rano Raraku. Scores of partially buried moai littered the lower slopes of the volcanic cone, with nearly 400 moai catalogued nearby. Further up the slope lay the quarry. Ancient craftsmen used hard basalt chisels to carve the statues from the relatively soft volcanic tuff. A number of incomplete statues, including a 22-metre giant, lay in situ. The excessive demands of its construction may have contributed to the revolt against the elite, as in "Enough is enough!"

While Jet strolled about the lower slope searching for an inimitable statue portrayed on a postcard, I scrambled up to the lip of the crater. As on the exterior, half-buried moai were strewn about the inner slope above a lake of fresh water and reeds. Climbing past deep notches from which the statues had been hewn, I came to a gap in the crater's wall presenting a bird's-eye view of the 15 silent sentries at Ahu Tongariki. While archaeologists speculate that the moai were delivered either prone on rollers or "walked" with ropes, it is an enduring mystery how they were transported up the steep slope and over the crater's lip.

Returning to the crater's exterior, I joined Jet in the search for his elusive moai. Each moai has distinctive features, save for the common characteristic of elongated ears. A distinctively configured moai with its head inclined at an angle to the torso attracted our attention. Following extensive comparison with the postcard, it proved, when viewed in profile, to be the moai of Jet's quest.

My friend Gary Anderson, who had accompanied Jet and me to Libya, had visited Easter Island some years previously. He suggested that if I were alone at this incredible site I would hear spirits, as he had. Whoo! Whoo! Well I neither heard nor felt the presence of spirits, but I most certainly observed evidence of a society run amok in a spiral of self-destruction. What was the man thinking when he ordered the last tree felled? Then it was off home and a look in the mirror.

*Note 1 : The Globe and Mail -23 October 2014

Genetic data on 27 Easter Island natives indicated that interbreeding between the Rapa Nui and native people in South America occurred roughly between 1300 and 1500. "We found evidence of gene flow between this population and Native American populations, suggesting an ancient ocean migration route between Polynesia and the Americas," said geneticist Anna-Sapfo Malaspinas of the Centre for GeoGenetics at the University of Copenhagen, who led the study.

"Birdman" Isle

Jet & Moi in situ

Jet at Tongariki

Dick & Moi

Chapter 18
In the Footsteps of Alexander Mackenzie

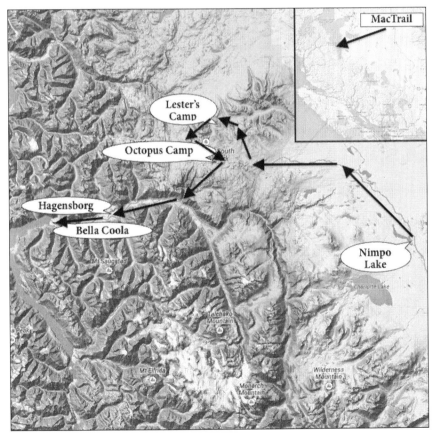

Canada – August 2007

Alex MacKenzie
from Canada
by land
22ᵈ July 1793

So reads the inscription Alexander Mackenzie painted on a rock near Bella Coola after his epic journey from Montreal to the Pacific. The subsequent publication of his journal motivated contemporary politicians to expand Canada's boundaries "from sea unto sea." It also inspired the Americans to launch the Lewis and Clark expedition to the Pacific. My objective was to follow in Alexander's footsteps, along the route of his penultimate trek across the Cariboo.

North to the trailhead

To that end I met with "Blue," of Wild Earth Adventures, at Jericho Beach in Vancouver. Joining us for the short briefing were my friend Steve Mackey from the Irish Wayfarers hiking club, as well as two lady hikers from England, Janet and Chris. Steve and I departed to buy a few missing supplies, including bear spray and bug repellent.

Next morning we drove to Squamish, picking up Blue's assistant Jessica, and continued past Whistler and Pemberton to Lillooet on the Fraser River. Most notable since my last journey through this area, 10 years prior, were great swathes of dead trees killed in the recent pine-beetle infestation. Forest fire suppression has resulted in an excess of the mature pine on which the beetle feed, and today's higher temperatures have resulted in 80% of pine beetle larvae surviving the winter compared to 10% previously. After lunch at Clinton we continued our drive north to Williams Lake, then west to Nimpo Lake for dinner and cabin lodging.

Trailhead

Following breakfast and a short drive to the Rainbow Range Trailhead in South Tweedsmuir Park, we met Dave and Joyce Dempsey, the outfitters contracted to carry our gear and supplies. I had to cut introductions short to apply bug repellent as a cloud of ravenous mosquitoes descended. Dave, part first-nation and legendary third-generation horseman of the Chilcotin, was to lead the horse train carrying gear and supplies, together with an attractive young lady Eileen and her 13-year-old sidekick Ida. Each of the nine packhorses would carry about 70 kg.

After depositing our gear for repacking in horse-friendly duffle bags, we began a steady climb up a narrow path of roots, rocks, and mud, with brown lodgepole pine eventually giving way to spruce. When I leapt over a small stream, my bear spray inadvertently discharged into my belt pouch containing sunglasses, small tripod, bug spray, etc. I washed the mess off in the stream and continued the trek. A two-hour hike brought us to a broad plateau where we stopped for lunch under the bright sun. After donning sunglasses I experienced an irritation about my eyes, and after a wipe with wet tissue the irritation increased to the point that I became blind. My sunglasses had picked up bear-spray residue from my pouch. Fortunately, I restored my sight by application of copious amounts of water directly to my eyes. I rinsed my pouch carefully before continuing the trek.

High-pitched whistles of marmots emanated from a nearby hill. Whistling while you walk is not recommended in bear country, for the grizzlies like nothing better than snacking on a plump marmot. Two marmots were spotted on the hill, seemingly sentries alerting their brethren to our presence.

Lester's Camp

As we trudged on, the horse train overtook us on the descent. Crossing a wide meadow, we arrived at Lester's Camp, where we retrieved our gear and pitched our tents amid another cloud of voracious mosquitoes. Fortuitously, at dinnertime the day-shift mosquitoes departed giving a brief respite before the night shift arrived. The next morning both Steve and Janet sported a mass of red welts from multiple mosquito bites. Apparently they had applied their European bug repellent instead of the local repellent, as a heavy dosage of DEET is the only effective defence against monster Canadian mosquitoes.

Breaking camp, we continued our northwest trek, climbing to an alpine meadow nestled between low rolling hills. A profusion of wildflowers spread every hue of the rainbow over the landscape.

Beyond, the Rainbow Range, named for the intense and varied hues of its volcanic lavas, also rendered a nearly full spectrum of colour.

A brief shower interrupted our restful lunch at Crystal Lake. Brief, but enough to coat the broadleaf plants, which then soaked us thoroughly as we descended a narrow path through the brush. Blue continually shouted "Hello bear, hello bear" so as not to surprise a beast in the thick foliage.

Horse Camp

Crossing a small river on a fallen tree, we slogged through a soggy meadow to Horse Camp to await the horse train laden with our gear. We had arrived at our first objective, the valley, which Alexander had trod after storing his canoe at Blackwater River to the northeast. After erecting my tent, I found a deep hole in the river fit for a full bath. DEET washed off, I dashed to my tent to escape the voracious mosquitoes.

While Steve and Jess enjoyed a day of rest, we hiked northeast along the valley in search of game, as Mackenzie's party would have done; truly now in the footsteps of Alexander Mackenzie as he trod on his return journey. Although we saw abundant sign of wolf, bear, and moose, we spotted no large animals. Blue could forego his "Hey bear" calls because Chris's unique staccato laugh rang out frequently: "ha-ha-ha-ha," like a woodpecker tapping "ta-ta-ta-ta."

Yellow Cone Mountain, across the river, blazed under a blue sky as we returned to camp along the Grease Trail. So-called grease trails were common in the Northwest, where coastal Indians traded eulachon, a small oil-rich fish, for the furs, copper, and obsidian of interior tribes. Indians from the Fraser guided Mackenzie along this, a prominent route later renamed the Mackenzie Grease Trail, or the MacKenzie Heritage Trail.

The following morning we returned across the soggy meadow. Soon the "F..k" expletives resonated in rapid succession as first Janet and then Jess slipped into a waist-high stream. The girls crossed the river to Rainbow Cabin and stripped off to dry their gear in the sun. Continuing our climb, we again met with roots, rocks, and mud until we reached open alpine meadow, with Mount Mackenzie looming to the north. While the others rested, I pressed on to Caribou Pass, named for the animal Mackenzie's party had shot here. Lying back against a rock, I enjoyed the solitude amid the stunning scenery. When the others approached, I hefted my pack to join Steve and Blue as they pressed on, leaving the ladies to rest. Crossing several deep snowfields, we gained the height of Mackenzie Pass. So close to the sea, we could almost smell the salt air from where Mount Stupendous rose to the clouds with its hanging glacier poised over the Bella Coola Valley, our ultimate destination.

An abnormally cold spring having left deep snow at the pass, Dave had earlier decided it was not feasible to bring the horses on this route. Two years earlier, Blue had descended from here and found the path in a sorry state. Since it lies outside the Tweedsmuir Park boundary, there had been no maintenance. There is also some doubt about the exact route Mackenzie followed. Reluctantly, we turned about and retraced our steps to Horse Camp for a dinner of steak and another refreshing bath in the river.

Park rangers

Breaking camp next morning, we again plodded across the boggy marsh to Rainbow Cabin. There we met park rangers Wes and Chris, who had flown in by helicopter the previous afternoon. They would be following us to Octopus Lake, leaving their gear behind for Dave to load on the packhorses. Once above the valley, we were much relieved to find the trail largely devoid of rocks, roots, mud, and, most curiously, mosquitoes. Presently we reached the sub-alpine, skirting a snowfield to top the ridge. We halted for lunch, enjoying a spectacular vista of mountains, snowfields, and valley.

Binoculars in hand, Chris reported what she thought to be a goat on the mountain across the high valley. Seeing no movement, I declared it a rock. Meanwhile, Jess spotted a large black wolf staring at us from the adjacent hill. It then moved to a snowfield, where it patiently sat and waited, presumably for a marmot to materialize near recent tracks in the snow. Eventually the wolf gave up and moved on in search of other prey. Subsequently Steve said the "goat" was moving. After careful observation, I also saw minuscule movement, and apologized to Chris for doubting her visual acuity. The rangers arrived, and Wes informed me that the goats typically stay rather still so as not to attract predators as they quietly graze. When the packhorses passed, we continued our hike downhill to Octopus Camp, where the mosquitoes returned with a vengeance. Already settled at the camp were two student rangers, Erin and Stephanie, who had backpacked in the previous afternoon. I pitched my tent, washed in the stream and after a meagre meal again dived into the tent to escape the mosquitoes.

With supplies almost exhausted, a sparse breakfast preceded our 16-km hike to the trailhead. Expecting a soggy march along a string of lakes, we were pleasantly surprised to find the trail much better than expected, traversing the hillside well above the lakes. At a small river, Jess and Blue waded across, soaking their boots, while Janet and Chris exchanged boots for sandals. Steve and I found a large log upstream on which to cross. Unfortunately, a scraggly branch barred the way, and when grasped it fought back. To keep from falling into the drink I sustained numerous scratches to my bare knees, for as is my hiking custom, I was wearing shorts. As the horse train passed, little Ida showed her expertise as she convincingly bent two stubborn packhorses to her will.

To Bella Coola

Arriving mid-afternoon at the trailhead on the Bella Coola River, we posed for a group photo at the information sign. Apart from two hikers seen on the first day and the four rangers, we saw no other human beings throughout this vast scenic wilderness. Blue proved an energetic and affable leader, often adjusting his pace to accommodate the short legs of our English ladies.

An hour's drive brought us to Hagensborg, a farming community cut from the rain forest by Norwegian settlers in the 1890s. Thence on to Bella Coola, reaching the sea as Alexander Mackenzie had done more than two centuries previous. A short flight on Pacific Coastal Airlines returned me to Vancouver, contemplating the fulfilment of my long-held objective in a most rewarding hike, mosquitoes notwithstanding.

Trailhead

Steve & Jen at Caribou Pass

Chapter 19
Jordan Journey

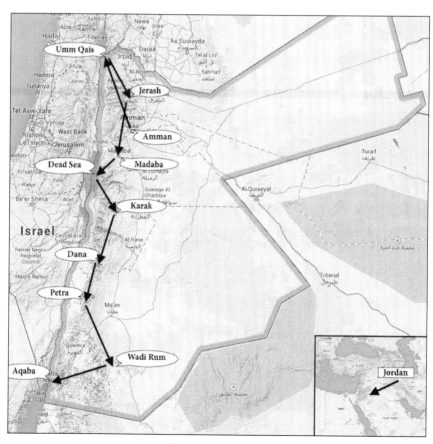

Jordan – October 2007

Amman

"The 23rd day." So read the Jordanian Times article that Bob Hyndman pointed out on our flight from Paris to Amman. Oops! My research had been rather inept. We were arriving during the last week of Ramadan, the holy month when Muslim faithful fast during the day. Another article mentioned many vehicle accidents, for drivers bereft of water and sustenance were crashing at an astonishing rate. Our primary goal was to explore the remarkable city of Petra, and to understand how the ancient Nabataeans came to carve the city out of solid rock.

Having booked through the Internet and blindly paid in advance; we were relieved to be greeted by our driver Abdullah when we emerged from Jordanian Immigration. Crash barriers at our hotel were also a welcome sight, for coordinated bombings at three hotels in 2005 had killed more than fifty people, mostly local Muslims attending a wedding. The King ordered a crackdown, and Jordan was now probably the safest country in the Middle East.

Decapolis

After an overnight rest, we drove north along a fine divided highway, passing a multitude of construction sites. Jordan's economy seemed to be booming, fuelled I suspect by the more affluent refugees from Iraq. Many new buildings have concrete half-pillars on the roof, the owners obviously intending to add another storey soon.

After stopping at an army checkpoint manned by machine-gun-toting soldiers, backed by a humvee armed with a heavy-calibre cannon, we came to Umm Qais, the biblical Gadara. Established by the Greeks in the fourth century BC, it was a city of the Decapolis; the ten cities that later enjoyed limited self-rule under Roman jurisdiction. Perched on a hilltop overlooking the Jordan Valley and the Sea of Galilee, Gadara commanded the principal trade routes from Syria to Palestine.

While Bob remained below to drop the coin, I climbed to the upper row of the black basalt seats of the Odeon. As in all Greek theatres, the acoustic effect was exceptional, for I clearly heard the clunk as the coin hit the paving stone. We then strolled along a colonnaded street where an archaeological team toiled under the blazing sun, the workers somewhat aghast as Bob blatantly slurped from his water bottle. Replicating my test at Olympia in 1976, I tasted an olive from a tree, and again found it completely inedible.

Jerash

Our next stop was Jerash, another Decapolis city and site of some of the best-preserved ruins of the ancient world. After earthquakes, water, and time had taken a toll, much of the ruined city lay buried in sand, which accounts for its remarkable condition.

A notable exception to earthquake-induced toppling was the splendid array of Corinthian columns at the Temple of Artemis, which have remained erect for 2,000 years. Our guide showed how these massive columns resisted recurrent earthquakes. He placed a small pebble as a fulcrum at the base of the 27-tonne column and placed his car key on it as a lever, one tip under the base. As the column, supported by a lead-filled base, swayed gently in the wind, the key slowly oscillated up and down. An impressive demonstration!

At the majestic Odeon, undoubtedly the finest-preserved of ancient theatres, Jordanian Army bagpipers gave an impromptu performance for a modest tip. Passing through the imposing Hadrian's Arch, we drove to our hotel at Madaba.

The Dead Sea

As I inspected a series of old photographs on the dining room wall, the proprietor of the hotel explained his family's genealogy. Bedouin Christians, they had lived at Karak until a dispute with Muslim neighbours forced their move to Madaba in the last decade of the 19th century. During the conflict the Muslims kidnapped the Patriarch's sister. The Patriarch then mounted a punitive expedition, during which he killed his sister, ostensibly to restore the family's honour. My recollections from Sunday school do not include lessons whereby Jesus sanctioned such action, but hey, this is the Middle East!

After a short visit to St. George Byzantine church to view the famous biblical mosaic map, we drove to Mount Nebo, reputedly the resting place of Moses, and site of a 4th century monastery rediscovered and excavated in 1933. On a promontory north of the monastery, I gazed like Moses across the Dead Sea to the "promised land," and like Moses could not cross, for the far bank is Israeli-occupied.

The Dead Sea lies along the Great Rift that runs from Syria through the Jordan Valley, Aqaba, and the Red Sea into Africa. I will never attain the earth's highest point, but southwest of Madaba we descended a steep, switchback road to its lowest, 410 metres below sea level. Donning a bathing suit, I waded into the shallow water for the obligatory swim and mud bath. I had expected rather grungy-looking water, but to my surprise it was crystal clear, presumably because the salt and minerals kill all organisms, which then fall to the seabed. After floating on my back for a while, I flipped over for a proper swim. Big mistake! My eyes burned, and I scampered ashore to wash the salt away. One dip in a lifetime is enough. We then checked into the Dead Sea Spa, the lap of luxury with five swimming pools and a bar pouring draft beer.

After a hearty breakfast we drove 65 km south along the east bank of the Dead Sea, then ascended to the imposing castle at Karak. Its thick walls and formidable defences, built by the Crusaders to control the trade route between Syria and Egypt, failed to prevent its capture several times over the centuries, including by Saladin and later by Mongols from Asia and Mamelukes from Egypt.

Hike

One night in the lap of luxury, the next at a "rustic" hotel perched over a gorge at Dana. Our rooftop dining afforded a grand view of the setting sun but, alas, no beer.

After breakfast we met our local guide, Abdelazeeh, and set out for a hike down the gorge. Jordan is a dry and dusty land, but given water the greens will grow. So it was as we passed a prolific spring, its waters channelled to irrigate the terraced fields on the upper reaches of the gorge.

Descending over treacherous terrain, I understood why your man Moses is always portrayed with a stout staff. At first exceptionally steep, the slope moderated as we reached the wadi and traversed its banks.

Our descent encompassed a 1,400-metre journey through geological time, for we passed recent lava flows, ancient sandstone, and, at the stream bottom, red granite of Precambrian age. Invited to tea at a Bedouin tent, we declined, using Ramadan as an excuse, but truthfully because I care not for the heavily sugared teas customarily offered.

Our 19-km trek ended at a modern eco-hotel, providing respite from the 33°C heat. The manager gave a short tour, perhaps to entice us to stay in the spacious rooms, quoting rates of 15 dinars for locals and 80 dinars for foreigners. The Jordanian dinar had diverged from the U.S. dollar and was now essentially at par with the euro.

Boarding a four-wheel-drive truck, we bounced along a rough track to the main highway, where a journey full of apprehension began. We sped at 110 km/hr across a landscape as barren as the moon, then up and over a ridge of hairpin turns, knowing full well that our driver was not in top form. Thankfully we arrived unharmed at the village of Wadi Moussa, near the ancient city of Petra.

Petra

In the morning it was but a short walk to the ticket office, where we met our site guide. Petra is Greek for stone, and this remarkable city is carved out of solid rock, albeit soft sandstone. Declining many hawkers of horse transport, we walked 1.2 km to the head of the Siq, the narrow entry passage winding nearly a kilometre between sheer sandstone cliffs towering 120 metres above the floor.

Originally nomads of the desert, the Nabataeans were masters of water management. With camels and secret sources of water, they monopolized the lucrative transport of frankincense from southern Arabia to the Mediterranean. The ancients used frankincense as medicine and as a food preservative, but primarily as offerings to the gods. The plethora of gods ensured an insatiable demand for the aromatic pitch. Becoming increasingly affluent, the Nabataeans surrendered their nomadic way of life twenty-four centuries ago, and occupied this hidden and easily fortified bastion.

They built a dam and bore a tunnel to divert flash floods from the Siq. Over the years the dam deteriorated, and in 1963 twenty-one

French tourists died in a flash flood. Belatedly, the government rebuilt the dam to prevent a recurrence.

The Siq is in places only three metres wide. Carved along each cliff face are channels designed to transport water to the city within. The left trough, originally covered, is now open. The right trough held tapered ceramic pipes to deliver water under high pressure. This technologically advanced hydraulic feature of two millennia ago was engineered when my forefathers were carrying water in leather buckets.

The Siq opened into a wide wadi with the so-called Treasury immediately before us, its red sandstone facade brilliantly lit by the morning sun. Undoubtedly designed to impress, it comprises an eclectic mixture of Greco-Roman features, including a statue of Aphrodite flanked by the twins Castor and Pollux. Regrettably, the carvings were defaced as recently as 1930 by Muslim iconoclasts. As we moved on, the scale of the city far exceeded my expectations. Many grand tombs line the cliff face, overlooking a 5,000-seat amphitheatre also carved out of solid rock

Beyond the theatre lay a long street once flanked with the decorative columns of enormous temples. After browsing the small museum, I climbed past several superbly decorated tombs, including the Soldier's and the Renaissance. From the Lion Fountain I accompanied two Kiwi ladies ascending a steep staircase to the Place of High Sacrifice. The hilltop had been levelled to host some type of assembly near a round altar surrounded by a channel, presumably to receive the flow of sacrificial blood. Having left my knife at home, I could not slit the ladies' throats to demonstrate the flow! However, there is no evidence that the Nabataeans practised human sacrifice. Descending the opposite staircase, I quickly reentered the Siq and proceeded to the dam, where in the guise of Indiana Dick I hired a horse to gallop back to the entrance.

After stopping briefly at the youth hostel to buy beer, we drove the truck to a saddle between two hills. Mattresses and sleeping bags laid on a large carpet were our accommodation for the night. When we took to bed after sunset and dinner, the serene tranquillity was broken only by the incessant yapping of dogs at the Bedouin camp across the valley. Periodically, I awoke to admire the canopy of stars, as Gemini, the Pleiades, and Orion rotated about the polar axis in a heavenly arc. Streaming arrows of meteors left trails of lingering incandescent dust.

Awakened at 6 a.m. as Abdelazeeh recited his morning prayers, I donned my eye mask and continued sleeping until 8, at which time Abdelazeeh restarted the fire to heat water for our morning tea. After a simple breakfast, we loaded the truck and drove a short distance to Little Petra. The village is similar to Petra, with an entrance through a narrow slit in the cliff providing secure protection for the inhabitants. After Abdelazeeh explained the configurations of several tombs, he entered one where he had lived as a Bedouin boy during the winter months.

At the end of a rough and rocky track, we disembarked and began our hike up and over numerous intersecting gorges and ridges on a back route to Petra. In places the traversing ledges were very narrow, with the valley floor some 300 metres below. The final traverse was across a ledge one-third of a metre wide along a sheer drop of 200 metres. From there it was a short walk to the edifice known as the Monastery, an impressive structure similar to the Treasury but simpler in design. The name derives from its conversion to a church during the Byzantine period. Its facade, the largest of the rock-hewn structures at Petra, is 70 metres high by 43 metres wide. Descending the steep staircase to the museum, I detoured into a small wadi to view the Lion Tomb, so named for the carving of a large lion that fronts it.

After lunch I returned to the Treasury to ponder its mystery. Among the grand facades built as tombs and for hosting funeral ceremonies, the Treasury is unique, with a large central chamber flanked by two smaller rooms. The floor plan is very similar to the library at Ephesus and one hypothesis postulates that the edifice was a library, designed to impress visitors with the grandeur and sophistication of the city.

Bound for Wadi Rum, we drove to the ridge overlooking Petra, where, binoculars in hand, we could clearly see the Siq entrance and the High Place of Sacrifice.

Wadi Rum

Leaving the main highway, Abdelazeeh engaged the four-wheel drive and deflated the tires, speeding across the desert to a huge arch chiselled by wind and water. While Bob remained below, I scrambled up the steep incline for a photo from the top. Thankfully, my hiking sandals gripped the coarse sandstone firmly as I descended. Despite four-wheel drive and soft tires, we became stuck several times in the extremely fine sand.

Beneath a nondescript concrete pad lay a jewel of the desert. Abdelazeeh lifted a lid to reveal an immense underground cistern carved by the ancient Nabataeans. Channels from the nearby hills funnelled precious infrequent rain into this reservoir of 3,000 cubic metres. It was knowledge and management of scarce water resources that gave the Nabataeans the means to control this arid land, and eventually settle in Petra.

A grand sunset of flame-red clouds obscured the new moon signalling the end of Ramadan. Stowing our gear at the last of several desert camps, we watched the opening celebrations of the three-day Eid al-Fitr, the Festival of Breaking the Fast. After a short burst of fireworks, boys danced with boys and girls with girls to the accompaniment of discordant Arab music, an acquired taste. As I strolled to our tent, a young lady invited me to hers. She and her sister, students from Kuwait, merely wanted to practise their English. Comfortably reclining beside her on her bed, I thought to myself, "I would be stoned for this in Saudi Arabia!"

Aqaba

On our drive to Aqaba we crossed the railway tracks along which T.E. Lawrence harassed the Turks during World War I and passed the Seven Pillars of Wisdom, the range of hills at whose base Lawrence and the Bedouin plotted strategy. At Aqaba beach, throngs of celebrants frolicked in the Red Sea. It was from these waters that the destiny of Petra was sealed in the first century AD. A Greek sailor bound for India, instead of clinging to the coastline, braved the open sea to sail the northwesterly monsoon, returning on the southeasterly monsoon. His voyage revolutionized transport, and thenceforth the sea route to India, directly from Suez at the northwest tip of the Red Sea, eclipsed that of the desert caravans. Deprived of trade revenue, Petra lost its dominance, and after a devastating earthquake in 363 AD was abandoned to wintering Bedouin.

A swift drive returned us to Amman along the King's Highway, a route that lay over an ancient pathway and later a paved Roman road. Our quest accomplished, Bob flew to Frankfurt and I to Paris.

Awaiting the coin drop

The Dead Sea

The Treasury at Petra

Desert Cistern Wadi Rum

Chapter 20
Death at Dingle

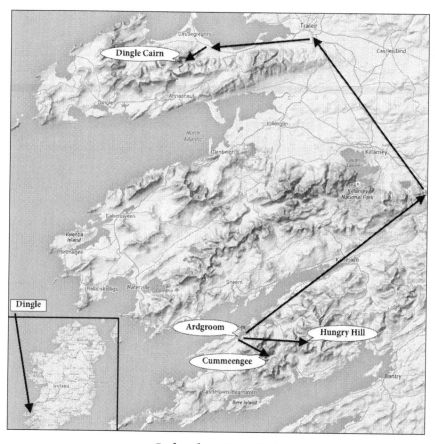

Ireland – May 2009

Dublin

Keith Mooney of the Wayfarers hillwalkers met me at Dublin's Heuston Station for the short drive to his home after my overnight flight from Vancouver via London. After Jane's delicious supper, it was early to bed in an attempt to mitigate my jet lag. Late the next morning, a Friday, we picked up Mary and Marion for a swift journey to the Beara Peninsula on the southwest coast. After stopping at Lauragh for dinner, we found our well-appointed accommodation midway along the peninsula at Holiday Homes, steps from Ardgroom village centre.

Beara Peninsula

With a sunny day ahead and hard rocky hills about, I donned shorts and decided to forgo my gaiters. Keith and Ted McGrath arranged for a minibus to shuttle us to the start point of the Cummeengeera Horseshoe walk. At the first glimpse of my skinny legs, one of the ladies began the "slag." That's Irish for good-natured disparagement.

Disembarking from the minibus, Keith led us through a verdant forest of soft, moss-covered trees to the foot of a low valley. Ascending on the left, I soon regretted my decision to forgo my gaiters. The ground was little less wet than that of the Wicklow Hills.

Reaching the first low summit, we split into two groups, Keith leading the first and Ted the second. A steep climb brought us to the summit of Coomacloghane, at 598 metres the highest point of our walk. Below lay a splendid view of the surrounding peninsula and the Ring of Kerry on the far shore to the north. Our intended track stretched before us in a great arc of three summits, your renowned Bantry Bay lying beyond to the south.

We headed west on rocky ground to the next summit. The terrain is reminiscent of the Aran Islands, with sharp jagged spears of rock where ancient tectonic forces had folded the mudstone strata to the vertical. Above a steep col, we sheltered from the cool breeze for our drum-up. That's Irish for lunch. Tiring of the incessant slagging about my bony legs, I told of an incident at my 2008 Air Force reunion at Quebec City. As I was about to enter the hotel elevator (lift to the Irish) a stranger in the crowd sized me up and said, "Are those your legs, or are you riding a chicken?" Well that brought a chuckle from my fellow hikers, and gave me a couple of hours respite from the slagging.

Gazing back at the deep col, we could see no sign of Ted's group. We learned later that they had diverted north, and thence back to the start point. Continuing, we climbed to two more magnificent viewpoints, and began a steep descent on a razorback ridge toward Glanmore Lake. With cliffs ahead, we turned north, making our way down a steep slope as Frank Keady and Adrian Ryan paused to yank out young shoots of the ubiquitous rhododendron. They soon abandoned their mission as futile, for the lower slope was awash with thick groves of this invasive pest.

A 1.5-kilometre road walk brought us to the rendezvous with the minibus and a short ride to Ardgroom. That evening we boarded the minibus again, as John, the driver and the proprietor of virtually every business in the village, drove us to Josie's Restaurant overlooking Glanmore Lake for a fine dining experience.

Sunday dawned bright and Alan King and Keith led separate groups on diverse routes to Hungry Hill, while Ted led a short hike to nearby hills. Mindful of the beating my knobbly knees endured on Saturday's downhill plunge, I decided to take a day of rest. After changing my flight itinerary at John's internet cafe, I walked to the promontory overlooking the final hairpin curve of the International Rally of the Lakes, of which this was the final stage.

Presently all hikers returned and in early evening proceeded to the local pub, where Jim Coogan had arranged a fine meal for the 30 Wayfarers. Predictably, the elegant attire of Veronica Ryan, Noreen O'Sullivan, and other lasses eclipsed that of the lads. As the evening progressed, Jim entertained with a few songs, including the applicable lyrics "Oh, from Bantry Bay up to Derry Quay ..."

Dingle

Monday morning we were on our way, some to Belfast, some to Dublin, and a group of 18 to a fateful valley on the Dingle Peninsula. After we had cooled our heels for an hour and a half awaiting errant Wayfarers, Keith led us up the valley on a gentle path, passing ewes, lambs, and a herd of ponies. Under a soft drizzle, 18 Wayfarers assembled in front of an orange tarp as Keith said a few words on the tragic death of Maurice McLaughlin two years prior. Maurice, an experienced hiker, had been last to leave after a lunch on the sloping bank of a mountain stream that was in flood after recent rain. It is speculated that he may have become unbalanced as he hoisted his pack, and fallen into the raging stream. It carried him about a kilometre to the flood plain and beyond.

Keith then unveiled the plaque, which reads:

In Memory of Maurice McLaughlin

Clontarf, Dublin

Who lost his life in a tragic fall

close to this spot

June 2nd 2007

Erected by his many friends

Wayfarers Hillwalking Club 2009

Ar dheis De go raibh a anam

I believe the last line translates as:

"May his soul be on God's right side"

Keith and Jane had affixed the solid bronze plaque to a large flat rock the previous week. It reminded me of the ancient Egyptian belief that a person lives on if his or her name is spoken. Like a pharaonic cartouche, the well-secured plaque will ensure that Maurice's name is spoken for many years to come.

Eileen Kavanagh then recited lines of Ewan MacColl, from the last verse of his song "Joy of Living":

Take me to some high place

Of heather, rock and ling

Scatter my dust and ashes,

Feed me to the wind

So that I will be

Part of all you see,

The air you are breathing.

I'll be part of the curlew's cry

And the soaring hawk

The blue milkwort

And the sundew hung with diamonds.

I'll be riding the gentle wind

That blows through your hair

Reminding you how we shared

In the Joy of Living. (*Note 2)

As Eileen paused, a small bird burst out of a nearby nest, flying straight toward the head of the valley. Good company for Maurice. We learned later that the bird was a wheatear, a migrant species wintering in Africa.

Keith then led us across the floodplain to the now-placid stream. Wading across the shallow water, we stood before the cairn where Maurice came to rest after falling into the torrent a kilometre upstream. After silent contemplation, we turned about for our respective onward journeys, mine back to Canada after a brief, bittersweet interlude on the open hills of Ireland.

*Note 2: Extract from 'The Joy of Living' by Ewan MacColl

Reproduced with the kind permission of Ewan MacColl Ltd.

View from Hungry Hill

Keith Unveiling the Plaque

Chapter 21
Tim and I in Timbuktu

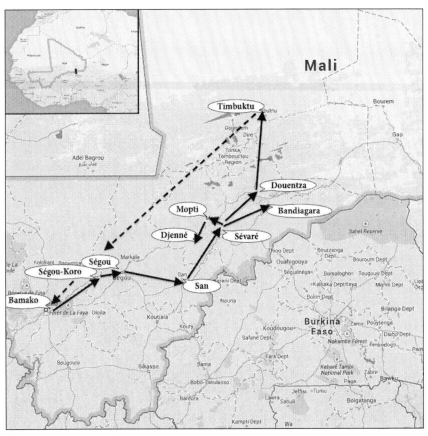

Mali – October 2009

Bamako, Mali

Five hours after departing Paris, our Air France Airbus descended in the dark to the Niger. Lightening and thunder to the north presaged the end of the rainy season here in the Sahel, the continent-wide band sandwiched between the arid Sahara and the humid equatorial jungle of Conrad's Heart of Darkness.

Disembarking at Bamako, capital of Mali, Jet Johnson and I passed swiftly through the formalities of customs and immigration, only to wait patiently for our luggage in the sweltering heat. A 30-minute ride on a shuttle bus brought us to our hotel perched on the north bank of the Niger. Finding no room at the inn, we reboarded the bus for a short ride to a sister hotel, the Libyan L'Amitié, formerly the Sofitel. We soon learned that Colonel Gaddafi had his hand in many enterprises and projects throughout Mali.

Although Mali ranks among the poorest countries of Africa, the land is rich in history. Over a span of 15 centuries, traders from the Mediterranean, Phoenician, Roman, Moor, exchanged salt for gold, weight for weight. Pound for pound, libre for libre, shekel for shekel, or whatever. Our self-appointed task was to meet "Tim" where these seemingly absurd transactions occurred, a place synonymous with "remote," the legendary city of Timbuktu. You've no doubt heard the infamous Timbuktu Newfie poetry contest joke, so I'll not repeat it here. It's available on the Internet.

Bereft of reservations save for two nights at our hotel, we planned to wing it. An ill-advised modus operandi, given recent kidnappings in this 90% Muslim country. However, possibly because of a dearth of tourists after a recent French government travel warning, we were able to book a guided itinerary at a reasonable price.

The next morning we met our guide, Ali, and Abdullah, driver of an antiquated Land Rover. Having sadly neglected African geography 101, I received my first surprise when we crossed the river in daylight and saw it flowing away from the Atlantic. The Niger rises about 200 kilometres from the Atlantic in the hills of Guinea and flows in a great arc northeast and then southeast to the tropical Atlantic, 4,200 km from its source.

A quick pass by the Africa Monument found us driving parallel to the river as we exited the sprawling city. Dilapidated trucks, buses, cars, motor scooters, and donkey carts shared the road, along which stood numerous small shops supplying diverse goods and services. As we drove out of the city, we found the two-lane paved road surprisingly good, save for the occasional array of potholes dug by heavy traffic during the wet season. The terrain is as flat as the proverbial pancake, a plain of grassland interspersed with brush and trees up to 10 metres high. Where farmers cultivated the land, vast fields of two-metre-high African millet and sorghum replaced the grass of the savanna.

Millet, high in protein and drought-resistant, was domesticated in Africa about 6,000 years ago. The tiny grains lie in a long husk resembling a bulrush. Women, often with babies strapped to their backs, would pound the stalks with a large post to free the grain. As Jet remarked, "There is no day care here." Throughout our journey we sighted neither tractor nor plow, for planting is entirely by hand hoe and harvesting by a short sickle or knife. The produce is transported by donkeys, or occasionally a horse-drawn cart. With the rainy season at an end, harvesting had begun. Great piles of watermelons lined the road at the small villages.

Ségou-Koro

Our first stop was at Ségou-Koro, formerly the capital of an extensive medieval empire. A wall enclosed the village of mud dwellings and granaries. With no rocks or stone on this ancient floodplain, all structures, including the mosque, were of unfired mud bricks with roofs of wood sticks and thatch. The bricks were coated with a plaster of mud, donkey dung, and straw. The outer plaster needs to be refurbished every two years or the structures will wash away during the rainy season. Restored by UNESCO, the king's "palace," overlooking the Niger, was little different from the dwellings of his descendants, save for a coating of paint and a sturdier roof. Under a broad tree, women repaired gourd bowls and pounded millet. At water's edge, fishers repaired nets, women washed clothes, and naked children frolicked in the mucky water.

As we entered another small village, a pair of piglets and stray dogs gave the first sign that this was not a typical Muslim community. Although Mali is mainly Muslim, isolated tribes practice traditional rituals of their ancient animist culture of ancestor veneration. The headman showed us their sacred well, where chickens, pigs, goats, or dogs were sacrificed on auspicious occasions.

He then led us into a mud hut, the village bar, and beyond it to the brewery, where millet mash was heating in six large pots embedded in a clay oven. After several days of fermentation, mellowing patrons would drink the potent brew from communal gourd bowls. Departing the village, we posed beside a three-metre-high mud shrine, its parapet crowned with dog skulls.

We stopped for lunch at Ségou, a sprawling administrative centre noted for its French colonial architecture. At an obligatory visit to a cloth factory, I found it intriguing that while traditional cloth is in subdued tints of brown, grey, and rusty-red, modern dress is invariably in bright colours, save for the hand-me-down rags you might have donated to your local charity.

The main highway diverged southeast away from the Niger. As Ali played a tape of local musician Ali Farka Touré, Jet remarked that he had the album at home and the song was one of his favourites. Crossing the Bani River, we continued to the small town of San. With no beer available at our modest but adequate hotel, we drove to a nearby restaurant for a simple meal. The onion soup was great, the beef as tough as shoe leather. But then we had not come to Mali for a gourmet dining experience. Three ladies from Cornell University who were working on a local water development project shared information on the land tenure system, in which the local chief allots communal plots to families on a yearly basis.

In what was to be our sparse morning fare throughout our journey, breakfast consisted of tea, instant coffee, bread, and jam. "Big voices make big men," and seven of them competed for attention resplendent in colourful djellabas as two World Bank officials attending the same "UN circus" looked on in amusement.

Sévaré

Our departure from San was delayed briefly at a police checkpoint, for although a bribe seemed to be expected, our driver refused to pay. At Sévaré, we strolled through a great regional weekly market, a chaotic jumble of vendors offering goods and produce of every description. Departing the town eastward, we passed an extensive block of concrete houses recently built with Libyan funding. The land gently rose above the plain, scattered boulders of sandstone appeared, and vegetation diminished. Dotting the landscape were huge pyramidal mounds resembling deteriorating mud granaries. They were homes to industrious termites.

Ten metres to the right of the road, bareheaded teams toiled with pick and shovel to dig a metre-deep trench for a fibre-optic cable. Seemingly a make-work project, the 700-km line from Bamako to Mopti is actually a viable commercial enterprise, for the existing microwave system is at maximum capacity. We stopped to examine a point where the trench had cut through a three-metre-high termite mound. I had thought the root of the mound would be deep, but it extended only about 30 cm into the rocky soil.

The land continued to rise, bringing us to the base of the Bandiagara Escarpment and the Land of the Dogon.

Land of the Dogon

The Bandiagara Escarpment is an imposing cliff running south to northeast for about 200 km. Uplifted 500 metres by ancient tectonic forces, the flat-lying sandstone plateau dominates the surrounding plain. Early inhabitants lived in cliffside caves to escape predatory animals. After centuries of abandonment, the caves were reoccupied sometime in the 11th century by the Tellem, a sub-Saharan group. Sometime in the 15th century, the Dogon, quite possibly migrating from the Nile Valley, displaced the Tellem in turn. When the Dogon refused to convert to Islam, they found refuge in defensible positions along the walls of the escarpment.

On the plateau some 3 kilometres from the cliff, our courtyard-style hotel at Camp Sangha overlooked a shallow depression. Next morning after Abdulla changed a flat tire, our local guide Amassagou led us to the district diviner. Barefoot, in a short cloak and floppy hat, the wizened seer stood beside a rectangular plot of earth bounded by a low border of rocks, within which were piles of small sticks. With his long pointed staff, he pointed out fox pawprints. During the night, foxes from nearby dens, attracted by millet flour sprinkled on his amah, or holy rock, had knocked over some of the sticks he had placed the previous day. Examining the disturbance, the seer would interpret the answers to his patrons' questions: "Should I get married? Should I move to Bamako? Should I build a new granary?" Quite bizarre, but I guess no more so than tea-leaf or tarot-card readings, or stock market forecasts based on images of heads and shoulders on price charts.

We strolled through a vast sandstone cavern, to be greeted on the far side by a troupe of about 30 children. Colourfully clothed, walking sticks in hand, they sang in a fine harmony of melodious voices, for which the eldest received a modest tip.

Our guide showed us a baobab tree, two metres in diameter, the bark of its lower trunk long since peeled for cordage. Its dried leaves, rich in vitamins, are pounded into a powder for soup and its fruit is squeezed for a nutritious juice. In the nearby field, a family toiled at harvesting the sorghum crop. Everyone pitches in, from the elderly to small children. Although slim, the Dogon seem well-fed. Their subsistence farming, supplemented by livestock, provides adequate sustenance.

After a photo op overlooking the precipice, Jet reboarded our vehicle and I followed Amassagou on foot along the lip of the escarpment, passing dwellings, granaries, goats, and children. The local buildings were more substantial than those of the plain, for beneath the mud plaster were walls of solid sandstone blocks. Ornately carved gates, doors, and shutters displayed animist themes. Three kilometres along the escarpment, we turned and descended a narrow cleft, gaining respite from the blazing sun and 42 C heat. A small spring-fed pool provided a cooling head soak. Amassagou remarked that he had climbed to his home the previous night with torch in hand to illuminate any snakes slithering about, for diverse vipers and cobras nest in the rocks during the day. At the bottom of the 500-metre descent, we passed three young women climbing with heavy loads balanced on their heads.

Crossing a small stream, we rejoined Jet and drove 10 kilometres along the base of the escarpment. A short climb through a village brought us to a broad ledge. Fifty metres above, stone and mud dwellings lined the cliff wall, deserted save for one inhabited by a family visible only with binoculars. Baobab bark ropes dangled from the rocks. The ancient dwellings of the Tellem, barely visible on a smaller ledge high above, were now burial sites for the Dogon.

Continuing along the side hill, we came to the Toguna, or Parliament House, where elders would shelter from the oppressive heat. Stout stone pillars supported a heavy roof of eight layers of millet stalk. The ceiling is deliberately low, 1.5 metres, so that someone who became frenzied in an argument would knock his head.

As we continued we found ourselves marching to drumbeats, whose faint volume increased as we approached a village where seemingly the entire adult populace was assembled in a courtyard. They were there for a funeral ceremony commemorating a death some 12 days earlier. It was not unlike an Irish wake, for it was a Christian gathering. The Dogon are remarkably tolerant, with animists, Muslims, and Christians living harmoniously in proximity. At the local hostel at the base of the cliff, we dined on a dish of rice and vegetables and quaffed a refreshingly cold beer, not necessarily in that order.

Ascending a steep road of jagged rocks, we stopped to gaze across the valley at a narrow waterfall plunging 400 metres to the valley floor. Much of the water evaporated during the fall, leaving only a thin stream to reach the cliff base. Rounding the top of the valley to the plateau, we found women washing clothes and bathing in a stream below a low concrete dam, the stream that fed the aforementioned waterfall. I hiked to the cliff edge for a photograph of its abrupt drop over the cliff, taking care not to get too close.

As we descended to a narrow bridge, we came upon two drivers arguing over who was to blame for the plight of a pickup truck lying on its side below the bridge. Although the truck had the right-of-way climbing the far side, its driver spooked when he encountered a big SUV sporting diplomatic licence plates. He backed up, too fast, and tumbled off the bridge, fortunately with no injuries. I talked with the occupants of the car, and lo and behold they were none other than staff of our Canadian Embassy and visiting parents on a little sightseeing junket. Since they were staying at our hotel, we learned later that the embassy recompensed the driver of the pickup. Your tax dollars at work!

As we enjoyed an afternoon rest, a thunderstorm arrived and the heavens poured forth. The downpour lasted only about half an hour. After it passed, I donned my boots and followed Amassagou to a nearby village of about 3,000.

A two-metre-high amah stone stood in the centre of a large plaza. Celebrants would circle the stone during festive occasions, somewhat like pilgrims at Mecca. Beyond was the "palace" of the village chief, an elder living alone in an ornate dwelling with sculpted mud facade. His courtyard was bounded by a metre-high wall defining the forbidden area.

Nearby, an elderly gent remarked that he had been a soldier. I replied that I too had been a soldier, in the "armée de l'air." When I suggested that we have a photo taken of us as brothers-in-arms, he scooted inside his house and emerged with his soldier's tunic, whereto I helped him affix his medal. As a large group of youngsters looked on, I suggested to Amassagou that he could give some pens to the children and I handed him a bag of pens from my packsack. Big mistake! When I looked up I saw our guide engulfed in a feeding frenzy, youngsters grabbing pens like piranhas on a wallowing cow. In retrospect, I should have asked the soldier to line up the children by size and give a pen to each.

As we continued through the village it became evident that it was zoned into separate areas for meetings, dwellings, and work, with a quarantine section set apart at a distance for women menstruating. During a brief visit to the village blacksmith, my guide told of a ritual that took place every three years at a site I would see in a later excursion.

Next morning we left the plateau, driving along the plain below to a trio of high promontories, clearly of the same sandstone formation as Bandiagara. Among them nestled the sizable village of Songo. A local guide led me up to a cavernous overhang, its interior rock face completely covered with red, white, and black paintings. He explained some of the drawings: a founder of the village, a centipede, a black boa, and a crocodile, the local totem. Once a wetland swarming with crocodiles, the village now straddles a dry riverbed.

Two low, flat rocks lay in the centre of the cavern. Every three years, as foretold at the blacksmith visit, all boys aged 11 to 13 would line up for a mass circumcision. The blacksmith, the man with the sharpest blade, would sit on one rock while the boys filed by and sat on the other rock for the operation. A large boa constrictor placed near the boys beforehand gave substance to the admonition that should they cry, their fate would be entwined with the snake. According to Ali, the boys never cry! Apparently, tourists visiting the village at the time of the ceremony may watch the proceedings. I would give it a miss, thank you!

The boys then spend three weeks in an adjacent cave learning their tribal duties and the responsibilities of manhood. A nearby cave held a vast store of musical instruments, mostly made from the calabash, or bottle gourd. Since it is taboo to play the instruments except during the circumcision ceremony, I know not the sound. Descending to the edge of the village, I found Jet being serenaded by a chorus of youngsters.

Mopti, "Venice of Africa"
Dropping from the slightly elevated plain at Sévaré, we reached the 10-km raised causeway leading to Mopti, the "Venice of Africa," at the confluence of the Niger and the Bani. On either side of the causeway, flooded rice fields reached as far as the eye could see. Standing erect, boatmen used long poles to plow slowly through the paddy. Near town, children frolicked while women washed clothes in the muddy water.

Disembarking, we strolled through a bustling market where fishmongers shovelled rather unappetizing-looking miniature dried fish from straw mat to basket. Dining at a restaurant overlooking the busy port, mindful of the foregoing, I chose the onion over the fish soup. Scanning the menu, Jet said, "You can't go wrong with spaghetti bolognese." Wrong idea, wrong choice. Before the day was out he suffered the tummy trot.

In a scene reminiscent of Hong Kong, a ceaseless parade of boats ferried passengers and goods across the 100-metre-wide harbour mouth. As we walked through the market, Ali stopped to buy a half-kilo block of crystalline salt. Thence to our hotel, the Ambedjele, at the landward end of the causeway. Enclosed in a spacious garden, comfortable thatch-roofed huts stood around a swimming pool ringed by palms.

Ferry to Djenné

Market day dawning, we set off early to avoid a lengthy delay crossing the Bani at the Djenné ferry. At the ferry landing, trucks, buses, motorcycles, and horses queued to cross the shallow river. Once docked, the ferry loaded swiftly, with vehicles in the centre, horses to the right and people to the left. When we reached the far shore, a short drive brought us to the marketplace in front of the Great Mosque.

One of the sub-Sahara's oldest cities and a natural hub for trade, Djenné declined in importance as Mopti arose under French colonial administration. Djenné's claim to fame is now its Great Mosque, reputedly the largest mud structure on the planet.

A climb of three flights of stairs to a rooftop overlooking the Grand Mosque gave us a good bird's-eye view of the edifice. Since the site is often flooded during the rainy season, the mosque sits on a platform about three metres above the marketplace. Three stout minarets fronted the market square. Metre-long posts protruded from the mud walls like pins from a pincushion. Apparently, the palm posts relieve expansion stress resulting from the extremes of daytime heat and nighttime cool. The posts also provide secure scaffolding for the yearly refurbishment.

As Jet headed to the restaurant, Ali arranged for a local guide to show me around town. Grey, grey everywhere, save at the smaller port at the north side of the town, where colourfully garbed women disembarked from long canoes balancing goods on their heads.

Signs around the Mosque forbade entry to non-Muslims. This is a deviation from Muslim tradition, for non-Muslims are typically welcome in a mosque, provided they are respectful and modestly dressed. Having visited mosques in Jeddah, Istanbul, and Casablanca, I was curious to see the interior. Five thousand francs doled out to a local guide and another 5,000 to the son of the Imam gained me access. Entering through a side door, I doffed my shoes, treading on the earthen floor. Unlike the aforementioned mosques, renowned for expansive interior space and ornate geometrical designs on walls and ceilings, this was a labyrinth of narrow aisles amid massive pillars. As mud lacks inherent strength, the high flat roof of palm was supported by a hundred 1.5-by-3.5-metre pillars. The only worshippers who see the Imam are dignitaries kneeling in the reserved front row. The interior is dimly illuminated by 104 small ventilation holes in the ceiling. The walls are without ornamentation. A rear door led to an open courtyard where rows of cylindrical mud bricks, about the size of a beer mug, lay drying in the sun.

I rejoined Jet for soup and a beer at a pleasant courtyard restaurant. Returning to our vehicle, we passed the one and only farm tractor we saw on our journey, an Indian Mahindra. Towing a four-wheel cart, it clearly transported goods, and pulled not the plow.

Mopti river cruise

Next morning we returned to Mopti and boarded a 12-metre shallow-draft riverboat. Comfortably reclining on soft cushions, shielded from the blazing sun by a canopy, we motored downstream. Presently we came ashore at a small mixed village of Bozo fishers and Fulani herders. The boat's high prow allowed us to disembark on the muddy bank with dry shoes.

Passing between high mud walls, we came to the house of a Fulani family. Surrounded by small goats, women spun cotton as a man sat weaving a long, narrow blue and white scarf. At water's edge, students of the Islamic religious school, wooden platters and pen in hand, wrote and recited the Qur'an. Ali remarked that despite their diligence they would benefit little from their studies, for they learn nothing but the Qur'an by rote.

As we strolled back to the river, the accompanying gaggle of children sought to hold our hands. I kept my hands in my pocket, for as an American doctor later reported, many have sores, lesions and parasites from drinking and swimming in the fetid tropical water. As we reboarded our boat, Jet posed with a youngster clad in a star-spangled "Obama" T-shirt.

The captain's helper prepared a fine meal of grilled fish and rice, with the motor providing enough speed to elicit a cooling breeze as we returned upriver. As I sipped a cool beer with Bizet's "Les Pêcheurs de Perles" on my iPod, fishers in narrow canoes cast diaphanous nets, doubtless to catch the tiny fish sold at market. The slate-grey water of the broad Niger, dead calm, met the hazy grey sky at a nearly imperceptible boundary.

The Journey

Next morning from our hotel outside Mopti we drove to the airport for a flight to Timbuktu. Arriving two hours before the scheduled 8 a.m. departure, we found half a dozen tourists already in the queue. The tedious waiting ended suddenly when a convoy led by a luxurious vehicle flying the Mali flag rolled up on the tarmac. As a coterie of dignitaries and military officers swept into the VIP lounge, I thought, "Oh, oh, this looks like trouble."

About 11 a.m. a plane taxied in and the provincial governor disembarked to inspect the assembled dignitaries and officers. As the convoy drove off, the airport staff began to weigh luggage and issue boarding passes for the much-delayed flight. A late-arriving group of 12 Dutch tourists, obviously warned of the delay, received immediate attention. As envisioned, the governor's entourage had commandeered many seats. Jet and I watched helplessly as the aircraft taxied away.

Ali had departed, so I borrowed an agent's cell phone and contacted our tour director in Bamako. The cheeky agent then demanded 4,000 francs for the telephone call. "No way, don't pay," said another tour guide. Employed by the same company as Ali, he coordinated a switch to his more robust vehicle when Ali returned to accompany us on our quest.

As Homer observed, "The Journey is the Thing," or as the line is sometimes translated, "The Journey is the Reward." Throughout history, reaching Timbuktu has been a challenge. History repeats, as we set off on our 550-kilometre journey.

Finale - Timbuktu

A mass of potholes on the drive east morphed into a construction zone of trucks and graders laying fresh blacktop. Pausing at the village of Douentza, nestled in a gap between the Bandiagara Escarpment and the Tondo Mesa Range, Ali and the driver dined on searing hot beef from a roadside grill. Wary of Jet's tummy complications, we sustained ourselves on biscuits and my emergency rations of mixed nuts brought from France.

Leaving the paved highway behind, we exited the village northbound on a dusty red-dirt track, skirting the spectacular cliffs of the towering Mesa. On the north flank of the Mesa, thick gorse marked the boundary of the Gourma Elephant reserve. About 700 elephants forage here for water and food on their annual migration from neighbouring Burkina Faso.

Back on rolling open terrain, our progress slowed as the bumpy track crossed countless dry watercourses. A halt at a toll checkpoint gave the opportunity for a welcome stretch. Jet posed beside a red and white road marker inscribed "95 KM FLEUVE TBTOU." En route again, we dared not stop to photograph a brilliant crimson sunset, for nighttime travel was ill-advised as cattle and goats graze along the track.

As the cloak of night descended, we reached the landing of the ferry that would take us across the Niger, within a few kilometres of Timbuktu. And as the Newfie would say, "There was the ferry, gone!" Ali contacted the ferry company by cell phone and said we would have to wait an hour or so for its return. A most welcome message, for we had visions of spending the night in this mosquito-infested habitat. I whipped out my insect repellent to spray my bare arms and legs, for malaria is endemic on the Niger.

Stick and mat hovels lined the causeway, where half-naked children scampered about. Eventually we heard the guttural chug of the engine as the ferry approached, invisible, devoid of navigation lights. Although bright lights beckoned across the broad river, the ferry turned west, motoring 10 km upriver to the new port. Crocs and hippos lurk in these waters, unseen in the pitch-black night. On the other side, a drive of about 15 km brought us to our hotel on the outskirts of the legendary city. Famished, we dined under a canopy of brilliant stars. A nearby fluorescent bulb diverted swarms of mosquitoes, allowing us to dine in comfort. Now to find Tim, as I will call our local guide, to illuminate the enigma of salt and gold.

Next morning Tim led us to the nearby mud mosque and began to recount the history of Timbuktu, or as the archaeological sign spelled it, "Tombouctou." Once a thriving centre of trade, religion, and scholarship; today a dusty, moribund outpost. Founded about 1100 AD, the city became exceedingly rich from the taxation of goods passing through. Caravans of camels, or more precisely of one-humped dromedaries, "ships of the desert," laden with salt from mines near Fez in Morocco, trod the hard impediment of the Sahara for 90 nights, resting by day. Here their 1,900-km journey ended.

The Roman statesman Cassiodorus observed, "Some seek not gold, for there lives not a man who does not need salt." Hence the willingness of the Niger peoples to exchange life-sustaining salt for gold, weight for weight. On those terms, the half-kilo block that Ali bought in Mopti would have been worth $18,000 at the prevailing gold price of $1,100 an ounce. Ali paid but 500 francs, about a dollar! Today the salt still arrives by caravan at Timbuktu, but from a source half as far away. Local merchants at Mopti resell the salt blocks up and down the length of the Niger.

While medieval Europe languished in ignorance and strife, Timbuktu became a magnet for scholars. At its peak, the Sankoré Madrasah, or university, had 25,000 students and one of the largest libraries in the world. Recently rediscovered in desert caches, hundreds of thousands of manuscripts, many damaged from the ravages of time, water, and termites, are now available for research. A modern library financed by South Africa, opened shortly after our visit, will catalogue, restore, and preserve the historic documents. Tim arranged a visit to the archives, where we examined some of these ancient manuscripts. Not confined to religion, the texts are a compendium of mathematics, medicine, chemistry, and astronomy, to name but a few of their subjects.

A stroll along a wide paved street brought us to the house where a British officer, Major Gordon Laing, recuperated for five weeks in 1826, having sustained many grievous injuries, as well as losing his interpreter, in an attack by Tuareg nomads. His epic journey to the mythic city, believed to be brimming with gold and precious gems, took more than a year. The authorities, distrusting his motives, had him killed shortly after he left the city.

We then examined the plaque on a house where the French explorer René Caillié lodged for two weeks in 1828. Traveling alone, disguised as a Muslim, fluent in Arabic, he later wrote an unembellished account of his journey. By then Timbuktu was an unimportant, impoverished village giving no hint of a fabled past. The city never recovered from the Moroccan conquest of 1591.

At the next house, a woman perched on a high stool meticulously copied ornate plaques. I bought one of her works: four lines of Arabic script bordered with an exquisite gold and copper geometric motif in an embossed leather frame. The English translation of the ancient proverb: "Salt comes from the North, gold from the South, but the word of God and the treasures of wisdom come from Timbuktu."

Late in the afternoon I mounted a camel for the obligatory ride into the desert. "Hut, hut" said I, trying to remember whether to lean back or lean forward as the beast ascended a steep sand dune. Recalling the French government warning of recent kidnappings, I decided to forgo the trip to the caravan campsite and returned to our hotel, skirting the 15-kilometre ditch excavated by Gaddafi to bring water from the Niger.

Throughout our tour I had struggled to understand the physical geography of the Niger Basin. Next morning as we lifted off on the flight to Bamako, our bird's-eye view revealed all. Great swaths of green alternated with desert brown. A Swiss agricultural scientist in a nearby seat explained that this area of the Niger constituted a rare "inland delta." When the river rises in the rainy season, the waters spread out to deposit fertile sediments in a fan shape much like that of the Nile delta, except that being landlocked, the main channel resumes its flow downstream. Farmers plant the vast fertile wetland with African rice, a native species cultivated for thousands of years. In contrast to eastern Africa and the Indian subcontinent, currently suffering severe drought, the rains here have been abundant and crops are bountiful.

Homeward bound, we had time to ponder our experience. The people of Mali are self-reliant, warm, friendly, and tolerant. Their greatest vulnerability is a shortage of clean water, which diverse aid groups are presently addressing by boring deep wells. Vulnerabilities differ, and we have ours, such as our dependency on electricity and computers. A massive solar flare like that of the 1859 Carrington event would fry electrical circuits and computer chips. Our society could come to a standstill as refineries shut down and agricultural production plummeted from lack of fuel. Famine would be a possibility. Meanwhile the primitive farmers with hand hoe and the fishers of the Niger would carry on as they have for thousands of years. (*Note 3)

*Note 3: December 2013 issue of the journal Space Weather. The paper, entitled "A major solar eruptive event in July 2012," describes how a powerful coronal mass ejection (CME) tore through Earth orbit on July 23, 2012. Fortunately Earth wasn't there. Instead, the storm cloud hit the STEREO-A spacecraft.

"I have come away from our recent studies more convinced than ever that Earth and its inhabitants were incredibly fortunate that the 2012 eruption happened when it did," says Baker. "If the eruption had occurred only one week earlier, Earth would have been in the line of fire.

Brothers in Arms

Niger Cruise

Hut, hut

Chapter 22
Careening Copper Canyon

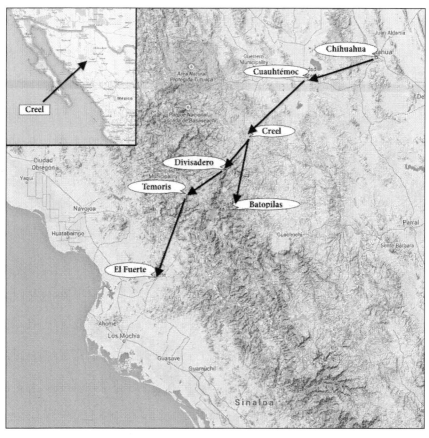

Mexico – March 2010

Chihuahua

Several friends had recommended the Copper Canyon Railway of Mexico, world-renowned for its spectacular views. The Chihuahua al Pacifico, known locally as El Chepe, is an engineering marvel. Although its construction began in 1863, it was not completed until 1961, after interruptions including revolution, the Great Depression, and two World Wars. Conventional tourist access is from Los Mochis near the Pacific, some six hours by bus north of Mazatlan. Jet Johnson and I chose to ride the rails from the northern terminus of Chihuahua, the city that gave its name to the tiny breed of dog.

It was a blue-sky day as we flew out of Dallas across the desolate west-Texas landscape, dotted with oil-well pads and vast arrays of wind turbines. At Chihuahua our quest for train tickets proved fruitless: the station was closed on Sundays. Our taxi driver dropped us at the Quality Inn, a fine hotel near the cathedral. On the plaza fronting the cathedral, an award-winning cast-iron gazebo was flanked by four smaller gazebos replete with shoeshine stands. On the nearby pedestrian street, multitudes of shoppers perused restaurants and stores, seemingly every third one a shoe shop.

Creel

Arising for a 6 a.m. departure, we bought tickets for the first-class train. Our seats were comfortable and reclinable. Two locomotives pulled a dining car, a bar car, and two passenger coaches. Gliding out of the railyard, surprisingly devoid of trash, we passed idle freight cars. Three well-armed Federales patrolled our train, ostensibly providing protection from the drug-cartel violence endemic to northern Mexico. Picking up speed, we soon came to the town of Cuauhtémoc, centre of an inter-montane district of apple orchards and grain fields farmed by about 50,000 Mennonites.

A steady climb through sparse pine and oak forest brought us to Creel, known as the Gateway to the Copper Canyon. Although the name is singular, Copper Canyon is a complex of three major and three lesser gorges, their depths and combined area exceeding those of the Grand Canyon. Unlike the Grand Canyon's slice through two billion years of geological history, the rock here is relatively young, a

25-million-year-old assemblage of flat-lying volcanic strata. The name derives not from mineral deposits but from the copperish hue of rocks and lichen. On disembarking we were taken by local touts to a couple of nearby hotels. We chose the Cascada, only a short walk from, but at half the rate of the Best Western, reputedly the finest in town. Creel is rather nondescript, somewhat reminiscent of any interior British Columbia town. The main street parallels the railway. To the southeast the village opens to an industrial area where lumber mills predominate.

After lunch we chatted with two American bikers. They told us they had awoken to gunfire that morning, and gave directions to the targeted house. We strolled about 500 metres down the main street to a two-storey house peppered with hundreds of bullet holes. The gunfire had hit four family members, including a child who later died. This shoot-up followed a massacre of five at a small town to the north the previous day.

I arose early to take my morning tea before our 7:30 a.m. bus departure. With our hotel closed, I walked to the Best Western, glancing at a pickup truck with its headlights on just across the road. The Best Western was closed. Typical of a "sleepy Mexican town."

Half an hour later I tried again, this time with success. Returning, I found a police vehicle barring the road near our hotel, three officers armed with submachine guns standing guard. With the scene now in daylight, I noticed a bullet hole in the side window of the truck. Shortly afterward about fifteen police arrived, including a detective with notepad in hand. Two officers donned latex gloves to lay a blood-soaked body on a blanket, then hoisted it into the back of a red pickup truck. Forget breakfast, it was time to get out of Dodge!

Batopilas
For a 24-hour side trip to the town of Batopilas, we boarded a rickety old "school" bus along with six other passengers, Jet and I commandeering the front seats. We detoured to a back street to avoid the police blockade of the main, speeding out of town at a brisk but unknown speed, for the speedometer read zero.

Soon the driver pulled over and crawled under the bus, wrench in hand, fiddling with something around the differential. On the move again, we made good time along the two-lane paved highway, descending and ascending about 700 metres several times. The bus stopped at a junction where a modest snack relieved the hunger from our missing breakfast.

Ten new passengers boarded, including a couple of native Tarahumara in their distinctive attire of waist-length brightly coloured cloaks, white triangular loincloth, and thonged sandals. We turned south from the main highway along a good but under-construction road for about 25 km, when it suddenly became a narrow gravel and dirt track.

At a widening of the track, the driver stopped briefly for picture-taking from the top of the steep face we were about to descend toward the Batopilas River. Just before plunging down through the multiple hairpin turns, the driver made the sign of the cross. Not an encouraging portent. Thankfully we met no other vehicle on any of the many blind corners, for on most of the track there was no room to pass.

Jet later called it the most frightful journey of his life. The driver rotated the steering wheel left and right continuously as the bald tires skimmed along the dry track. I would definitely give this trip a miss in the wet season. As the temperature rose during the 1,800-metre descent, from near zero to 25 Celsius, the vegetation changed to cacti and scrub.

Crossing the bridge at valley bottom, we again climbed and descended repeatedly along a road paralleling the river between 20 and 200 metres below. Contented cows lay on river sandbars, apparently well-fed, although it is a mystery to me what they found to eat on the steep banks. An immense dump of yellow tailings perched above a precipitous slope near an abandoned mine. Refreshments were available here as the driver chatted with the shop proprietor. Further along, our two Indian passengers disembarked with their modest possessions at a narrow footpath rising from the valley.

Jet noticed a stone aqueduct on the far side of the river just before we crossed a sturdy steel bridge to Batopilas. Bounded by the river and a steep slope, the town has but one narrow street, lined with shops and houses along its two-kilometre length. At the far end of the town the terrain opened up, giving space for two more streets, a town square and a large church, terminus of the bus trip. Our planned hotel, the Riverside Inn, was closed. A helpful local led us across the square to a pleasant inn within a courtyard.

After lunch we toured the village museum, learning the history of this fabled mining town. Spanish soldiers discovered veins of pure silver here in 1632, promptly enslaving the native people to mine the lode. After intermittent primitive mining over the next few centuries, Alexander Shepherd, former governor of Washington D.C. arrived in 1880 and established a modern mine and mill. One hundred and ten kilometres of drifts and tunnels pierce one of the richest silver deposits in the world.

All inbound goods and the outbound silver had to be carted by mule train in packets no heavier than 35 kg, two packets per mule. The journey to Chihuahua took five days by mule and another two days by wagon. Skilled workmen manufactured parts in a foundry in Batopilas and cobbled together diverse pieces to assemble the mine and mill machinery.

Locals still fondly remember Shepherd, who died from appendicitis in 1902. His extraordinarily enlightened enterprise included a hospital, resident doctor, company store, and high wages for the workers. During his tenure he introduced an intensive program of smallpox inoculation, and is credited with eliminating the disease in the area. Shepherd's sons took over the operation after his death, but mining went into a permanent decline beginning with supply disruptions following the Mexican Revolution of 1910. Today tourism supports much of the town, although an illicit cash crop in the surrounding fertile fields and benches is reputed to contribute to the economy. Soldiers in full combat gear disgorging from a truck lend credence to such speculation.

While Jet returned to the hotel, I walked to the bridge to examine the aqueduct. Its water, dropping 4.5 metres over its 5-kilometre length, powers a Pelton Wheel that generates enough electricity for mine, mill, and town. Its installation in 1890 made Batopilas the second town in Mexico to receive electricity.

Across the steel bridge, also built by Shepherd, stand the ruins of his adobe mansion and mill works. Pausing for only a brief look, since the site was now densely overgrown with bougainvillea, I hiked 2 kilometres to a mine portal, finding it dark and dangerous. I turned about and hitched a ride on a flatbed truck, desperately hanging on to steel posts as we bounced along the rough road. At dinner we met an Aussie group that had arrived by private van. They too had experienced apprehension on the descent, their anxiety somewhat mitigated by smoky windows obscuring the view.

El Chepe

The 5 a.m. bus back to Creel left with the punctuality of a Swiss train, the predawn departure scheduled to allow connection with El Chepe. The return trip was largely uneventful. The hazardous blind corners were less frightening than during our daytime arrival, since headlights illuminated the way. It was only as we climbed out of the canyon to meet the rising sun that trepidation returned. Driving with one hand, the driver shielded his eyes in a feeble attempt to penetrate the glare.

After breakfast in Creel, we boarded the train for the onward journey. Creel is near the highest point of the line, at 2,340 metres. An ascending 360-degree tunnel brought us to the continental divide at Divisadero, with spectacular views of grand scenery. A 15-minute stop allowed the obligatory photo over a sheer cliff plunging 1,800 metres to the Urique Canyon floor. As the first whistle sounded, I bounded back to the train, passing native women selling food and wares. Many tourists from the northbound train overnight here at a rustic cliffside hotel, returning south the following day.

The railroad crosses 36 bridges and traverses 87 tunnels. Emerging from one, I looked down to see a train about 300 metres below on the left. We entered another tunnel and upon emerging saw the lower tracks on the right! It later became apparent that the line made a 180-degree descending turn within the mountain. At the Temoris station, three distinct levels of the line are in view. A scenic dome car would be a real asset on this railway. Without one, tourists jostled uncomfortably for position at open windows on the bouncing platform between coaches.

El Fuerte

The route paralleled the Rio Fuerte from Temoris, twisting down from 1,000 metres as the vegetation changed to exotic subtropical plants and shrubs. A span of 560 metres across the Fuerte reservoir marked the end of the mountainous terrain. Beyond lay the piedmont and El Fuerte station, where we disembarked for a 10-minute taxi ride to town. A pleasant colonial town, El Fuerte is the birthplace of Don Diego de la Vega, better known as the legendary Zorro. It is worth a day visit. However, we planned to return on the northbound train next morning.

Attired in shorts awaiting the 8:40 a.m. train, I was beset by a swarm of near-invisible mites dining on my bare legs. It took five days for the 100 or so large red welts to subside. We were unable to buy tickets; the station was inexplicably shuttered. As the train approached, now with four locomotives attached for the steep climb ahead, a mass of tourists queued along the platform. Chaos ensued when the train stopped and then reversed to allow those with tickets to board first. Near the last to board, we were directed to the bar car. Eventually we found vacant seats in the forward passenger coach.

As predicted, the return journey was as interesting as the descent, if not more so, for fresh aspects unfolded with the morning light. At Divisadero, mindful of foreseeable tummy consequences, I quashed the urge to buy the delicious-looking food grilled by the ladies.

After overnighting at Chihuahua we flew to Dallas and home, reflecting upon the great dichotomy between the average, kindly disposed Mexican struggling to make a living and the abhorrent barbarity of a small minority of drug dealers. The existence and preponderance of the drug cartels are only possible because of the insatiable demand for their products north of the border.

Death in the Morning

Thar be Silver

El Chepe

Chapter 23
Arctic Watch

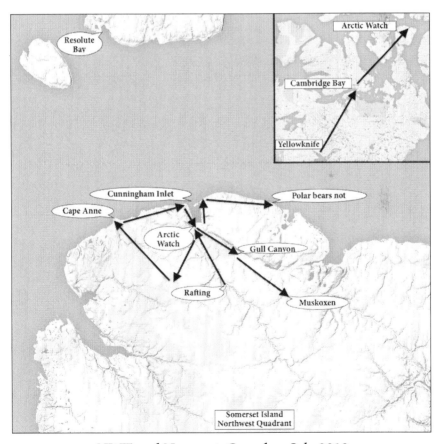

NWT and Nunavut, Canada – July 2010

Yellowknife, N.W.T. and beyond

In mid-July my friend Gary Anderson called to offer a position on an excursion to the Arctic. One of his group had cancelled. After a quick look at the destination, I immediately signed on and scrambled to assemble the required gear for departure two days later.

Awaiting an early morning flight to Yellowknife, I met two other members of our group, Willem Stronek, who had organized the expedition, and David McCann. At Yellowknife we spent a day and a half looking at the local sights, notably the very fine museum, the outstanding Legislature and the Information Centre of the Diavik Diamond Mine.

Friday morning we assembled at the Summit Air hangar for our charter flight to Somerset Island. Joining us were Fred of Toronto and Blanche of Ottawa, as well as Andrew and Matt, who were to upgrade the website of Arctic Watch Wilderness Lodge, our destination. Josée Auclair supervised the loading of freight and supplies for the lodge.

As we boarded the Dornier 228 for a 2 ½-hour flight, Willem asked the pilot if he could detour to the Diavik mine. Since our intended track lay closer to the Ekati mine, co-founded by my friend Stewart Blusson 20 years before, he instead descended and circled its gargantuan pits.

Stretching our legs at a brief refuelling stop at Cambridge Bay, I recalled my friend Dale Horley, who some years previously had arrived here, taken one look at the desolate landscape and promptly reboarded the plane for a return flight. Viewing the land from on high, I could understand why. This quarter of Victoria Island is a flat wasteland of shallow lakes and rocky tundra, the only modest rise topped by a Distant Early Warning Line radar dome.

Somerset Island, Nunavut

As our aircraft reached the north coast of Somerset Island, our pilot carved around Cunningham Inlet, presenting vertical views of multiple whale pods below. Upwards of 50 white belugas swam in the shallow water. Touching down on a gravel strip between channels of a river, we came to a stop and disembarked to meet our host, Richard Weber. While his staff loaded our gear onto a vehicle, we donned our rubber boots and hiked half a kilometre to a narrow but swift river channel where a raft waited to ferry us across.

On a level bench 15 metres above the river lay Arctic Watch Wilderness Lodge, the planet's most northerly at 74°05'. The spacious lodge consisted of modules in a Y configuration, each with a glossy plywood floor and steel frames supporting double walls of a white poly fabric.

From the vestibule, "Boots off please", the left door led to a spacious dining room with attached kitchen, the right to the main lounge of 20 x 10 metres with comfortable sofas and chairs, an artifact display, and a library. Off the lounge was a private office beaming wi-fi Internet access via satellite. The other arm of the Y led to a heating room and to men's and women's showers.

As Richard introduced the staff, it became apparent that this was essentially a family operation: Richard's wife Josée, their sons Tessum and Nansen, and friends or cousins Sven, Catherine, and Virginie.

Assigned to our individual tent-cabins of construction identical to the main lodge, I found mine to be a room with a view. It measured about 3.5 x 4 metres; its furnishings consisted of a double bed with single bunk above, a cold-water sink with a mirror, hanging shelves, an enclosed marine toilet, and a window looking over the inlet.

After a gourmet dinner, we walked to the mouth of the estuary to watch about 20 beluga whales cavorting in the shallow waters. This "toothed" whale, sometimes known as the sea canary for its high-pitched chirping, reaches a length of 5.5 metres and a mass of 1.5 tonnes. Apparently the belugas congregate at the river for its relative warmth, about 10 C warmer than the ocean, and to shed their moulting skin by grinding against the river gravel.

Thence to bed in my unheated tent. Josée had provided a hot water bottle to warm the bed of flannel sheets and a heavy duvet, which kept me snug and warm throughout the bright, cold night. I awoke shortly after midnight, observing the sun due north and about 5 degrees above the horizon as it began climbing again, for this is truly the Land of the Midnight Sun.

The Northwest Passage

Following a hearty breakfast, Richard, shotgun over his shoulder, led us on a hike inland, across a small stream and thence to a cliff overlooking a pristine waterfall. Climbing the barren hill, we stopped to examine a seemingly vacant lemming burrow. The resident ground-nesting snowy owl needs about 1,500 lemmings to feed her brood and likely relocated because of fluctuations in prey population.

From the brow of the hill, a gentle descent brought us to the bank of a stream bounded by patches of peat, not unlike the upland peat bogs of Ireland. And what of bugs, mosquitoes, and black flies, scourges of the mainland barrens? None, zilch, zero! The high Arctic is thankfully devoid of these pests.

After lunch, we mustered on the old airstrip above the camp for instruction on All-Terrain Vehicles or ATVs. Instantly proficient, we set off northbound in convoy, passing the enormous jawbones of a bowhead whale that Richard had salvaged the previous year. Continuing, we arrived at the bank of the legendary Northwest Passage, grail of European explorers from the 15th to the 19th centuries, including the ill-fated Franklin Expedition of 1845. A jumble of pack ice littered the shore. Giant icebergs, calved from the glaciers of Baffin Island, drifted slowly westward. Eighty kilometres across the strait lay Resolute Bay, from which Richard and Sven had started a remarkable endeavour five years before. Richard told of a week-long journey across the ice on a bulldozer, with frequent stops to test ice thickness. That journey would now be impossible, for there is open water on the strait throughout the winter.

Westward along the pebble beach, we stopped to examine the bleached bones of a bowhead whale that had washed ashore two years previous. Filtering plankton through immense baleen jaws, about a third of its overall length, the bowhead can reach 130 tonnes and 20 metres in length. Its blubber being rich in oil, it was hunted

A Journal of Journeys

almost to extinction before its protection in 1966. Retracing our route, we returned to camp for another gourmet meal.

Kayaking

Richard changed our itinerary to take advantage of a blue sky and dead calm on the water. Out came cumbersome "dry" suits with elastic cuffs that we donned in the main lodge. The initial plan was to remove the suits, hike 2 kilometres to the bay, suit up again and board the waiting kayaks. "How about we use the Unimog," say I. Déjà vu for me, for when I was stationed in Germany as a young fighter pilot, our ground crew used a smaller version to tow our aircraft. Occasionally we would hop aboard for a ride to distant dispersals. With massive tires and periscope-like intake and exhaust, a Unimog truck can ford deep water or traverse almost any terrain.

The two experienced kayakers, Gary and Willem, chose to crew together, leaving neophytes David and myself as partners, with Tessum and Fred in the third kayak and Blanche and her son Sven in the fourth. Our flotilla paddled the 3 kilometres across the inlet to a shingle beach. After dragging our boats well above the waterline, the tidal range is about 2 metres, we doffed our uncomfortable suits and trekked inland to the mouth of a sandstone canyon. Tessum and Sven had hauled along boxes from which issued a very fine lunch including hot homemade soup. The flat-lying strata provided ideal seats and tables.

I hiked upstream to view the spectacular waterfall surging from a narrow slit, abruptly diverting 90 degrees as the flow splattered against the opposing face. While David and Gary napped, several of us climbed the slope to view the canyon from above. On descending I hiked directly to the kayaks to kit up for the return.

On our outbound crossing my right foot had slipped out of the rudder pedal and my long legs could not regain purchase, leaving us rudderless approaching the shore. For the return journey we switched places, David taking the helm.

Arctic weather can be irregular, and so it was. A brisk wind was now blowing from the southeast. Waves quickly rose, approaching a metre in height as we surfed to the far shore. Paddling furiously to prevent broadside broaching, I constantly exhorted David, "More right rudder." Belatedly I recognized the need for the cumbersome suits!

Beaching, we removed our suits and walked to the estuary mouth, where countless stark white belugas and their grey calves frolicked in the shallow water. Had they somehow stopped moving, we could have walked across their backs to the opposite bank.

After dinner, we gathered in the lounge for a slide show. Richard's slight build, warm smile and soft blue eyes belied steely determination within. He soon captivated us with tales of his seven treks to the North Pole, including a two-man unsupported journey to the pole and back in 1995. An Arctic feat never replicated. The two explorers carried, or dragged in sleds, all supplies for that four-month expedition. Obstacles included 7-metre high-pressure ridges and lengthy leads of open water.

Gull Canyon & Muskox

Ferried across the river by raft, we mounted the ATVs and set off southeast, crossing multiple river channels. At narrow Gull Canyon, we dismounted and followed Richard along the shallow water. Around a bend, the ubiquitous grey-brown rocks gave way to a verdant green landscape. The droppings of gulls nesting on the cliffs provide rich nutrients for this prolific vegetation in an otherwise stark land.

After lunch we drove south, stopping briefly for tire repair and re-inflation, then ascended a long esker rising 30 metres above the plain. After speeding along the ridge for about 10 kilometres, Richard spotted a herd of muskoxen across the next valley and called a halt. Dismounting and descending, we crossed a stream and made our way up the hill to peer at a herd of 17 muskoxen grazing about 200 metres distant. Weighing about 300 kg, with long horns and shaggy coats almost touching the ground, they appeared much larger than they were, for they stand only about 1.5 metres at the shoulder.

Quietly, with the wind in our face, we closed to within 70 metres, at which point the herd alerted and slowly ambled off. A distinctive reaction of muskoxen is to form a defensive circle when threatened. Over the years the animals have learned that a circle provides no security from bullets, and now they merely move away.

Returning to our ATVs, we charged along the esker, returning across the delta by again fording the many small channels.

The appropriately named All-Terrain Vehicles easily negotiate steep slopes up, down, and sideways, as well as sharp rocks, round boulders, sand, gravel, mud, ice, snow, rivers, and the sea. The throttle on the ATV is a lever, unlike a motorcycle's rotating grip. Eventually my thumb became numb from the constant pressure. As I commiserated on my affliction, I then thought of the tars of Sir John Franklin's expedition dragging their heavy sledges across rough ice. They would laugh and roll in their graves at the thought: "Poor Dickie has a thor thumb!"

After another gourmet dinner, Tessum gave an engrossing slide show featuring his and Richard's recent journey to the North Pole, a one-way trek that culminated in an airlift to Norway by a Russian plane.

Polar bears not

Throughout the night I thought my tent would blow over from the howling wind. In the morning, fog lay thick, obscuring the river. It lifted as the morning progressed. After crossing the river by ferry, we set out by ATV along the east bank of Cunningham Inlet on a quest for polar bears. Our journey was timed to coincide with the ebb tide. We sped north along the shingle beach, slowing only for a gingerly diversion into the sea around a rocky promontory. Once clear, we made good time to the north coast and turned east. An impassable cliff compelled a diversion up and around the hill and back to the beach. With the west wind still howling, we hunkered behind a gravel berm for lunch. Offshore, bergs of azure blue, brilliant white, and gravel-laden dirty brown sailed eastward, driven by the wind against the current.

With no bears about we turned for home, stopping for photos on grounded ice floes. Racing along the pebble beach, Tessum stopped to pick up a well-worn shaft of a broken oar. Undoubtedly from one of Franklin's boats. Anyway, that's my story and I'm sticking to it despite the lathe marks on the grip.

Gravel deposited by the westward current formed a narrow isthmus that turned a small island at the mouth of the inlet into a peninsula. At the southern extremity of the peninsula we stopped to examine a Thule-era dwelling, its collapsed walls strewn with whalebones. Returning to the east side of the inlet, we left our vehicles and hiked to a deep canyon to view another spectacular waterfall incised from the flat-lying sandstone strata. Voluminous though the stream was, its flow was gobbled up by beachside gravel before it reached the sea. At the rocky promontory we had circumnavigated on the way out, the incoming tide now blocked our beach access. Mindful of our inexperience, Tessum and Virginie shuttled the vehicles along the steep incline above while we walked over the obstruction.

After dinner, three of us played Willem's esoteric "Learn as you lose" card game, while Gary amused himself with the innovative features of his new iPad.

Rafting

Next morning we boarded the Unimog and crossed the river to head south. About 15 kilometres out, we disembarked and began hiking. Shotgun over her shoulder, Josée led us across the tundra, identifying and explaining diverse flowers and plants. The "willow tree" I found particularly absurd, for only a botanist could call this minuscule four-centimetre twig a tree. Occasionally Josée would bend to pick up clumps of the inner wool of the muskox, which is exceptionally fine and much sought after. Later at the lodge, the resident photographer Gretchen would card, spin, and knit the fine wool.

Climbing a gentle slope, we spied muskoxen in the distance. At our feet lay a vast conglomeration of seashells. The land we were walking on was about 60 metres above sea level, having risen from isostatic rebound when glaciers from an earlier age melted.

The melting glaciers had deposited fine silt. During the wet season the previous year, Nansen had become mired in deep mud, extricating himself only by leaving his pants and boots behind. The boots and pants are still there, locked in the now cement-like clay. At the top of the rise lay the inverted skull of a bowhead whale. A hundred metres further lay another head, much of its skeleton extant. Both were from a time when this land lay beneath the sea; geologists have estimated their age at about 8,000 years.

The plateau ended abruptly at a steep declivity falling to the river. On the riverbank below, the crew had erected two large yellow rafts as a windbreak. As I reclined against a raft munching on lunch, Andrew, who had arrived by ATV, approached and asked, "Are you squashing around in your boots today?" "Yeah," I replied, "they are very sloppy, but we were walking slow enough." Ever the diplomat, he said, "Here, try these," and handed over my rubber boots. I had inadvertently donned his boots, matching but larger, leaving him to hobble about with cramped toes.

Paddles in hand, we boarded the rafts, Richard manning the oars of the first and Tessum the second. Drifting with a swift current through the narrow canyon, Richard rowed hard to avoid the overhanging cliff rising 30 metres above us. Beaching the rafts, we climbed a low escarpment to view the muskox herd spotted earlier. Unfortunately, the herd had moved over the hill, so it was back to the rafts to continue downstream on cold clear water. Negotiating a 180-degree meander; we emerged from the canyon to face a cold north wind. With the wind blowing us broadside, it was time for the reserve power; all passenger hands to the paddles to keep the bow pointed downstream. All hands save for Gary who not unlike an oriental potentate transported by his slaves, sat immobile, arms folded around his paddle.

With the camp in sight, Gary grumbled "None too soon, for I am really cold." A little energetic paddling would have hastened the trip and warmed the blood, thought I as we came ashore at our now-familiar docking rock. By Willem's calculation, Richard had powered the oars through 3,800 strokes.

Thule

A record low of 980 millibars had brought foul weather. Against a biting wind from out the west, we donned all available layers of clothing for a drive to ancient Thule sites on the northwest shore of Somerset Island.

I climbed aboard the comfortable seat on the Can-Am ATV behind Tessum. No more thor thumb for Dick. Our route took us southward, then northwest up the Red Valley along the return leg of the annual Northwest Passage Marathon. Unlike conventional marathons at which monitors distribute cups of water, here they ride shotgun on ATVs. Two years ago, when the aforementioned bowhead carcass attracted bears like bees to honey, the nine runners encountered 13 polar bears along the route! At the bottom of a ravine, we stopped for respite from the bitter wind. Richard stomped about, remarking "My feet are colder than when I skied to the North Pole!"

From high ground we espied the icebound shore, with pack ice as far as the eye could see. Tessum said he had never seen so much ice at this time of year. The abundant ice likely accounted for the dearth of bears, for they would be prowling the pan, dining on seal pups. Apparently the polar bear has limited success in hunting adult seals, and depends on spring-born pups to sustain it through the remainder of the year. After exhausting this easy prey, the bears come ashore and wander the breadth of the island scavenging for carrion, or maybe stalking unwary trekkers.

Diverging from the river, we headed northwest across the tundra to the prominent river delta at Cape Anne. Half a kilometre inland, overlooking a deep ravine, lay well-preserved ruins of ancient Thule-culture dwellings. This was the highlight of my Arctic experience. Two years before, Stewart Blusson and I had planned an airborne survey of mysterious boat-shaped sites on the Ungava Peninsula. Using Stewart's ultra-sensitive mine-finding geomagnetic detectors, we would attempt to find iron artifacts that might lend credence to the unconventional hypotheses of Farley Mowat. He speculated that these were stone foundations for overturned skin boats, shelter for "Albion" walrus hunters who predated the Vikings. Similar structures are said to be scattered about the high Arctic.

However, recent research has convincingly established that the Thule, predecessors of the Inuit, were iron-age hunters who came across the Bering Sea around 1100-1200 AD. With iron-tipped harpoons and weapons, including a re-curved bow of Mongol design, they hunted the mighty bowhead whale and killed or displaced the previous inhabitants, known as the Dorset or Tuniit. The presence of iron would therefore not have been determinative in confirming Farley's Mowat's hypotheses and we abandoned the quest.

Now here I was, scrambling over the pits and walls of what were clearly dwellings. Circular, about five metres in diameter, they were arrayed in a line much like a row of town houses. Each had elevated sleeping platforms and low passages connecting adjacent dwellings. There were about five such chambers here and eight at a larger site two kilometres east that we visited after lunch. The massive bowhead bones that once supported the roof are long gone, having been appropriated by present-day Inuit for their "Eskimo" carvings.

The sturdy stone abode afforded the Thule hunters a warm winter refuge, and protection from bears attracted by the immense carcass of a bowhead kill. Each room had a "souterrain," or underground entrance that acted as a "cold sink" but also, I suspect, served to deny entry to prowling bears. An outlying structure was probably a secure cache for meat and blubber. Although from the air these structures would resemble the shape of Farley's artifacts, they are in no way similar, and perhaps his boat-foundation hypotheses should be revisited.

Our return to camp took us along the north coast, where we stopped briefly to examine two massive bowhead skulls, one upside down, the other with gigantic eye sockets staring seaward. Richard was not sure whether these were recent depositions or had been washed from the slope above and were of the same vintage as the 8,000-year-old skulls we had seen inland. Draped with vegetation fertilized by nutrients leached from the bones, they both appeared very ancient.

In his ceaseless quest for the perfect photograph, Gary diverged from the leader's route and almost came to grief. He managed to stop just before plunging into a metre-deep hole. No harm done, we sped along the sloping beach, taking advantage of low tide and avoiding the bucking-bronco ride of the rocky ledge inland. As I read the odometer at camp, our circuit clocked in at just less than 90 kilometres.

That evening we dined on Sven's fresh-caught Arctic char. Willem gave a short address thanking the team and our hosts Richard and Josée. As Willem presented the team with a modest gratuity, David expressed special thanks to the youngsters for their solicitude, energy, and enthusiasm.

Departure

Our last day dawned as bright and clear as the day of our arrival. I packed my gear and vacated my tent to allow cleanup for incoming guests. Equipped with the mandatory pepper spray and radio, I walked up the track to photograph the bowhead baleen and jawbones we had viewed earlier, then hiked straight up the hill for an expansive view overlooking the inlet. At the summit I met Willem, Blanche, and Fred, who had taken the direct route. Wind at our backs, we descended to prepare for our departure. After lunch we donned Inuit fur garments and posed for photographs with a three-metre narwhal tusk purloined from the lodge's artifacts. Richard had found the tusk washed up on the shore; the narwhal is a protected species indigenous to the surrounding waters.

Early evening at river's edge we bade farewell and thanked this most remarkable family for an enthralling experience. After Andrew (almost) zip-lined across the river, we boarded the raft to meet the incoming plane for Yellowknife.

After crossing the Northwest Passage to the mainland, I asked the pilot for the name of the prominent river on the left. I was thinking of the attempt of Franklin's survivors to reach the Great Fish River, now called the Back River. In an earlier day, navigation in the vicinity of the North Magnetic Pole required considerable skill and navigation aids were few. Today the task is made simple by a GPS moving-map display. Our position determined, out came the topographical map, and after some searching, the pilots identified the river as the Burnside, which Franklin had traversed by canoe in 1821-22.

On the floor of the arrival-departure lounge at Yellowknife airport lies a striking polar map. It shows historical positions of the North Magnetic Pole, beginning in 1831 when its location was first determined by James Clark Ross of the Royal Navy as 70°10'N just west of the Boothia Peninsula, and ending with its position in 2007.

When the Norwegian explorer Roald Amundsen determined its location in 1903, the magnetic pole had moved north only about 55 kilometres, about 0.75 kilometres per year. Today it is at 85°N and is galloping along at 50 to 60 kilometres per year! The earth experiences a polar reversal approximately every 250,000 years, although the last was 780,000 years ago. Is a polar flip looming?

Arctic Watch Lodge

Bowhead Bones

Bowhead gazing Seaward

Inuit Not

Chapter 24
Planes, Plains, and Planes

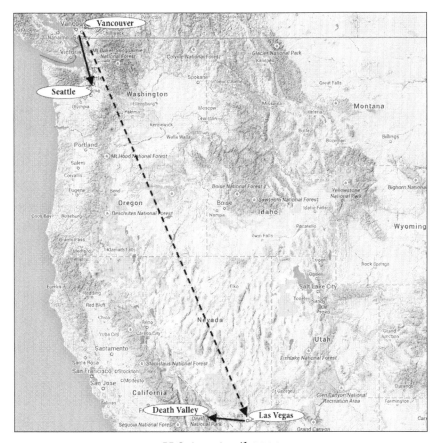

U.S.A. – April 2011

Seattle, Washington

Early in April, Bill Marr, retired Air Canada captain and wartime Mosquito pilot, organized a bus trip to the Museum of Flight at Seattle's Boeing Field. Vancouver aviators and aficionados assembled at a hotel just south of the Fraser River, picking up the balance of the passengers near the border. U.S. Customs inspection was quick, taking about half an hour to process the 51 passengers.

Just before noon we cruised through downtown Seattle and arrived at Boeing Field. After paying our entrance fee and receiving schedules for Air Park visits, we sat down for a brief lunch. With a little more than an hour before my scheduled time at the Air Park, I chose to visit the World War II exhibit hall with its superb displays of aircraft, historical narratives, and short videos. Particularly noteworthy were displays featuring Doolittle's Tokyo raid and the ambush of Admiral Yamamoto. The Battle of Britain zone, with Spitfire and Bf-109, offered a comprehensive analysis of that critical battle.

Crossing Memorial Bridge to the Air Park, I met up with Bill Marr, who had been appointed tour guide for the Lockheed Super Constellation. With its porpoise-like profile, this aircraft is arguably one of the most attractive ever built. This Connie had been trucked from Toronto to Rome, N.Y., for structural repairs and fresh paint in Trans-Canada Airlines livery, thence to Seattle where it was undergoing interior restoration. An earlier tour of duty as a bar in Toronto had left its interior without seats or furnishings. We entered by the rear stairs to a cavernous empty fuselage, but the fully restored cockpit was a fit backdrop for Bill's recall of his flights across the Atlantic on this very aircraft.

Another Connie pilot, Alex Bull, pointed out the sextant port where he had had to extinguish a mid-Atlantic fire resulting from an electrical short. Bob Bogash, a key museum volunteer, was still awaiting the Performance Manual promised him by a retired Air Canada pilot some years ago.

Our next stop was the Concorde, where Peter Duffy, retired British Airways Concorde training captain, gave personal insights into the Concorde operation. Supersonic flight was forbidden over Europe or the U.S.A., but on flights to Bahrain they would routinely cruise at Mach 2 across the Iraqi, Syrian and Saudi Arabian deserts. British Airways had a team on the ground whose sole function was to dish out cash to any herders who complained of a cow, camel, or goat stillbirth attributable to the 60-kilometre-wide sonic booms. Careful handling was required to avoid a combined double boom in a turn or during a descent.

Twenty-five years before, during Expo 86, I had organized a 427 Squadron reunion in Vancouver. Privileged to have friends in high places, we enjoyed VIP treatment at major pavilions and, at the Abbotsford Air Show, guest access to the Boeing chalet on the flight line. On the final day of the reunion, I chartered a 25-metre schooner for a harbour tour. After lunch on the lawn at the Royal Vancouver Yacht Club, we motored into False Creek. Just as we turned under the Granville Bridge, a Concorde appeared on a low-and-slow pass down the length of the Expo site. There were exclamations of "Dick, how did you arrange that?" Blind luck, of course, but I recently learned that Peter was on the flight deck that day!

After a quick look at the Air Force One B-707, I returned to the museum to spend the rest of the available time in the main hall. The variety of aircraft and exhibits are truly exceptional, rivalling that of the Smithsonian, if not in quantity then surely in quality. The museum website proudly proclaims, "Come and see the largest and most comprehensive air and space collections in the United States."

Boarding the bus, we returned to Vancouver, myself with a certain commitment to return for a more thorough visit.

Death Valley, California
Next day I flew to Las Vegas and met Dale Horley for the United States Air Force Sabre pilots reunion. With a day in hand, we rented a car for a trip to Death Valley. Saturday morning we drove northwest to the small town of Beatty, once a booming mining town, now a rather forlorn and desolate backwater. As we fuelled up, the proprietor remarked that there was snow just to the north of town. Shivering, I wondered what I was doing in shorts! We departed the town, climbing slightly to the pass at 1,250 metres and then began a

descent to the valley. It soon became much warmer. At the rim of the valley we stopped at an area known as Welders, where miners extracted a considerable quantity of gold in the 1860s. The entire area is cordoned off, for it is underlain by a dangerous honeycomb of shafts and tunnels.

At the valley floor, we drove on to the Ranger Station at Furnace Creek to register and pay a $20 vehicle fee. Despite a vast amount of information at the Ranger Station, some of the volunteers were rather ill-informed. I asked about what looked like a steam engine just across the road, and the volunteer said it was not a steam engine but a water wagon hauled by 20 mules.

When we went back to reexamine the artifact, it was clearly a steam boiler with a piston and rod. The volunteer was obviously referring to another exhibit somewhat further away that included two wagons and a water tank.

The Pacific Coast Borax Company gathered borax from the dry lakebed and hauled it with the iconic Twenty-Mule Team to a processing plant 265 kilometres across the mountains and desert. Later the steam tractor did the hauling.

As we were departing, a Ranger came out of the building, armed with a rifle, a taser on one hip and a pistol on the other. "Who are you going to shoot today?" I asked. "Hopefully nobody, but there are a lot of crazies hiding in the hills," he replied. Apparently, many antigovernment folk inhabit hillside caves and occasionally take potshots at the Rangers.

Leaving town, we took the advice of another Ranger and diverted onto the one-way loop road known as the Artist's Palette. We parked a short way into the hills and I climbed to a lookout point offering a vista of contorted rocks, their colours ranging from crimson through brown and yellow to greenish and bluish.

The one-way loop took us back to the highway and then descended to the very bottom of the valley at the Golf Course, a vast field of jumbled crystalline minerals. Rejoining the highway, we continued to Badwater, the lowest point of North America, 86 metres below sea level. A white sign on the cliff above marked the elevation of sea level at 282 feet.

Now well-warmed by the sun, we strolled a few hundred metres on the dead-level salt plain for a photo op. Continuing southbound, we passed the end of the salt flats and climbed out of Death Valley, returning to Las Vegas for the cocktail hour.

USAF F-86 Sabre Reunion, Las Vegas, Nevada

The next morning, Sunday, we assembled on the convention floor of the Gold Coast Hotel to register for the 18th United States Air Force F-86 Sabre reunion. The welcoming package included an attractive coloured medallion emblazoned with four Sabres fronting the U.S. flag.

At the evening meet-and-greet Danielle and I joined 427 (Lion) Squadron members John and Susi Shute, as well as Dale and Marilyn Horley. Also joining us were Honorary Lions Kay and Bob Custer, inducted at the recent Penticton SPAADS reunion. (*Note 4). It was at the Las Vegas Sabre reunion of 2007 that Dale had first met Bob. "What squadron were you with?" Bob had asked.

"I'm just a visitor from the RCAF," Dale replied.

"What base?"

"Zweibrücken."

"Wow! That was the party of the century!"

The Soviets erected the Berlin Wall in the early 1960s at the height of the Cold War, triggering the activation of Bob's unit, the 197th Fighter Squadron of the Arizona Air National Guard. Transferred from sunny Phoenix to the U.S. base at Ramstein, 30 kilometres northeast of Zweibrücken, their F-104 Starfighters often tangled with the Canadair Mk VI Sabres of #3 Wing, Royal Canadian Air Force. In keeping with a time-honoured aviator tradition, our Wing Commander invited the 197th pilots to the party at Zweibrücken.

Next morning bright and early, we boarded buses for the short drive to Nellis Air Force Base. On arrival we broke into two groups, mine heading to the flight line to examine the F-22 Raptor and the F-15

Eagle, the other to the briefing. Further down the flight line, the F-16s of the Thunderbird aerobatic team prepared for takeoff. A close examination of the Raptor revealed aspects of its stealth technology, including concealment of all weapons in internal bays.

We walked over to the briefing at the Weapons School, formerly known as Fighter Weapons. There were now so many diverse units involved that it had become merely Weapons School. Following a short video explaining air power from World War I to the present, the briefing colonel gave a comprehensive overview of the school's role.

During the question period, I remarked that "In the upcoming election in Canada, the F-35 purchase is somewhat of a political football," and asked, "Could you shed any light on the relative merits and capabilities of the Raptor versus the F-35 and the Chinese J-20 stealth fighter?" The colonel prefaced his reply by saying he would express his own opinion and not necessarily that of the U.S. Air Force, but felt that the F-35 program was a complete waste of money and resources. The program was well behind schedule, he said, and the actual cost per aircraft was not yet known. The capabilities of the Raptor were superior to those of the F-35 and it had two engines. The government cut the Raptor program from 750 aircraft to 350 and then again to 186 and the production line was now closed.

He thanked me for my question and we boarded the bus for the return to the hotel. The comparison is rather moot from the Canadian perspective, for early in the development program Congress prohibited export of the Raptor.

That afternoon we attended a talk by the legendary aviator Bob Hoover. Scheduled to speak for an hour, he held us enthralled for three hours with stories of his flying career. Having started flying as a teenager, he was already a skilled aerobatic pilot when he joined the U.S. Army Air Corps shortly after Pearl Harbor.

Although an enlisted man, he took charge of a group of 67 pilots shipped overseas on the Queen Elizabeth. Lacking adequate aircraft, the U.S. Air Corps assigned the unit to the Royal Air Force, flying Spitfires. Two months later they shipped out to North Africa.

Although Bob was keen to engage in combat, his extensive experience kept him test-flying recently assembled aircraft offloaded from U.S. ships. Eventually he joined a U.S. combat squadron flying Spitfires from Sicily.

When he was jumped by four Fw-190s, his external tank failed to drop, resulting in severely degraded performance. A lucky, or perhaps a skilful 90-degree deflection shot hit his aircraft. Fished from the drink by the Germans, he wound up at the notorious Stalag Luft I. Near the end of the war, after many attempts, he managed to escape, commandeering a German Fw-190 that he flew to Holland and freedom.

After the war he joined another renowned aviator, Chuck Yeager, as a test pilot on the Bell X-1 program, and later flew as a test pilot for North American Aviation, manufacturer of the F-86 Sabre. It was while testing an innovative control system on the Sabre that he proved his phenomenal skill. On taking off from Los Angeles, he found himself with a frozen control column.

As he describes the flight: "Immediately after the landing gear was retracted, the nose of the airplane pitched straight up. The airplane was out of control. I pushed forward on the stick with all my strength, but it could not be moved fore or aft. Somehow both the normal and the emergency systems had failed.

"The F-86 then pitched up, stalled, started to spin, and headed straight down. It was difficult to keep my bearings, but then the rudder control, which was mechanical, permitted me to stop the spin. The horizontal tail was free-floating and completely out of control, but the plane recovered, barely missing the ground. The plane climbed right back up, and the same process started again. I called a Mayday, unsure of what response would come next.

"For the next forty minutes, it was stark terror. I was so certain that a crash was inevitable that I asked Los Angeles Airport to stop all air traffic. An airliner that was ready for takeoff on the other runway was told to hold his position, leaving one clear runway for me in the event I could regain control.

"I went through all sorts of gyrations to figure a way to gain control." (*Note 5)

Eventually Bob managed to find the "sweet speed," the airspeed at which the vertical downward force on the horizontal stabilizer equalled and balanced the upward force from the airfoil. Gently he climbed over the coastal mountains to the Mojave Desert, a dry lakebed not unlike the previously visited Death Valley. A plane on the plain so to speak! Meanwhile, Joe Lynch, a fellow North American test pilot, had scrambled a Sabre and was flying Bob's wing.

Bob continued: "I had been increasing the power in an effort to get the nose up for landing. Joe had advised me to bail out before I set up the approach. Now he was telling me that I was going 240 knots and wouldn't survive the landing at that speed.

"Instead of the hard landing I expected, the swept wings on the F-86 picked up ground effect. To my surprise, I experienced one of the smoothest landings I've ever made even though I had no real control of the airplane. Later, after some further inspection, I found that I couldn't have ejected even if I had wanted to. The ground crew had not pulled the safety pin on the ejection seat. I'd have gone down with the F-86.

"People have asked me over the years what's the most terrifying ride I've ever had. There have been many, but none scarier than the one in that F-86."

After that memorable tale, we adjourned to make ready for the evening formal dinner. Bob and Kay joined our table, as well as two Norwegians who had trained in Canada and two very amusing Americans. As the honour guard marched in, we rose for the obligatory question, "Oh, say can you see ...?"

Following his introductory remarks, James Alley, the president, asked all those who owed their life to the ejection seat to stand. About forty pilots popped up, including one of our Norwegians.

With the RCAF ensign proudly flying over our table, several pilots stopped to chat. The conversation of fighter pilots encompasses a universal language, with two-handed depictions of aerial manoeuvres. And so to bed, and thence home.

*Note 4: SPAADS: Sabre Pilots Association of Air Division Squadrons (Membership restricted to those who flew the F-86 Sabre with one of the 12 squadrons of the RCAF's 1 Air Division in England, France and Germany, 1952 to 1963.)

*Note 5: With the kind permission of Bob Hoover, extracts from his book "Forever Flying," ISBN 067153761X (1996).

Bill Mar & Connie

Death Valley Steam Engine

Dick & Dale – Death Valley

Chapter 25
Utah Mountain High

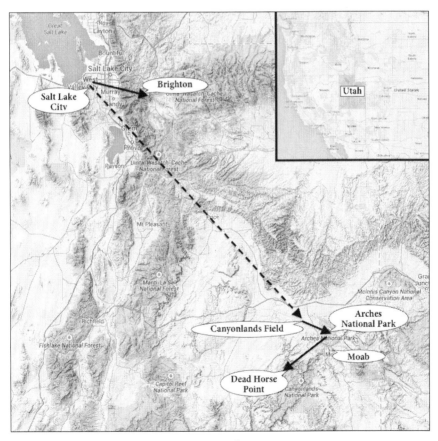

U.S.A. – October 2011

Salt Lake City

In mid-October Jet Johnson and I accepted Susan and Tom Horne's offer to visit Salt Lake City. Susan's father, Lt. Lamar Barlow, had died in the 1954 crash of a United States Air Force F-86 Sabre on Grouse Mountain, overlooking Vancouver. In 2009, Susan, her mother, and 10 family members had visited the crash site.

Susan met us at Salt Lake City airport, smartly dressed in a business suit. She was a member of the airport's board of directors and had been attending a board meeting. We drove into the heart of Salt Lake City, sited on a gentle slope above the valley. Broad streets arrayed in a north-south grid were the first notable feature of the city. Parking in front of the Mormon Cathedral, we had a quick look around the Latter Day Saints Church's History Museum. My knowledge of the Mormon religion was minimal, so it was not difficult to increase it considerably. I asked Susan about the meaning of a model baptismal pool. She explained a rite unique to this religion, the baptism of the dead by proxy. The rationale is to give the deceased equal rights, enabling their souls to enter the Kingdom of Heaven. Thus the Mormon's passion for genealogy.

We attempted to visit the Genealogical Center, but it had closed at 5 p.m., for Mormons are encouraged to meet with their families each Monday evening.

With some time in hand, Susan gave us a quick tour of the family business, a steel fabricating factory with an impressive inventory of high-tech machinery. Thence to meet Tom at the Alta Club, Salt Lake's foremost club for executives. A fine dinner followed. Mormons do not consume alcohol. When offered wine, we decided to do in Rome as the "Romanians" do, and declined.

For those whose families have flown the coop, the optional Monday evening activity is to meet with friends. Tom and Susan invited us to join an empty-nesters' gathering at a friend's luxurious mansion on a knoll overlooking the city.

With bright lights sparkling below, about 30 guests gathered in the spacious living room, facing a jazz quartet and grand piano on a mezzanine over the front door. After a short prayer from our host, the quartet struck up. Our task was to identify the Broadway musical song from the jazzed version. I recognized a few tunes but could not put a name to any. Susan identified nearly all of them.

Post concert, we helped ourselves to strawberries and ice cream in the prodigious kitchen. Our hostess, widow of a local multimillionaire, was interested in the circumstances of our meeting with Susan and Tom. Fortunately, I had my iPad in the vehicle and showed her photos of the family visit to the F-86 crash site.

We then drove to Big Cottonwood Canyon, climbing to 2,500 metres and what was billed as a modest cabin. It turned out to be a luxurious five-bedroom ski chalet, complete with dry sauna and a high vaulted ceiling over the living room.

Flight to the Badlands
After breakfast at the local restaurant, we drove to the valley floor through vibrant yellow aspen and, lower down, fire-red maples. On the corporate aviation side of Salt Lake City airport, we boarded Tom's six-seat Piper Lancer. Flying southeastward, we left the broad valley behind, skirting the bright-yellow-cloaked slopes of Loafer Mountain.

Below lay the historic tracks of the Union Pacific Railroad, the first to cross the nation, its Golden Spike driven in 1866 at Promontory Summit, well to north of our flight route. Three locomotives pulled a long line of cars laden with coal. They were headed to nearby power plants, unlike the coal of the Canadian Rockies which is shipped to China and Japan. Presently the terrain transitioned to a broad upland plateau. bisected by the ancient cut of the Green River. We followed the Green through amazing formations of sculpted sandstone, the epitome of badlands. After circling over the confluence of the Green and the Colorado, we set course for Canyonlands Field, 25 kilometres northwest of Moab. Moab, where the historic Spanish Trail crossed the Colorado River, became "Uranium Capital of the World" during the Cold War.

All eyes to the sky as we searched for parachutists, who had first dibs at the airfield. On landing we boarded a rented SUV and drove to the Ranger station at Arches National Park for a synopsis and geological explanation of its fantastic rock formations: arches, windows, bridges, pillars, and hoodoos. Beneath the stratified rocks lies a mile-thick salt bed, deposited eons ago by the evaporation of a vast inland sea.

Parking the vehicle, we set off on a rough track to the striking Double Window. At a steep incline we left Jet behind, as he could not climb the slope. We climbed through one of the holes and descended on the far side for a view of a landform that looked to me like two eyes with a nose between. Retrieving Jet, we drove to another spectacular formation known as the Grand Arch. Again, Susan and I left Jet behind as we made the lengthy climb to a gorge overlooking the impressive Delicate Arch, depicted on the Utah licence plate.

A half-hour drive took us out of the park to a promontory known as Dead Horse Point. Wild horses were herded across a narrow isthmus to a mesa bounded by sheer drop-offs on every side, then barricaded in to be captured as and when needed. One hot dry summer the barricaded horses all died of thirst, hence the name. From the cliff edge we gazed down at the upper Colorado 600 metres below us. Since the river is visible, the view is arguably superior to that from the rim of the deeper and more famous Grand Canyon. Dusk fell as we landed at Salt Lake City.

Hiking the Silver Hills

Next day we drove up Big Cottonwood Canyon Road past Solitude Nordic Center to Brighton, nestled in a pristine alpine basin. In 1857 a Mormon congregation of 2,500 held a historic Pioneer Day celebration on the meadow. While Jet strolled the boardwalk around Silver Lake, I hiked to Lake Solitude. The entire area is pockmarked with tunnels, adits, and declines, for the hills are laced with rich silver deposits. I entered an adit in search of silver, but someone had beaten me to the lode.

Descending, I met a bloke decked out in camouflage and armed with a crossbow. "What are you after?" I asked. "Moose. Yesterday we saw a cow and calf, and then a bull charged us, forcing us to hide behind a tree." Snapping a photo, I hiked on to meet Jet. We dined at Silver Fork Lodge, the only restaurant in the valley open during the off-season.

Under a bright blue morning sky, I hiked along a small stream, climbing southward. When huge boulders blocked the way I scrambled up the steep bank, finding a narrow deer trail. Passing multiple groves of yellow aspen, I reached a small alpine lake at the base of Alta Peak, finding another adit barren of silver.

That evening Susan and Tom hosted dinner with her mother present. Susan remarked that her mother's visit to the Grouse Mountain crash site had transformed her. Until I told the details of the crash, Gloria had known nothing of how her husband had died. And so to home.

The Colorado from Dead Horse Point

The Eyes

Silver Search

Chapter 26
Panama Low

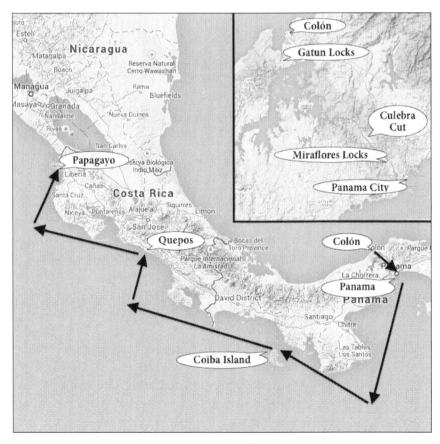

Panama – April 2012

Panama City

My flight from Houston, Texas landed in Panama City shortly after sunset. The taxi made swift progress on the toll road, passing near-vacant towers at water's edge and on through the hotel and business district to my modest hotel, in a no-man's-land between the luxury hotel zone and the old Spanish town.

I flew to Panama at the invitation of my friend Brian O'Sullivan to join his 41-metre yacht Komokwa on its voyage of delivery to Vancouver. Of the millions who have traversed the Panama Canal, the overwhelming majority have done so from the decks of a cruise ship or freighter. It had been a longtime objective of mine to traverse the canal, so I was pleased to be invited to pass through on a smaller vessel, viewing the operation from low in the water. Panama Low, as it were.

While Sarah, a fellow Komokwa guest who had been on the flight from Houston, flew to the San Blas Islands, I chose to stay in Panama City to get a feel for what is hyped as an ideal retirement destination, and to visit the Canal Museum to learn more of this monumental engineering project completed in 1914. The city's forest of high-rise towers is reminiscent of Miami Beach, although the beaches looked less than pristine. Banks and shops invariably had an armed guard at the entrance, suggesting that all was not as peaceful as advertised.

I boarded the hop-on-hop-off tourist bus to Miraflores Lock, where I viewed a short movie on the canal's construction and toured the interpretive centre. After lunch I joined the crowd at the gallery overlooking the lock to watch the first of the afternoon arrivals, a catamaran and a conventional sailboat rafted together, followed by an enormous "Panamax" container ship, a vessel of the largest dimensions that will fit through the canal.

Although the locks are twinned, congestion in the narrow Culebra Cut constrains traffic to one-way only from Gatun Lake to Panama City. Beyond the locks, just visible over the ridge, was the construction site of the new canal. The new 180-foot-wide locks will accommodate the many supersize vessels that cannot transit the current 110-foot chambers.

Reboarding the tour bus, I rode out to the end of a 3-kilometre causeway to several preexisting islands in the Pacific. Rock from the the Culebra Cut, the excavation through the continental divide, was used to build a barrier against silting of the canal approaches. The three outermost islands, now hosting marinas, upscale hotels, and restaurants, sprouted remnants of military fortifications on hilltops.

Canal transit

I had planned travel by rail from Panama City north to Colón, the Caribbean entrance to the canal, but the passenger train operates only weekdays. Completed in 1850 with funds generated from the 1848-49 rush to California gold, this historic line, the first transcontinental railway, now conveys mainly freight containers.

I made plans to take the bus, but Brian's agent recommended strongly against it. The next day, a Saturday afternoon, he provided a vehicle, and driver. Arriving in Colón, I had my first taste of red tape, for the Canal Zone is an entity separate from the Republic of Panama. I had to clear immigration for the zone. Colón is a rather shabby town and apparently a dangerous place. Strolling around with suitcase in tow, I would be easy pickings. Presently I boarded the tender and motored around Cristóbal Harbour to Komokwa, anchored in front of enormous cranes and gantries.

I climbed aboard and Captain Chris introduced me to the crew: first mate Alex, second mate Chris the younger, Theo the cook, Abbi the stewardess, Will the engineer, and Noli the Filipino deckhand. Guests included Sarah, her Californian friend Jeremy, and Cindy, Mike, and Hayden, all from Vancouver. Abbi escorted me to the stateroom that I shared with Chris the younger, and then gave a quick tour of this luxurious vessel.

While awaiting the Canal inspector, Captain Chris had little rest day or night, repeatedly resetting the anchor as a 20-knot wind dragged the boat along the slippery silt bottom. Will announced that we would have to restrict fresh water consumption; the silt had clogged the filters of the water-maker. A competent agent is a crucial element in a successful transit, and the consensus, including the inspector's view, was that our agent was somewhere south of the D team. For instance, when Will requested 3,000 litres of fresh water, he asked, "What size bottles do you want?"

After the inspector departed, Will was able to arrange docking space at the nearby Shelter Bay Marina. At the narrow marina entrance, Captain Chris and crew delicately pivoted the boat and reversed to the outer dock. While Will boarded 3,000 litres of fresh water, ending our water restriction, Jeremy and I went ashore to explore the jungle-shrouded gun batteries of Fort Sherman.

On Tuesday morning the captain received belated instructions regarding the lines needed for the transit. There are three categories of vessels: under 65 feet, requiring only an "advisor"; up to 125 feet, requiring a "pilot"; and over 125 feet, classified as a large commercial vessel. Since we were in the third category, we were required to have four 125-foot hawsers of about 3 inches diameter. They arrived in a large coil at 1 p.m. The crew promptly laid out four lines and made the required loops at either end, stowing the lines just in time for our 3:15 p.m. rendezvous with the pilot.

After a short delay we motored to the first Gatun lift lock. As we approached, a tender came to our starboard side and transferred ten linesmen aboard, four at the stern and four at the bow, and of course each of these teams needed a supervisor! A rowboat neared the port bow and slung aboard two "monkey's fists," small weighted lead lines. When attached to the hawsers, shore workers hauled them to the electric "mules" that ran on tracks the length of the lock; two on each side at bow and stern.

The 125-foot hawsers lay idle on the deck, the linesmen munching chocolate bars, and the mules shunted along the dockside tracks with lines slack, for we moved through the lock under our own power. The three locks raised the vessel a total of 26 metres, after which we motored into Gatun Lake, an artificial body formed by the damming and diversion of rivers. Along the muddy shore crocodiles lurked, and in the fields grazed a sounder of wild boar, a European species introduced by the Spaniards.

The freighter that had preceded us sped away, soon lost from view. We made our way across the lake at 10 knots, entering the Culebra Cut and then the first down-lock. About 11 p.m. we cleared the Miraflores Locks, entered the Pacific, and tied up at a nearby fuelling dock.

The fuelling representative arrived promptly at 8 a.m., but after negotiations regarding couplings and liability it was past 10 when the fuel began to flow. The gauge ticked off 217 barrels, about 9,000 U.S. gallons. Confusion reigned, for from the days when I cached "barrels" of fuel for my helicopter, I recalled a barrel as equivalent to 54 U.S. gallons. I learned later that a barrel of petroleum is defined as 42 U.S. gallons, while what I called a barrel is a "drum." During the delay, Cindy and Hayden decided to go shopping for Panama hats. Despite their risky straddle across the unstable ladder, they were unsuccessful, for the gatekeeper refused to open the gate of the compound. After a further wait for a pilot to depart the Canal Zone, we motored to the open sea.

Costa Rica cruise

Early Wednesday morning I arose for my scheduled 6-to-10-a.m. lookout watch. Shortly after I reached my post, with Chris the younger at the helm, a 10-metre log passed close off the port bow, emphasizing the need for a keen lookout. We made good time, a 3-knot following current giving us a speed of 13 knots. I noted a fuel imbalance on the monitor. When Will investigated he found that a seal on the centre tank had popped, spilling diesel fuel into the bilge below the lower guest rooms.

We anchored early afternoon off Coiba Island, formerly a penal colony, now a national park. To quote from the guidebook:

"Coiba's underwater topography is linked by the underwater Cordillera mountain chain to Cocos Island [800 km southwest, out in the Pacific] and the Galapagos Islands [1,000 km west of Ecuador]. Scientists from the Smithsonian Tropical Research Institute have proclaimed it an unparalleled destination for discovering new species."

Some of us boarded the tender, Mike at the helm. Wading ashore into soft sinking sand, I recalled with some trepidation a visit to another tropical isle where poisonous snails inhabited the soft sand. A sign in front of a derelict building identified the island as a park. Theo and Jeremy harvested a modest crop of limes from a nearby tree. After a short, unsatisfactory snorkel in murky water, we re-boarded the tender and motored to anchor near a low headland for another session in clear, but shallow, water. I saw neither coral nor fish, just the odd bit of algae. Sarah, standing on the tender, pointed to a turtle 20 metres off. I swiftly swam to that point. No turtle. So much for the great turtle chase.

We returned to Komokwa, whereupon Chris the younger and Will decided to inspect the beach. I explained there was very little to see, and expected them to return within the half hour. They departed about 4 p.m. At 6, with the tender in view on the beach, we assumed something had gone amiss. Shortly afterwards smoke appeared from a fire that the "Castaways" had lit to alert us to their stranding. Alex, on Komokwa, had been attempting to start the sea-doo, whose battery needed a jump start. Eventually he powered it up and raced to the beach, returning shortly afterward to say, "We need water, beer, chocolate bars, cigarettes, and a lighter." I was not sure whether Alex was kidding, but he returned to the beach and retrieved the castaways in time for dinner. As Chris told it, he and Will had explored inland for about 20 minutes, and upon their return found the tender grounded by the ebb tide.

Meanwhile, Jeremy and company cast fishing lines and, aided by the underwater stern lights, soon landed a good catch. A 15-inch bonito was slated for next day's sushi lunch. A disagreeable number of venomous sea snakes slithered among the swarming fish.

About 8 p.m. Alex and Chris the younger set out on the sea-doo to the beach, sans compass but with a powerful light provided by Will. Despite their shallow draft, they grounded on a sandbar. About 10 p.m. I listened to radio discussions of the ongoing foul-up. Captain Chris, having located the tender on the radar, directed them to proceed 300 metres to their left. The lads stumbled along the beach, most of the time without radio contact, and eventually found the tender. They then waded out to retrieve the stranded sea-doo, which presumably would not start because of the faulty battery. As Alex towed it to the tender, I heard a loud exclamation on the radio: "Shaaark!"

With that shriek, I became increasingly concerned that the fiasco would turn into a tragedy. I climbed to the bridge looking for the captain but found him on the bow with Abbi, radio in hand. I gave my opinion: essentially, that the guidebook listed the island as a former penal colony surrounded by shark-infested waters. In my extensive experience in tropical waters, having lived on Jamaica, Bermuda, Samoa, and other tropical islands, I was well aware that sharks feed in shallow water at night. I suggested that he give orders to get out of the water. I then retired to my stateroom. Captain Chris immediately sent Abbi to retrieve the eavesdropping radio and, as he later recounted, transmitted, "Get out of the water. Now!"

About 30 minutes after midnight, I arrived at the stern just as Alex and Chris returned from the beach. Chris said he had been in waist-high water at the dinghy when he saw a large fin pass within an arm's length, followed by fish leaping out of the water, at which time he jumped straight into the tender. Tragedy had been averted, and although the lads made light of the incident they both appeared somewhat shaken. As an airman, it mystified me that these seamen seemed blissfully ignorant of tides, the time it would take to refloat the tender, and the hazards of nighttime activity in tropical water.

The following morning Captain Chris manipulated the crane to raise the small dinghy with Alex standing precariously astride. I helped stow it, and shortly after 10 we weighed anchor and motored northwest to Costa Rica. "Dolphins off the port bow," said I as twenty leaping dolphins formed up port and starboard, giving a grand demonstration of speed and agility.

At 3 p.m., it was "slow ahead" as an overheating gearbox compelled an engine shutdown. We dropped anchor offshore from the village of Quepos at 8 p.m., for there was no dock. Will and Mike set to work on the gearbox. They later found it had been contaminated by small crabs, most likely from the Mediterranean where the boat originated.

At 8 a.m. the next morning, not long after we left our anchorage, the hitherto calm sea gave way to 3-metre rolling swells on the port beam. Prone to seasickness, I would have been heaving over the side but for the yacht's excellent stabilization, its ride remained dead-level. Late in the afternoon, Jeremy spotted a sailfish 500 metres off the port bow and instructed the crew to slow for trolling. Alas, the sole result was another tiny bonito.

At midday the next day, a Saturday, we docked at Papagayo Marina on the northwest coast of Costa Rica. There is always someone with a bigger something, and so it was here: a Bermuda-registered superyacht towering over Komokwa. Immigration officials cleared crew and passengers late that afternoon, but since Customs declined to work on the weekend, boat clearance was delayed to Monday. Giving "Captain Cook" a respite from his induction stove, I treated crew and guests to dinner at the dockside restaurant.

Promptly at 10 a.m., marina staff came to convey me to my taxi for the trip to nearby Liberia airport and my return flight. Mission accomplished!

Komokwa

Battery Mower at Fort Sherman

Gatun Lock Lighthouse

Chapter 27
In search of Genghis

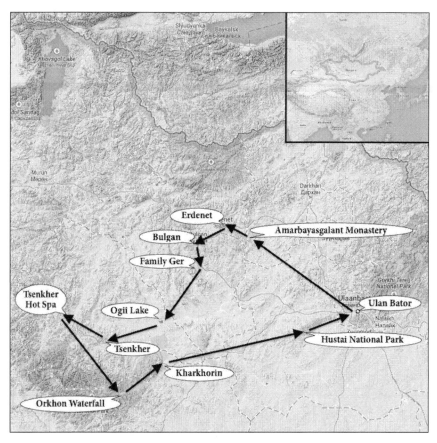

Mongolia – July 2012

The Quest

My travelling companion Roger Sylvestre, an affable, full-bearded French-Canadian, can make friends promptly, as was his nature during his 40 years of contract diamond drilling around the globe. His company opened a gold mine in Mongolia shortly after the 1990 departure of the Russians. They poured their first 15 gold bricks in 1997, whereupon the government expropriated the mine.

Roger's return to Mongolia was motivated by a wish to revisit the mine and view the changes of the intervening 15 years. As for myself, I was interested in seeing at first hand the land that spawned the conqueror of most of Eurasia in the 13th century, and to take a stab at finding the tomb and treasure of the legendary Genghis Khan.

Awaiting our morning flight from Beijing to Mongolia, Roger struck up a conversation with a fellow passenger. Paul, formerly an officer of the Australia Special Forces, was now leading a team of instructors tasked with training the immense work force needed for Mongolia's rapidly expanding mining projects.

Our Air China flight crossed the smoke-shrouded mountain range just to the north of Beijing and set out on a two-hour traverse of the barren Gobi Desert. Low hills appeared as we approached Ulan Bator, capital of Mongolia, nestled in a bowl and somewhat obscured by smoke and pollution.

Ulan Bator

Our guide Luna and driver Nick of Ayan Trails met us at the airport with a generously sized Toyota four-wheel drive. A curious feature of Mongol society is that a person has only one name, given at birth to evoke the infant's bright future. The modern world now requires the addition of a clan or family name for travel abroad.

On our short drive into Ulan Bator, we passed roadwork and numerous apartment towers under construction. "Under construction" is the operative phrase, for both city and nation are in a state of rapid change. The city's population had exploded from 500,000 when Roger was last here to about 1.5 million. That was almost half the population of this sparsely populated country, which encompasses an area about three times that of France. Passing a modernistic tower across from the imposing Parliament and its square, we came to our modest hotel just outside the city centre.

Next morning we drove to a monastery complex on top of a nearby hill surrounded by makeshift shacks. The monastery is one of only two that survived the Soviet purge of religion following the establishment of the People's Republic in the early 1920s. In the central temple, Buddhist monks chanted and recited from the 108 volumes of Tibetan codices. Genghis Khan himself worshipped the Sky Father, but was tolerant of all religions. A close affiliation with Tibet developed early in the reign of his dynasty.

Next stop on our city tour was the Winter Palace of the Manchu Priest-King of the late 19th century. At the time the country was a sectarian Lamaist (Tibetan Buddhist) state. "Palace" is a bit of a stretch; it is essentially a two-storey wooden barrack-like building with central steam heating. It is now a museum displaying the Khan's possessions, including an eclectic collection of stuffed fauna.

The imposing Zaisan Memorial, perched on a prominent hill with an outstanding panoramic view of the city, honours Soviet-Mongolian military campaigns. Twin spires tower over a circular mosaic in socialist realist style, portraying scenes from the 1920s through to the postwar space age.

In 1921 the Manchurians were dislodged by a White (anti-Bolshevik) Russian force allied with the Chinese. Shortly afterward the new rulers were ousted in turn by a combined force of Mongolians and a Red (Bolshevik) Russian army. The city's name is Mongolian for "Red Hero," the nickname of the Russian liberator. Liberation was short-lived, for Mongolia became a puppet of the Soviet Union. All reference to the Great Khan was suppressed to avoid the use of his name and memory as focus for revolt.

When the Soviet Union collapsed, the Russians withdrew both their troops and their economic aid. When Roger's company began construction of the mine, goods and supplies were scarce. Most supplies including timber had to be imported from Canada or the

United States. A short visit to the former state department store showed that material shortages were of the past. Escalators rising from the floor of a soaring gallery passed five levels displaying a comprehensive range of consumer goods.

Roger arranged a meeting with Demby, his right-hand man during construction of the mine. The exterior of his Soviet-style apartment was predictably shabby, but its interior was decorated with tasteful local art. Dipping a finger in a glass of "Genghis" vodka, he flicked drops to the floor and the ceiling as a tribute to earth and sky.

Tourist camp and monastery

Next morning we drove north, roughly paralleling the railway that leads to Russia, passing metal scrap yards, fuel depots, and about 10 gas stations open or under construction. At a bridge where the road crossed a small stream, we stopped for several herds of horses thundering down to the water. A frenzied stallion ran up and down the bank looking for one of his errant mares. Continuing north, we stopped at a roadside cafe for an indifferent lunch. Amenities were rather primitive, the toilet being an outhouse with two planks lying over a deep hole.

The landscape was a series of treeless rolling hills, with wide, lush valleys providing excellent pasture for the abundant livestock. From youthful reading and western movies I had gained an abiding impression of continuous conflict between shepherds and cattlemen in the American West. There was no such conflict here. Horses, cattle, sheep, goats, and yaks shared the same pasture. Although a small amount of land is fenced, most is open range. The animals forage until they have exhausted the local grass, and then move with their nomad herders to fresh pasture.

We diverged west, passing vast fields of wheat and fallow. Somewhat more than 300 km later, we left the paved road and bounced along some 30 km of dirt track to a tourist camp. Enclosed within a white picket fence were 18 "gers," along with a shower-toilet building and a large dining room. What the Russians call a yurt the Mongols call a ger, a round dwelling that can be erected or dismantled in about an hour. Our ger was about 3.5 metres in diameter, its wood lattice frame composed of four sections. A ger could easily be enlarged by the addition of sections. Two central posts supported a ring frame from which spoke-like rafters sloped to the 1.5-metre-high walls, all covered with felt and canvas. A central opening provided light and a port for the chimney. The comfortable furnishings included two beds against the side walls, a chest opposite the south-facing door, and an iron stove in the centre.

As we awaited dinner, enjoying the afternoon sun, 400 sheep and goats passed along the perimeter fence. Their day of foraging done, they were returning to their pens for milking and for protection from marauding wolves.

Thunder, lightning, and heavy rain during the night foretold slippery roads for our morning drive to an ancient monastery. A four-wheel drive was unquestionably a requirement for the 15 km of rough track. The Amarbayasgalant Monastery, 300 years old, is the other monastery not razed by the Russians. Bypassing it, Roger and Luna climbed a long staircase to the imposing white stupa, a dome-shaped structure on a hill overlooking the monastery. The hill was topped by a modern construct of 37 marble Buddhas, each with a different pose, encircling a six-meter-high gold Buddha.

While Luna and Roger climbed the staircase to the stupa, I hiked to a nearby hill topped with an "obo" or shamanist shrine. A pile of rocks anchored a few wooden posts swathed in blue, representing the sky or Sky Father. The Mongols are mainly Buddhist, but the shrine clearly showed an attachment to their ancient beliefs. The monastery once hosted up to 5,000 monks; now only 80 remain. It was undergoing restoration after decades of neglect during the Soviet period.

Family ger
Leaving the chanting monks behind, we retraced our journey 45 km along the rough track to the main road, on which we continued to Erdenet. Site of an enormous Russian-Mongolian copper mine dating from the early 1950s, this city of about 150,000 is the second largest in Mongolia. Another mediocre lunch, and on to the small town of Bulgan.

Though our map showed a paved road southbound, the pavement ended suddenly about one kilometre south of Bulgan. My map, printed in Vancouver, soon proved worthless. The dirt track eventually morphed into what we termed an eight-lane highway, for when the wheel ruts became too deep the drivers veered onto the grass, resulting in a braided network of road scars. The adjacent slope sparkled like diamonds. Diamonds not, but plastic and glass bottles lit by the sun, discarded by travellers oblivious to the ecological eyesore.

Our itinerary listed a night's lodging with a family, but on arrival at the valley south of Bulgan we found no booking. On reflection this was quite logical, as nomads can and do move on short notice. So our guide and driver searched for a suitable family. Few gers and few people were important criteria, for in a larger community alcohol could be a problem. The chosen family comprised a widow, her two sons, and an infant grandson. A small cooking ger stood near the family dwelling. The family ger contained two beds that we appropriated for our use. A solar panel on the roof provided power for light and, incongruously, an LCD television. After a meagre dinner of macaroni and dried mutton, I climbed a nearby wooded hill for a panoramic view of the valley. Livestock were returning from pasture, the mares and cows to be milked and 200 sheep and goats to their pen. This small family was largely self-reliant, producing curd and yogurt from the milk, selling the odd sheep for cash, and slaughtering animals for meat as needed.

Shortly after we retired, the lads came to watch television, bedding down on the floor. A fitful sleep followed, as people snored, horses neighed, cows mooed, sheep bleated, and the dog serenaded his neighbours.

Sipping morning tea, we watched the daily routine unfold. One of the lads opened the gate and shooed the adults out, restraining lambs and kids. One lamb bleated repeatedly, answering the calls of its mother but to no avail. It was amusing to watch the kids, only four months old, rear up on hind legs and bash horns in an attempt to establish dominance. The adults milled about as mares and cows came for the morning milking, then all moved off to pasture. Separate pasturing for adults and young ensured that they would all return to the pen at night. Just before our departure, Roger presented the mother with his "Mongolian Gold" corporate pin, with intertwined Canadian and Mongolian flags.

We set off on a bouncing ride across a low pass, the land here without livestock or gers, for there was little water in this highland of sparse grass. We stopped between an ancient burial mound and an obo that looked like the frame of an Indian tepee, the wood enclosing the customary rock pile. Luna circled the obo three times, placing a stone on the pile with each circuit.

Ogii Lake

Midday we arrived at Ogii Lake, a roughly oval basin measuring about 5 x 9 kilometres. Multiple tourist camps dotted the gently sloping southern shore. As we relaxed in the afternoon sunshine, a violent storm moved in from the west. The far shore was obscured by the froth of windswept water as a classic gust-front rapidly approached. Camp girls feverishly scurried about to lower the chimneys, secure the ceiling flaps, and close the doors of the gers. We ducked into ours just before the pelting rain, thunder, and lightning arrived. That evening we dined on fish from the lake, a rather nondescript dish but a welcome change from the omnipresent fatty mutton. Living in a climate of harsh winters, the Mongols, much like the Inuit, crave fat, the more the better.

The next morning, as expected, muddy tracks were the norm along the north shore and through the western wetlands where we crossed the river draining the lake. After many kilometres of rough track, including two fords, we passed a jumble of heavy vehicles and reached a paved road to Tsetserleg. A small town nestled at the head of a narrow valley, bounded by granite hills, Tsetserleg had clapboard houses of Russian style sporting brightly coloured roofs. Among interesting artifacts in the museum, formerly part of an extensive monastery complex, was a collapsed ger loaded on an ancient wood-wheeled cart, yoked to a stuffed yak. The shaggy, ox-like yak copes well with the frigid climate. The Mongols prefer their milk for its high fat content. Another curious exhibit, dating from the mid-1920s, was a life-sized painting of a 2.75-meter (9-foot) giant, with photographs of him towering over Communist Party functionaries.

Tsenkher hot spa

After chatting with a trio of Hungarian motorcyclists en route to Ulan Bator, we drove on to the Tsenkher hot-spring spa, the local tourist attraction. Our camp was one of several at the head of a valley surrounded by forested hills. An unprepossessing concrete blockhouse housed the baths, no doubt a relic of Soviet days. Although the spa was not up to the luxurious standards of Baden or Banff, the shallow hot and tepid pools felt very refreshing after our bucking-bronco ride.

Orkhon Valley

Another late afternoon thunderstorm with heavy rain guaranteed a muddy drive to our next tourist camp, at the gateway to the upper Orkhon Valley. After lunch we set off up the valley, stopping for photos from the top of a vertical cliff cut by the meandering Orkhon. Over a history of human habitation reaching back 60,000 years, the Orkhon Valley has taken on a sacred quality for many. Its fertile volcanic basalt basin has provided rich pastureland for successive tribes of Huns, Turkic peoples and finally Mongols. We passed at least seven ancient burial mounds on the 30-km drive to our objective, the 20-metre-high waterfall described as the most scenic site in Mongolia. While Roger photographed from the rim, I clambered down a steep path to the river below. The sheer basalt walls are punctured with lava-tube caves, and on the gravel bar below the falls, a ubiquitous obo marked the shamanic reverence for water, rock, and sky. On our return journey, we stopped to help a group of local tourists whose vehicle had become stuck in a deep mudhole. Nick fastened a cable to the frame and slowly towed it free. Ladies in their finery huddled beneath a blue tarp as the usual afternoon shower began.

Considering Roger's gamey knee, we decided to forgo the planned 80-km drive and 3-km climb to another monastery. Retracing 60 km of rough track, we reached the paved road leading to Kharkhorin, the ancient capital. Here Genghis directed the establishment of a formidable city patterned on Chinese fortifications and dwellings. It was from this broad valley that he and his successors ruled their vast empire, until Kublai Khan moved the capital to present-day Beijing. The city fell into disrepair and was eventually destroyed by Manchu invaders.

Beneath a glass floor at the entrance to the exceptional museum lay the excavated remains of a circular kiln. Nearby, a 6 x 6-metre table mounted an archaeological model of the walled city. Our timing was fortunate, for we joined a lecture in English with a slide presentation of a recent tomb excavation, uncannily similar to those at the Egyptian Valley of the Kings. A gentle decline along walls of bright frescoes terminated at chambers filled with grave goods. The museum displayed these, including many gold coins of Byzantine origin, gleaming bright as the day they were struck. However, this was not the gold we sought, for the tomb, found about 150 kilometres to the northwest, dates from about 600 AD, well before the birth of Genghis.

Nearby, 108 stupas lined the towering white walls enclosing the Erdene Zuu monastery, built in the 16th century from the ruins of the former capital. Of the 62 temples within the wall, only three, converted to museums, survived the Soviet purge of the 1930s.

Exiting through a tall gate, we strolled to the nearby tourist market where I donned a leather glove and hoisted a huge golden eagle. As the bird spread its enormous wings, I needed both arms to lift it above my head for the obligatory photo op.

En route to our next tourist camp we passed through present-day Kharkhorin, a Soviet-style town of clapboard houses and a huge abandoned flour mill. At the camp gate, maidens in traditional dress greeted us with airag, the customary welcoming drink of fermented mare's milk. Definitely an acquired taste! Our newly erected ger at the back of the compound lacked stove, light, and power, but the helpful staff soon made it right. On this flood plain between the town and the Orkhon River, flies, hitherto rare, made their annoying appearance in black swarms. A pan of dung on the hot stove soon drove them from our ger, but it was some time before we could clear the smoke. After dinner, local performers presented an entertainment of folk music, dancing, and the peculiar "throat singing" renowned throughout Mongolia.

Takhi horse

Back on the paved road, we stopped at a roadside souvenir market where I bought a few trinkets, then stopped again to observe six giant condors feeding on the carcass of a pony. Presently we arrived at Elsen Tasarkha, an area of low sand dunes. Declining an offer to ride a Bactrian, or two-humped, camel, I instead mounted a lean pony and headed off to the dunes. Mindful of your "Superman" Christopher Reeve and his paralysis resulting from a fall, I was no Genghis Dick. I timidly restricted the pace to a brisk trot instead of a Mongolian gallop.

After checking into our rather austere tourist camp on the boundary of Hustai National Park, we drove to the Information Centre. The park contains widely diverse environments, from mountain range to open pasture, wetlands, and steppe. There is a remarkable variety of wildlife, of which the pride of the park is the Takhi, also called Przewalski's horse after the Russian explorer and naturalist who was the first European to describe it. War, hunting, and habitat loss contributed to the decline of this unique and never-domesticated species, thought extinct in the wild by the mid-1960s. In 1992 a cooperative effort led by the Dutch reintroduced it to its natural habitat from descendants of those collected for European zoos in the late 1890s. Of the 78 horses shipped by air, 50 survived. Nearly 300 now roam the park.

Early evening we set off to find the horse. Our local guide spotted a small herd silhouetted on a distant ridge. Binoculars in hand, Luna and I hiked up the slope for a closer look, stopping for photos of the 10 animals, including two foals, at the mandated closest approach of 300 metres.

Descending the slope smothered with colourful wildflowers and pockmarked with marmot burrows, we returned to the vehicle and drove farther into the park. We disembarked at a bubbling brook when we spotted a herd of 11 grazing in the nearby lush pasture, only 50 metres distant. A day-old foal suckled her dam as a yearling rubbed against a smooth rock.

Naadam Festival

Upon our return to Ulan Bator, Ayan Trails treated us to a delightful evening at the State Opera House. The show opened with a ballet of "archers," followed by a folk dance evoking images of galloping horses. Dancers in colourful costumes leaped about the stage mimicking battles of the past.

Our tickets for the National Naadam Festival allowed early access to the stadium at the portal of the Horse Guards' entry. Dressed in historic apparel and armour, the Honour Guard trotted into the stadium with gold yak-tail standards held aloft, planting eight low standards about the larger central plume as was the custom for the mustering of Genghis' troops. After the prime minister's welcoming remarks, the elaborate ceremony began, featuring military bands, dancers, athletes, and singers. Competitions followed immediately. "Naadam" means the "manly games," of wrestling, archery, and horse racing, though women now take part in the latter two sports.

The wrestling competition had but one category, with 512 competitors of varying ages and weights. In the first round, burly sumo types take on skinny young army recruits. The army lads are quickly dispatched, and the competition continues over three days until only one man is standing.

Leaving the stadium, we strolled to the archery pavilion, where competitors and spectators alike were clothed in their finest del (pronounced "deel"), long belted cloaks. Armed with a powerful composite bow, archers let loose at the targets, low walls of wicker cylinders. At a distance of 75 metres for men and 65 for women, the walls routinely toppled.

Luna had invited us to her home, a comfortable one-bedroom flat in a modern apartment complex where she lived with her 3-year-old son. She served a delicious mushroom soup and Roger's favourite Mongolian dish, buuza, a steamed mutton dumpling.

Next day Roger watched the horse races from the finish line outside the city. Boys and girls aged 5 to 13 raced along a cross-country course of 15 to 30 kilometres, depending on the age of the horse. A horn sounded at a distant starting point and the youngsters set off at a gallop. At the finish, the laggards struggled in at barely a trot.

The next leg of our itinerary was to have taken us to a mountain range 400 kilometres to the northeast, birthplace of Genghis and purported site of his tomb. When I telephoned home on arrival in Ulan Bator, our cleaning lady answered. "Danielle is in the hospital and her mother has died." I abandoned my trip. While Roger watched the races, I departed for the airport, reaching home via Seoul and San Francisco. My mission unfulfilled, the resumption of my quest awaits.

Family Ger

Luna circles an Obo

Orkhon Waterfall

Chapter 28

Costa Rica Repose

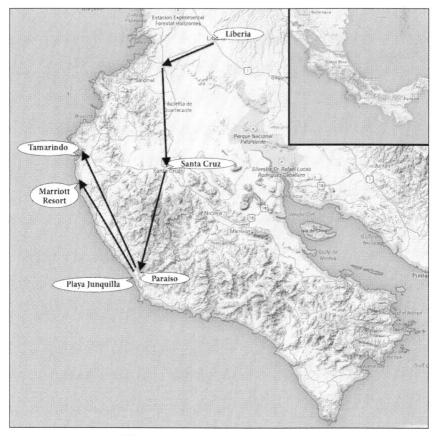

Costa Rica – December 2012 / January 2013

Playa Junquilla

Greeting us at Liberia airport in northwest Costa Rica, our Bermuda friends Kathy and Gerhard Lipp drove us 80 kilometres on paved road to the small village of Paraiso, then another couple of kilometres on gravel track to their gated condo complex at Playa Junquilla. Five exquisite two-story Spanish-style buildings at Las Villas Ventanas surrounded a lush garden with a waterfall amid a sizable swimming pool. The Lipps owned three units in the complex. We had rented a two-bedroom ground floor unit for a modest fee.

The area was rather rustic, with old farmsteads and shacks around the complex. A 150-metre track led to a broad black-sand beach, jungle-bordered, unspoiled, great for surfing though offering no snorkelling. You could walk the black sand for miles without seeing any development.

Despite the rustic setting, there were many fine restaurants in unlikely places, run by expats of origins ranging from France, Switzerland, and Italy through Argentina and the United States. All seemed intent on making a small fortune by starting with a large one! The French restaurant offered wine at up to $1,300 a bottle. One of the best, and cheapest, was a local Costa Rican open-air restaurant.

Our first excursion was to Tamarindo, a busy, chaotic beachfront town somewhat reminiscent of Karon Beach in Thailand. Surfing and souvenir shops abound, ideal for Dany to stock up on trinkets.

On New Year's Eve we dined at the beach club of the five-star Marriott Hotel, a half-hour drive on a dusty, bumpy gravel road. The food, open bar, music, dancing, and firework display ensured a most memorable gala.

Riding the bulls

All towns have a festival at this time of year. Paraiso's was held over the four days leading up to the new year. The village park became a fairground, with food concessions and rides for the kiddies. But the main attraction was in the stadium, a sturdy temporary structure of wood bleachers surrounding a bullring.

According to Gerhard, there is a religious element to the spectacle. The participants gather in a prayer circle before the event. Something about the conflict between good, and evil, evil being the tormented bull. Bull and rider burst out of the pen, the bull bucking until the rider falls off. The bull attempts to gore or stomp on the thrown rider, who is most of the time saved from serious harm by other participants distracting the bull.

Meanwhile, local lads try their hand at provoking and evading the bull. Most are wimps who generally linger near the fence, which they quickly climb when the bull approaches. But, again according to Gerhard, the lads become more courageous as the night progresses and the beer and liquor flow. When the bull tires of the game, three very skilful horsemen enter the ring and lasso it with one or two lines, then lead it to the exit gate. Some bulls, having been in the ring several times, know the routine and make their way to the exit unaided. We left after a half-dozen rounds, with the score at good 3, evil 3.

Riding and Kayaking

A few days later we set off on a horseback ride. Our German leader had two rules: (1) Do not pass her; (2) do not follow too close, as the horse ahead may kick back.

As we rode along the wave front of the black-sand beach, she suggested a little canter, which resulted in an exhilarating water-splashed ride. Rounding a promontory, we came upon the estuary of a small river. After a walk and trot though the dry-tropical forest we returned to the beach. As we neared the stable, our leader suggested another canter. I know not whether you have much riding experience, but picture this:

Of the four riders, only our leader-guide had a horse with a bit. Our own mounts had but a rope halter. Without a bit, a horse can pretty much do as it pleases. And so it was, as they sensed their time under the beating sun would soon be over. The canter morphed into a full gallop, our leader left far behind. So much for rule number one! Without proper riding gear, i.e. boots, my shins took a beating from abrasion at the stirrups.

Back home, at poolside, I heard what sounded like a cow under duress. I exited the back gate of our complex looking for the cow. There was none in sight, but high in a tree cavorted a troop of howler monkeys feeding on the leaves. Those little fellows can make a lot of noise.

We returned to the estuary, this time by car for a kayak paddle. As we rounded a turn in the forest, a speeding motorcycle on the wrong side of the road barely had time to swerve out of our way. Had we been five seconds later, he would have been a goner and our kayak ride a nonevent.

As we paddled upstream, the river narrowed and we had to navigate hanging vines. Thankfully they were bereft of snakes, though bugs became more annoying. The ebbing tide exposed the massive, tangled roots of a mangrove swamp, ideal habitat for the boa. Our kayak excursion ended uneventfully, no crocodiles sighted.

At the suggestion of our neighbours, I knocked on the door of the house directly across from the entrance to our compound. It was the home of the aforementioned motorcycle rider, who had been spear fishing at the mouth of the estuary. He sold us 1.5 kilos of lobster for $20, enough for a good dinner and a lobster salad for lunch the following day.

Visitors
Shortly after our Bermuda friends departed, Peter "Pedro" Jarman and Anne, his significant other came for a visit. Peter, a retired Air Canada pilot, lives in a small, gated community in the hills near San José, the capital.

"Pedro" is a man of many talents. He brought one of the model airplanes that he builds from scratch. Our broad beach proved to be the perfect place for the maiden flight of his 1:10 scale model of a De Havilland Hornet, the world's fastest piston aircraft. Our fellow condo dwellers showed considerable interest in the launches, flights, and landings.

Dan, another Bermudian, and I set off to view a four-metre crocodile lurking in a small river a few kilometres north. The resident fisherman was out to sea, but his wife led us to the river and gave a clap to alert the croc that a free fish was at hand. The beast must have been able to distinguish fake fish from real, for no croc appeared. Sunny, a native Hawaiian running a nearby B&B campsite, said a few dogs had recently gone missing, no doubt croc fodder.

Dan, a winter resident for 22 years and an erstwhile landowner, then directed me to a backcountry of grand estates now chopped into three-acre lots. Imposing mansions sat incongruously atop the high ground, seemingly miles from nowhere. A grandiose development scheme had fallen apart in the world financial meltdown of 2008. On one decaying concrete shell, a fading sign touted "Solid Investment Opportunity."

The Las Villas Ventanas complex was built by Mike, a developer from Edmonton, and most of the owners and guests were friendly folk from Alberta. In a conversation I joined with a couple of chaps at the pool, Bruce, a full-bearded beefy Coloradoan, mentioned that he had been in the bullring a couple of years before. His perspective: "There is no upside potential to going into the ring." His newfound caution was succinctly confirmed by a YouTube video of his encounter, with slow-motion repeats of his beer flying as the bull tossed him over its horns, fortunately without a puncture wound.

We drove to Santa Cruz for the Horse Parade on the penultimate day of its festival, the largest in the area. Unfortunately, we missed the parade because of misinformation about the time. We marvelled none the less at the expert beer-swilling vaqueros dancing their superb mounts along the streets, in and about the beer tents.

Despite, or perhaps because of the rustic environment, this place grows on one. After many hectic vacations in Mexico, Asia, and the Carib, we thoroughly enjoyed the tranquillity of our Costa Rica repose. The lush inland rain forest and volcanoes await a future visit.

Beach Ride

"Pedro" with his Hornet

Chapter 29

The Blue Danube

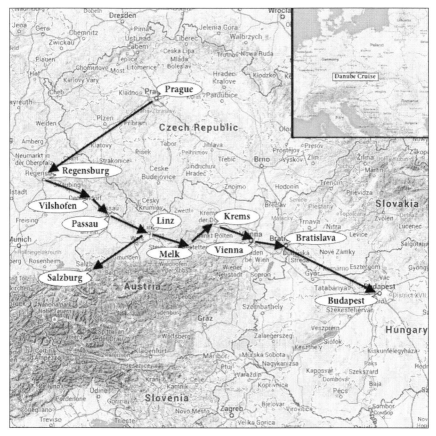

Central Europe – April 2013

Prague

In early April we flew to Prague via Frankfurt. Our hotel, the recently restored Century Old Town Hotel, well-located in the centre of Prague, featured high ceilings and an old-world charm. The nearby Palladium Shopping Centre gave Dany an opportunity to check out the local fashions.

A bus tour provided a good overview of the city, site of the infamous Defenestration of Prague. That outrage, the tossing of officials from a window in 1618, launched the Thirty Years' War, which eventually engulfed all of Europe. Initially a conflict between Protestants and Catholics, it later morphed into a power struggle between the Catholic French, supporting the Protestants, and the Catholic Habsburg Monarchy, ruling much of central Europe.

Dany had earlier bought tickets for Carmen at the National Theatre. We almost missed the beginning when our driver dropped us at the State Opera instead, but we got to the right venue in time. The elegant theatre proved a splendid setting for a stunning performance.

Regensburg

Next morning we joined the cruise group at the nearby Hilton and boarded buses for a three-hour journey to Regensburg, Germany. Passing an ancient steam locomotive on the approach, we crossed an even more ancient stone bridge into the historic town on the south bank of the Danube. Founded by the Romans in 179 AD as a fortress, Regensburg is one of Germany's oldest towns. Now a UNESCO heritage site comprising almost 1,000 heritage buildings, the old town escaped serious damage during World War II.

The U.S. Army Air Corps' disastrous Schweinfurt-Regensburg daylight bombing raid of August 1943 targeted the Messerschmitt aircraft factory a mere five kilometres east of the old-town centre. More often than not, U.S. "precision" bombing included many stray bombs, and it was just luck that spared the town.

Vilshofen

A further one-hour bus ride brought us to Vilshofen, a narrow peninsula between the Danube and Vils rivers. Following a welcome-aboard briefing, we stored our luggage in our comfortable cabin on the upper deck of the AmaDolce. After a delicious dinner, I stepped ashore to find a dockside tent hosting a Bavarian Oktoberfest. A fine little fest it was, even if it were either six months early or six months late. The lederhosen-attired quartet of violin, base, accordion, and tuba brought back memories of my arrival in Germany as a young fighter pilot in 1961. My days of oom-pa-pa, beer gardens and lovely lasses. Now it was to be a cruise featuring walking tours in the heartland of medieval and renaissance Europe, with a cornucopia of gothic and baroque churches all summarily bypassed on my first visit.

The lederhosen lads moved outside to give a demonstration of "whip cracking." A three-metre leather thong attached to a two-metre handle is waved in a circular motion, then snapped. The leather tip reaches the speed of sound, and the crack is a sonic boom. I tried my hand, but failed to get the crack.

Next morning we joined a walking tour in the old town, not quite as old as one would imagine, for fire almost completely destroyed it 220 years ago. The Stadtturm or City Tower with its clock escaped the flames. Gilt furnishings, marble columns, oil paintings, frescoes and stained glass adorned the interior of the opulent Saint John's church.

Passau

The AmaDolce departed at noon, and two hours later passed through the first of 12 locks we would encounter on our way to Budapest, our ultimate destination. Disembarking at Passau immediately downstream, the 146 passengers split into four groups for walking tours. This being our first river cruise since the Nile in 1981, I was pleasantly surprised by the audio feature of the tour. We all had a small radio with an earpiece that allowed us to listen to our guide without interference from traffic or hindrance by distance.

We entered the old town under the arch of the gothic town hall and tower. Passau is at the confluence of three rivers: the Ilz, a small stream from the north; the Inn, rising in the Swiss Alps above Innsbruck; and the Danube. The Inn is the most voluminous of the three, but since convention dictates that length determines name, the resulting winner is the Danube. Every August, meltwater from the Alps swells the Inn to a volume that backs up the lesser Danube, causing it to flood the lower town. Our guide pointed to marks on buildings showing flood levels to about 8 metres over a century of yearly floods. The city owns all the buildings prone to flooding, renting them to artisans and shopkeepers who remove their goods and wares when the waters arrive. Only five weeks after our visit, torrential rains resulted in severe flooding throughout the region. In Passau the water rose to almost 13 metres or 42 feet, the highest in records spanning 500 years.

Continuing our stroll, we reached a plaza at the top of a gentle rise. Passau was devastated by fire in the mid-1600s, after which Italian masters rebuilt the city in baroque elegance. The Cathedral of St. Stephan with its three green-domed towers holds the world's largest pipe organ.

Linz

A few hours later the AmaDolce slipped away for a night cruise to our next port, Linz, an overtly industrial town over the border in Austria.

The gothic and baroque buildings of the old town are blocked from view by modernistic museums and art galleries at river's edge. During our walking tour on the cobblestone streets, we stopped to view the plaque on the house where Mozart stayed in October 1762. The Hauptplatz or Main Square is the largest in Austria. It was briefly Adolf Hitler Platz, as Hitler considered Linz his home town. The Pestsaule or plague column towers 20 metres over the plaza. Like similar monuments in cities throughout Europe, it is a memorial for those who perished from bubonic plague.

Salzburg

Returning to dockside, we boarded coaches for a 1 1/2-hour drive to Salzburg, stopping briefly at a roadside restaurant with a splendid view over Mondsee, or Moon Lake, to snow-capped peaks in the distance. In Salzburg, our guide led us through the geometric garden of Mirabell Palace. Its ornate fountains and Greek-mythology-themed statues were featured in the movie "The Sound of Music."

We crossed Mozart Footbridge to the old town on the far bank of the Salzach, or Salt River. There is no salt here, but barges transported salt from the prince-archbishop's mines upstream. The massive revenue of "white gold" contributed to his wealth and to the town's coffers.

Strolling along Getreidegasse or Grain Street under the wrought-iron guild signs hanging above its shops, we came to Number 9, Mozart's birthplace. The third floor was his home to age 17. The entire four-storey building is now a museum dedicated to the life and music of Austria's exceptional musician and composer.

A funicular railway carried us to the lofty castle of the prince-archbishops, the Festung Hohensalzburg or High Salzburg Fortress. Throughout the Holy Roman Empire, which as Voltaire remarked was neither holy, nor Roman, nor an empire, its nobles combined the sacred with the secular, cross in one hand and sword in the other. The Salzburg castle is among the largest in Europe. Its interior is now a museum showcasing the luxurious apartments of the prince-archbishops. An audio guide allowed us to visit diverse sections, blacksmith's forge, torture room, and gun tower at a leisurely pace. The view from the top is spectacular, Salzburg and river below framed by snow-capped Alps.

Melk

Another overnight cruise brought us to Melk. Shortly after breakfast we boarded coaches for a short drive to the mustard-yellow Benedictine Abbey, perched on a promontory overlooking the town. Passing the garden, we entered a large courtyard surrounded by the high walls of the school included in the abbey complex, home to about 900 students. Modernistic murals adorn each of the walls representing the four virtues: Prudence, Justice, Fortitude, and Temperance.

Our tour took us through a series of themed rooms featuring historical displays, gilt statues, oil paintings, icons, ornate medieval manuscripts, priestly robes and other religious paraphernalia. It has been described in The Lonely Planet as "baroque gone barmy, with regiments of smirking cherubs, gilt twirls and polished faux marble." Each room is illuminated by lights of a single colour, blue, green, pink, etc. One incongruous display was a re-useable coffin. The deceased could be viewed in the coffin. Upon burial, a latch opened the bottom and the corpse dropped out. Functionaries later retrieved the coffin for repeated use.

The Marble Hall is crowned by an amazing and beautiful fresco giving the illusion of a high curved ceiling. The ceiling is flat. The hall leads to the Terrace with a grand view of the Danube and the narrow medieval streets of Melk below. It connects with the Library, where about 100,000 medieval and renaissance manuscripts are stored in an array of wood shelving rising 12 metres to the ceiling. A steep descent on a spiral staircase brought us to the cynosure of the monastery, the awe-inspiring baroque church, a splendour that words cannot describe.

A pleasant walk through the town, across a bridge, and through the woods returned us to the AmaDolce, where the crew prepared to cast off for Wachau Gorge.

Wachau Gorge

Wachau Gorge was undoubtedly the most scenic section of our cruise. Here, the Danube cuts through the rolling hills of an eroded ancient mountain range. Aggstein Castle high on the right bank dominates the approach to the gorge. A succession of robber barons, not content with collecting tolls for river passage, would loot passing vessels and imprison affluent travellers for ransom.

From a generally eastward flow as far as Melk, the river turns northward in a crescent-shaped curve. At the picturesque town of Dürnstein with its blue church spire, it turns east again. Six kilometres downstream, our ship docked at Krems on the north bank and we boarded coaches for Dürnstein. Strolling the narrow streets, we stopped at Hotel Richard Löwenherz or Hotel Richard Lionheart. I left Dany to continue browsing the shops and art galleries as I climbed the steep path to the ruins of the medieval castle on the promontory above the village.

The Danube has been an important transportation link for thousands of years, joining the Black Sea to the heart of Europe. And so it was in 1192, when Richard the Lionheart headed home from the Third Crusade. Duke Leopold V of Austria, whom Richard had affronted in Palestine, captured him and imprisoned him in Dürnstein Castle. To ransom him the English paid 100,000 marks, about 25 tonnes of silver.

The castle gave a bird's eye view of the village, the narrow flood plain leading to Krems, the hills of the far bank and the mud-brown Danube. And what of the Blue Danube immortalized by the Strauss waltz? Our guide gave two explanations. First, when the water is still, the reflected sky can give a blue cast to the surface. Second, when a division of Napoleon's troops crossed the Danube at Dürnstein in 1805 on their way to the great French victory at Austerlitz, a superior force of Russians and Austrians burst from the hills. With little room to manoeuvre on the narrow flood plain, thousands of French died and droves of blue uniforms fouled the Danube. Take your pick!

Vienna

Another night cruise brought us to Vienna, Wien to the German-speaking. Since both Dany and I had spent considerable time in Vienna on layovers with Air Canada, we chose the Hidden Vienna walking tour over the comprehensive city tour. Our coach drove along the Ringstrasse, then to the town centre. The Ringstrasse follows the arc of the defensive wall that withstood attacks by the Ottoman Turks in the 15th and 16th centuries. Capital of the former Austro-Hungarian Empire, the city boasts numerous grand palaces, monuments, and parks. We disembarked near St. Stephen's Cathedral with its Gothic spire reaching halfway to heaven. The roof of the choir is adorned by a mosaic of richly coloured tiles portraying the double-headed eagle of the Hapsburg dynasty.

Our walking tour took us through narrow streets and alleys to hidden courtyards. Plaques abound, dedicated to the illustrious who have lived or worked in Vienna; among them Haydn, Beethoven, Strauss, Einstein, and of course Vienna's favourite son, Wolfgang Amadeus Mozart. He was somewhat of a nomad, for in less than 10 years he lived in 11 different apartments. Great composer that he was, Mozart was often short of funds and compelled to move to lesser lodgings.

Crossing a small plaza, we entered a Jesuit Church, its rather austere exterior contrasting with a rich baroque interior. Twisted faux-marble pillars vied for splendour with an ornate gilded ceiling dome. Ah! Not a dome, but a trompe-l'oeil or "fool-the-eye" illusion on a flat ceiling.

After lunch a coterie of cyclists donned helmets and mounted the ship's bikes, pedalling along the path upriver. Crossing a bridge over the Little Danube, we continued to Klosterneuburg Abbey, sited on a slight rise above the plain. Built in the 1100s, it was remodelled in the baroque style in the early 1600s. In contrast to previous touristic visitations, we had the entire complex to ourselves. Our guide had keys to various rooms and exhibits including the famous Verdun Altar, a unique gold and enamel altarpiece that is reputedly the best-preserved artwork of the Middle Ages. The abbey is home to the oldest and one of the biggest wineries in Austria. Under a blue sky, we enjoyed a sample at the terrace cafe.

On our return journey we stopped to examine a grey armoured gunboat. Before World War I the empire had a substantial navy on the Adriatic. Present-day Austria, landlocked, has no navy, but the Federal Police operates a squadron of gunboats to forestall river piracy.

After an early dinner we boarded coaches for a private concert at one of Vienna's many princely palaces. The delightful gala included opera, ballet, and a soloist playing a Stradivarius.

Bratislava

Our ship departed at 8 a.m. for a leisurely cruise through locks and past riverside villages, stone fortresses, and dredging operations, docking five hours later at Bratislava, capital of Slovakia. Our upper-deck cabin and balcony notwithstanding, we drew the curtains, for with docking space limited our ship was rafted to another. It was but a short walk to the centre of the compact town, most of which is a pedestrian zone. Bratislava has made a remarkable recovery from years of neglect under Communism.

A twice-life-sized statue of Hans Christian Andersen gave the backdrop for our first photo opportunity. A onetime visitor here, this prolific traveller is memorialized in statues across the breadth of Europe. Nearby, the approach to the single cable-stayed bridge over the Danube lies over the remains of the city's medieval west wall. Construction of the linking roadway in the early 1970s demolished much of the old town, including nearly all the Jewish quarter. Two hundred metres north, St. Martin's Cathedral forms part of the city's fortifications.

At the nearby main square, a whimsical statue of Napoleon leans against a bench in front of the Old Town Hall, now a museum. Scattered about are other quirky statues, including the much-photographed Man in a Manhole.

Back aboard, we dressed for the Captain's Gala dinner, after which the ship set sail for Budapest.

Budapest

Below Bratislava the river passes through a gap in the Hungarian Hills and abruptly changes direction, from eastward to straight south. Hungary, home of the dreaded Hun, scourge of Europe during the Dark Ages, became a Christian kingdom in 1000 AD, though the Ottoman Turks ruled the country for 150 years ending in 1699. Buda on the right-bank hillside overlooks flat Pest on the left bank. Now a single city, Budapest rivals Paris in the elegance of its buildings and public spaces, albeit somewhat shabbily as the city also suffered neglect under Communist rule. Cameras clicked as we cruised past the Parliament, its design inspired by the British Houses of Parliament. We gazed up at Buda Castle and crossed under the Chain Bridge.

Disembarking, we boarded coaches for a city tour, with brief stops at Buda Castle, Hero's Square, and the huge market at the former railway station designed by Gustave Eiffel, of Parisian tower fame.

Returning to the AmaDolce, we prepared for disembarkation the following morning. One task at hand was to calculate a tip for the crew. Did I mention the food, wine, and service? All were absolutely first-class. Breakfast and lunch were sumptuous buffets of great variety; dinner was à-la-carte with delectable choices. English was the exclusive language of the ship and most of the passengers hailed from the U.S.A., Canada or the U.K. The crew was mostly from former east-bloc countries. We highly recommend AmaWaterways.

After dinner the ship cast off for a delightful evening cruise. A spectacular scene unfolded as we coasted past brightly illuminated monuments and public buildings; the city spares no expense for lighting.

The following morning we waited in the lounge until the concierge announced our taxi. Bidding farewell, we drove to our hotel on the Pest side of the river, well-sited just off the ring road that follows the arc of the long-gone defensive walls. We had three more days to explore this fascinating city.

Public transport is very efficient, with multiple tram lines and three underground metro lines with a fourth under construction. The M-1 line opened in 1896, the second in the world after London's. It was a relatively simple cut-and-fill construction project, unlike the M-2 that tunnels beneath the Danube.

Budapest has many thermal springs, where first the Romans and later the Turks built palatial spas. These hint at the complex geology underfoot. The construction of the metro under the Danube was an engineering challenge with fault zones, rock fissures, and methane gas hazards to be overcome. The nearby M-2 line would take us from our hotel to Buda Castle in about eight minutes.

The imposing Buda Castle has been expanded and rebuilt repeatedly, most recently after severe damage during World War II. Much of the artwork went missing or was destroyed during the war. An austere modernist style superseded the gothic and baroque interiors. The Castle now houses the National Gallery, the National Library, and the History Museum. Grand martial bronze statues embellish every exterior plaza.

Walking to the Buda town square, we passed a blockhouse pockmarked with bullet holes from the ill-fated 1956 Revolution.

Matthias Church, dominating the square like St. Stephen's in Vienna, is crowned by a gargoyle-laden gothic spire and a roof of brightly coloured tiles.

We crossed the square to Fisherman's Bastion, climbing steps to the parapet with its superb view of the Danube and the city below. Local fishermen were responsible for defense of this zone of the medieval wall. Today their bastion is a mock construct of pointed towers and turrets, built in the 1890s to mark the millennium of the Magyar conquest of Hungary. Serenaded by a fine string quartet, we enjoyed a good lunch under a warm sun.

Dany had bought tickets for the ballet at the elegant National Theatre, a short tram ride from our hotel. The lavishly appointed interior enhanced an amusing performance of The Taming of the Shrew. And then home, after a week in Paris visiting Dany's twin sister.

Melk - Baroque gone Barmy

Richard the Lionheart
- Incarcerated

Napoleon at
Bratislavia

Budapest Serenade

Chapter 30
Russian River Cruise

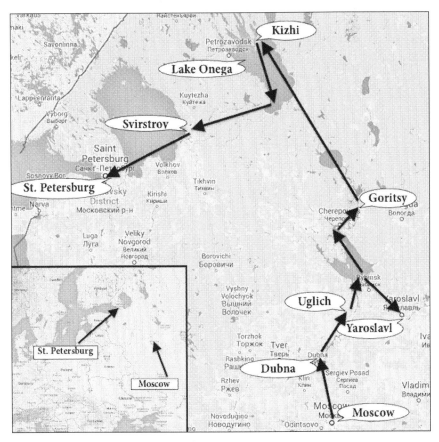

Russia – May 2014

Moscow

All went well with our flights to Moscow for an 11-day cruise to St. Petersburg. After an overnight at a Frankfurt airport hotel, we departed on Lufthansa. I had reserved a car at the Moscow airport. A good choice, as the express train would require a taxi to the hotel, and apparently random taxis can be rather predatory. There was a Metro very close to our hotel, but Dany is not into shlepping bags up and down escalators.

We sped along a good highway north to the city, but the southbound lanes were parking lots. A 45-minute drive brought us to the elegant Savoy Hotel, close to the Bolshoi Theatre and Red Square. The 67-room hotel, extensively renovated in 2005, is among the finest in the city.

Again I had failed to consult the local calendar: the following day was Victory Day. Sightseeing was out of the question; all public places would be closed for the celebration of victory in what we call World War II and Russians call The Great Patriotic War. On a stroll to Red Square, site of the reviewing stands, we met Nataly, a young lady who spoke excellent English. She guided us to the best viewing area for the common folk, at the bridge where the parade turns below Red Square. Red Square itself would be filled by veterans, officials, and of course military troops and weapons on parade.

Next morning we set out to view the parade under a blue sky at 21 C. Unfortunately, the street in front of our hotel was barricaded and we could not cross. We followed the crowd west, but that seemed to be a dead end. Danielle gave up, for she suffered a migraine from jet lag. I took her back to the hotel.

I walked up to Lubyanskaya Circle, adorned with pyramidal red stars. It too was blocked, for thousands of police and troops manned barricades surrounding Red Square. I boarded the Metro to Kitay-Gorod, the next station, about 500 metres from the bridge. All the station exits at Kitay-Gorod were blocked, so I returned to Lubyanskaya Circle and walked out the Metro's south exit and made my way to the river. I guess I was 200 metres underground when the tanks went by! However, I did get some good close-up photos and videos of the various units as they marched past to their dispersal area.

The keen, well-kitted troops, in crisp uniforms adorned with gold braid, holding Kalashnikovs in white-gloved hands, marched to the accompaniment of their own singing. Good singing must be a requirement for enlistment! Happy warriors all. And hats. Big peaked hats. Like Napoleon's guards in their bearskins, later appropriated by the British Guards, the objective seems to be to add a little height to appear more formidable. The flypast of 69 aircraft, helicopters, transports, a bomber trailing a tanker, Mig-29 fighters and an aerobatic team of supermaneuverable Sukhoi Su-30 followed. Mission accomplished!

AmaKatarina

The next afternoon we boarded the 135-metre AmaKatarina a at the Northern River Terminal, a decaying structure dating from the late 1930s and much in need of restoration. Our spacious cabin included an outdoor balcony, flat-screen TV, and ample storage space. We joined the 146 other passengers for a safety briefing given by a few of the 100 crew members. Then to dinner in the lower dining room, with à-la-carte service. The upper dining room had the same menu, served buffet-style.

We split into groups of 25 and were taken by Mercedes coach to Red Square, where our lovely blonde guide gave a brief overview of the history of the square and the Kremlin. "Kremlin" means fortress, and there are many kremlins throughout Russia. This one is "The Kremlin," political capital of Russia. The adjacent buildings and Kremlin walls are faced with red brick. The square's name comes from neither the red brick nor from the Red Army, victorious over the royalist White army of the revolution. Rather, the Russian word for "red" is also an old Russian word meaning "beautiful." And beautiful it is, the far end graced by the asymmetrical, colourful, varied onion domes of St. Basil's Cathedral.

Napoleon captured and his troops looted the Kremlin in 1812. But the Russians had vacated the city, burning much of it to deprive Napoleon's 500,000-man army of shelter and sustenance. In the subsequent long winter retreat, only an estimated 40,000 made it back to France.

We had free time to peruse the shops of the GUM Department store, pronounced "goom." From my first visit to Moscow in 1968 as a copilot on an Air Canada DC-8, I remembered long queues in front of each shop. At that time each shop sold only one item, shoes, hats, trousers, bread, meat, etc. Now the shops sport the logos and wares of the planet's foremost designers. The elegant edifice, built in 1893, consists of three, three-level galleries joined by arched glass ceilings.

We returned to our coach for a short drive to the Moscow River, where we boarded a barge for a cruise up the meandering river. The pusher-barge turned about after lunch, providing an opportunity to photograph the sights from the sun deck. These included the Academy of Science with its crown of solar panels, the huge nautical statue of Peter the Great, the Kremlin walls, and, at Gorky park, the prototype of the Russian space shuttle Buran.

The golden dome of Christ the Saviour Cathedral dominates the left bank. Tsar Alexander dedicated the original cathedral to the deliverance from Napoleon's incursion. Patterned after Hagia Sophia of Constantinople, it took 30 years to complete. In 1931 Stalin, espousing state atheism, ordered it dynamited. The state pocketed the 20 tonnes of gold salvaged from the dome. Subscriptions from citizens funded the rebuilding of the present cathedral in the 1990s.

Our afternoon tour took us to Moscow State University, a huge edifice perched on high ground overlooking the city. It is one of the Seven Sisters, or Stalin's Skyscrapers, built after the war to enhance the prestige of the city with high-rise buildings it had previously lacked. Constructed by gulag slave labour, it was, at 240 metres, the tallest building in Europe until 1990.

A short drive brought us to Victory Park, sited on a low ridge overlooking Moscow. From this hill Napoleon gazed at Moscow ablaze when the citizens chose to burn the city. The cast-bronze Victory Stela of 141.8 metres towers over the circle. Each 10 centimetres of its height represents one day of Russia's four years of struggle in World War II. St. George, patron saint of Moscow, stabs the dragon at the base. Nike, goddess of victory, floats near the pinnacle.

Our guide led us to the Metro for a three-stop tour of its renowned stations. Moscow's subway system is quite possibly the world's most extravagant. We descended a 120-metre escalator to a station built in 2009. Lacking the ornamentation of older stations, it is nevertheless a showcase of fine marble and granite panelling. At Kiev station, we perused lavishly decorative artwork featuring scenes from the Ukraine, illuminated by crystal chandeliers. Our final station, near the Bolshoi Theatre, featured larger-than-life-sized bronze sculptures in Socialist Realist style. Heroic soldiers, sailors, airmen, miners, workers, and farmers crouched under pink marble arches. Stopping at a soldier with a huge overcoat, a bolt-action rifle, and a faithful dog at his side, we followed local custom by touching the dog's much-polished nose for good luck.

The Kremlin

Next morning we returned to Red Square, now largely devoid of the Victory Holiday crowds. Passing through security, we strolled through the Kremlin grounds, past the government offices to the Armoury, repository of Russia's national treasures. The vast array of exhibits ranged from Catherine II's dresses to silver and gold gifts from European nobility, gilded coaches and sleighs, medieval body armour, exquisite clocks, gold drinking bowls, a full set of embossed dinnerware given by Napoleon to Tsar Alexander, and a display of eight bejewelled eggs, masterpieces of Peter Fabergé crafted for the Tsars as Easter gifts to their ladies.

A visit to the Dormition Cathedral within the complex revealed interior walls and columns completely covered with icons large and small. We strolled along a walk overlooking the riverside fortifications, crossed over to a garden of colourful tulips in full bloom, paused at a sturdy oak planted in 1961 by Yuri Gagarin, first man to orbit the earth.

Our next photo op was the bronze Tsar Cannon, the world's largest cannon at 39 tonnes. Although fired at least once, the cannon was never deployed. It was too cumbersome to manoeuvre. Likewise the six-metre-high, 201-tonne Tsar Bell. Shortly after its casting a fire broke out in the wooden scaffolding. Guards poured water on it to "protect" it. The still-cooling bronze cracked and an 11-tonne chunk split off. Is it really a bell if it has never rung?

As we returned to the entrance, I pondered the contrast of this delightful and historic site with my mental image of the Kremlin. As a fighter pilot at the peak of the Cold War, during the erection of the Berlin Wall and the Cuban Missile Crisis, I read the books and saw the spy movies of the era and had visions of a dark and dangerous place. Don't go there! Maybe then, but this is now.

Departing Moscow, our ship ascended and then descended through a series of nine locks on the canal, built in the 1930s, that connects the metropolis to the Volga 100 kilometres north. The Volga rises 200 kilometres northwest of Moscow, flowing east, north, and then in a great arc southeast to the Caspian Sea. Vikings sailed the Volga and the Don to the Black Sea and Constantinople, first for plunder and later for trade. Our 2,000-km cruise would take us along this ancient trade route in a great arc northwest to St. Petersburg on the Gulf of Finland.

Uglich – Hydro Museum

Early in the morning we docked at Uglich, site of a huge dam and hydroelectric power station. I joined a small contingent for the tour of the hydroelectric museum that opened in 2012. It gave a very comprehensive overview of Russia's hydro power system and grid, as well as models of hydroelectric projects throughout the world. One interesting graph compared the hydroelectric potential of various countries: China first, with its immense Yangtze potential, less than 20% developed; Russia second, with about half China's potential, also 20% developed; Brazil third; and Canada fourth, about 65% of its potential developed.

Russians today have fully acknowledged the brutality of the Stalinist period. An entire room portrayed conditions in the gulags, or slave labour camps, located throughout the length and breadth of Russia. Their inmates, some of them criminals, but most of them dissidents and ordinary citizens, toiled for years building the dam and canal system. Food was the hammer. A full, though limited ration depended on fulfilling one's work quota. Conditions were appalling, especially in distant Siberia. A chart showed the total numbers incarcerated, rising from 500,000 in 1934 to more than 2 million in 1945.

Yaroslavl

The ship docked at Yaroslavl, one of Russia's oldest cities, tracing its roots to the days of the Vikings. In 1010 Prince Yaroslav slew the bear of local Finnic tribes and gained control over this strategic location. Our walking tour took us along the river banks at the confluence of the Volga and the Kotorosl. Sited astride the primary trade route from the Baltic to the mid-East, Yaroslavl was known as the City of Merchants. Its burgers amassed great fortunes and vied in the building of stately mansions and the finest churches, of which there are about 50 in the city. Particularly colourful is the "Army Church" of St. Michael, patron saint of the military, tiled in orange and white and topped with a green dome.

A donation of $75 million from a local businessman facilitated the recent reconstruction of Assumption Cathedral, destroyed by the Soviets in 1937. Our stroll continued to the monastery, now a museum with only a handful of monks in residence. A local carillonneur gave a concert, striking an array of a dozen bronze bells. Dodging trams and buses, we continued to the town square and market. The city is spotless, for as in Moscow a fleet of street-sweeper vehicles makes the rounds several times per day. Although public trash receptacles are rare, there is little trash, and what exists is swiftly scooped up by an army of pickers.

Our final visit was to the elegant former governor's residence, where young ladies in period dress guided us as if they were the governor's daughters. After a short concert by a string quartet, the ladies began to dance, soon enticing the visiting men to join in a formal minuet. Attired in hiking shorts, I slouched to the back, content to quaff the champagne on offer.

Goritsy

A pleasant feature of our Russia cruise was its leisurely pace. In contrast to our Danube cruise the previous year, through densely populated Europe, here there were vast distances between our ports of call. It gave us an opportunity to make friends with our fellow passengers, Americans, Brits, Spaniards, a large contingent of Turks, and of course fellow Canadians. Our newfound Maritime friends included Dean and Mary Woodbury, Mike and Jane Wilson and Jim and Heather Eisenhauer of New Brunswick and Nova Scotia.

As we cruised through the seemingly endless boreal forest, our on-board professor Elizabeth Isaeva presented periodic lectures on Russian history, ranging from Viking times to the present. She gave an intriguing insight into the psyche of the Russian people, influenced in large part by Russia's 300-plus years as a vassal state of the Mongol-Tartar Golden Horde. That history partly explains the Russian predilection for serfs, slavery and strong leaders.

During the privatization, or as she termed it the "piratization," of the Russian economy after the breakup of the Soviet Union, every citizen received 20 shares of the "State Enterprise." The so-called oligarchs consolidated their ventures by buying those shares, often for as little as a bottle of vodka. Our professor kept her shares, investing in something like a mutual fund. In a few years the shares were worthless. As she ruefully remarked, "I should have taken the vodka." President Putin's current popularity is largely a result of his re-nationalizing of some industries, notably oil and gas. The resultant cash flow has benefited pensioners, who endured great hardship and poverty during the collapse of the ruble after the dissolution of the Soviet Union.

Docking at the typical Russian farming town of Goritsy, we boarded coaches for a short drive to the Monastery of St. Cyril on the shore of a lake at Kirillov. Founded in 1397, the modest monastery soon became a rich and powerful military centre. The 200 monks had 20,000 serfs at their disposal to look after their daily wants and to construct high towers and sturdy stone walls. The defences proved adequate to repel an early-1600s attack by renegade Polish-

Lithuanian brigands intent on looting the goods within. It is now a museum, although six monks inhabit the grounds. It displays some of the finest icons of Russia. The painted icons laced with silver and gold were works of men; the embroidery art was of the ladies.

Kizhi

A 125-kilometre detour took us to the midpoint of Lake Onega, where we docked at Kizhi Island, famed for its wood structures. I chose the walking tour while Dany joined the larger group touring the Kizhi Pogost, a UNESCO heritage site.

As we strolled past fenced graves to the water's edge, our guide gave a brief history of the island, only 6 km by 1 km. Formerly 3,000 peasants tilled the land. Apparently the soil is particularly fertile, for an obscure black mineral retains the sun's heat and results in bumper crops. Today, only 30 residents remain, including an 89-year-old woman who, like her neighbours, must chop through a half-metre of ice for water during winter.

Forcibly removed during the harvest season of 1770 and pressed into the development of mainland iron mines, the peasants revolted. The Tsar's troops brutally suppressed the rebellion. The population declined and eventually the island's villages disappeared. Most of the sturdy log houses on view originated from other parts of the region.

After a visit to a small hilltop church, we hastened to the Pogost, an enclosure of wooden fortifications surrounding two iconic churches and a bell tower. The 22-domed Church of the Transfiguration, rising 37 metres, is one of the tallest wooden buildings of the Russian north, albeit somewhat skeletal in its current state of extensive renovation.

At the souvenir shop I noticed small pyramids of a black stone labelled Shungite, the mineral that supposedly enriched the local soil. Much to my regret I did not buy any, as I had never heard of it. From a Google search I learned of the rareness of this mineraloid, found mainly around Lake Onega, with a small deposit also known in Katanga, Congo. Like graphite, one of the softest minerals, and diamond, the hardest, Shungite is 100% carbon. Peter the Great used it to purify water for his troops, much in the manner of our present-day activated-carbon filters. It is classed as a mineraloid because it is amorphous, that is, lacking a crystal structure.

In 1992, however, scientists discovered fullerenes in shungites. A fullerene, or "buckyball," is a crystal structure of carbon atoms forming a hollow sphere similar to a soccer ball. The name honours Richard Buckminster Fuller, developer of the geodesic dome, notably that of the U.S. pavilion at the 1967 Montreal World's Fair. Apart from the industrial uses of shungite, the web is now awash with outlandish claims of its curative power. For instance:

> *Shungite cures, rescues, purifies, heals, protects, normalizes, restores and even stimulates the growth. Amazing rock: it kills and devours anything that harms people and other living beings, and concentrates and restores all that is good. The scholars who have studied shungite in one voice declare, it is a miracle!*
>
> A. Doronina, Shungite: The Stone-Savior

Svirstroy

On the Svir River, draining Lake Onega to Lake Ladoga, the focus is logging. Many ships loaded with timber ply its waters. We passed through two locks and docked at Svirstroy, a community of 1,000. Another of the hydroelectric dams built with slave labour in the 1930s, it provides extensive employment for the residents.

Breaking into groups of 15, we trooped off for a visit with local families. We met our hostess Iryna and her daughter Sonja at their comfortable 100-square-metre bungalow. Her husband was at work at the local hydro plant, while her 18-year-old son was serving his compulsory year of service in the army.

St Petersburg by water

On our early-morning approach to St. Petersburg via the Neva, which drains Lake Ladoga to the Baltic, I became somewhat confused about our direction. Eventually it became apparent that we were circling around to fill time until our berth became vacant.

Boarding coaches, we sped off on the ring road to Peterhof, seaside residence of Peter the Great and later of Catherine the Great. The grand Summer Palace, a short distance inland, soon superseded the modest houses and gardens at the shore. The park's statues and 176 gilded fountains of various forms, modelled after those of Versailles, are fed by water under pressure from a source 20 kilometres distant.

After lunch in St. Petersburg, we crossed the Neva to the Peter and Paul Fortress, the island citadel built by Peter the Great to forestall any Swedish attempt to reconquer the delta. Never attacked, it served as a prison in both Tsarist and Soviet eras. Hobbling across a broad cobbled plaza, we entered the mustard-yellow Peter and Paul Cathedral under a bell tower with lofty golden spire. The splendour of the gilded baroque interior was overwhelming.

Great marble sarcophagi hold the remains of Russian nobility. A recent arrival was Leonida, wife of the great-grandson of Emperor Alexander II, whose remains arrived in 2010. Another cordoned-off chapel displays wall plaques listing the Romanovs killed after the revolution. They are not interred here, on grounds that the remains discovered in 1979 have not yet been authenticated as those of the royal family. In answer to the obvious question, "Why not, with DNA analysis now readily available?" Our guide replied, "The authorities probably do know, but this being Russia, they won't tell us."

Our city tour continued with a brief stop at St. Isaac's Cathedral to admire the 48 immense granite pillars of the porticos and the splendid gold dome. Our guide explained that the ubiquitous gilding on buildings and monuments needed refurbishment every couple of years. The exception is the dome of the Cathedral, gilded with an amalgam of mercury and gold in 1850. Heated, the mercury vaporized, leaving a layer of gold looking as bright today as when first applied. The toxic vapour killed 30 workers in the process.

After dinner on the boat, we boarded hydrofoils for a swift journey to the Hermitage. A string quartet greeted us as we made our way to the lavishly decorated marble and gilt theatre for a private performance of the ballet Giselle. From our front-row seats I could tell when the curtain would fall, for during the pre-concert tune up, one of the violinists played from a rather tattered score whose last page showed a distinctly visible hole.

Hermitage

Arising early, we again boarded the hydrofoils for a return to the Hermitage, the large complex of six historic buildings along the embankment of the Neva. One of them was the Winter Palace of the tsars, stormed by the Bolsheviks to launch the 1917 revolution. Founded by Catherine the Great as the Imperial Museum, the Hermitage Museum opened to the public in 1852 and took over the entire complex after the revolution.

Our cruise director had arranged for priority entrance an hour before admittance of the general public. We were fortunate to view the numerous interconnected galleries without hindrance from crowds. Catherine the Great and her successors had agents scouring Europe for the finest works of art. The resulting collections, of which only a small part is on permanent display, comprise more than three million items.

Suffice to say that one cannot describe all the treasures on view. Among the wonderful great masters, Rembrandt, Leonardo, Rubens, Titian, et al, my attention was attracted by a two-metre-high green vase on a pedestal, flanked by two gilded tables topped with the same green mineral. "Where could they find a rock that big?" I wondered. As our guide explained, and a close examination confirmed, the artifacts were composite constructions; thin slivers of malachite, a bright green copper mineral, held with near-invisible mortar.

Catherine Palace

On our early-morning drive to Catherine Palace at Pushkin, 30 kilometres south of the city, we passed markers, 16 kilometres from the Hermitage. These identified the furthest advance of the German army that encircled the city during World War II. Hitler's goal for the city, known as Leningrad during the Soviet era, was to occupy it briefly and then raze it to the ground. Thwarted by the Red Army, he ordered a siege to starve the population into submission. Upwards of a million civilians perished during the two-and-a-half-year siege.

The Catherine Palace is named for Catherine I, wife of Peter the Great. Rebuilt several times during the 18th century, the last iteration by Catherine II, the Great, it rivals Versailles for opulence and sophistication. The gardens are an eclectic mix of follies, bridges and monuments, seemingly erected at the whim of Catherine II.

In occupying the palace the Germans completely looted and gutted it, carting off the legendary Amber Room. Its fate is still a mystery, as the crates containing the "sunny stone" disappeared during the war. In a prescient move, all furniture had been photographed and catalogued by the late 1930s and a sample of each had been removed to storage east of the Ural Mountains. This helped in the reconstruction and refurnishing that began immediately after the war. In 1984 the Russians stopped searching for the Amber Room and began assembly of a replica. The replication, based on photographs and a few original pieces, took many years, for ancient skills had to be relearned or reinvented by the craftsmen.

We entered the recreated Amber Room midway through our tour of the sumptuous palace. I must confess I was somewhat underwhelmed. Neither Danielle nor I value amber as a gemstone. But I do appreciate it for the scientific value of the rare specimens that contain preserved ancient life, as in the Jurassic Park scenario.

Yusupov Palace

One of AMA Waterways' challenges in Russia is maintaining the company's very high standards. In contrast to their other cruises where the company owns and operates the ships, here the ship, crew, and all tours and coaches came as a rental package. Since the lunch and cruise on the Moscow River aboard a rust-bucket barge did not meet their standards, AMA offered as compensation a choice of optional tours at no cost. We chose the Yusupov Palace option, and that afternoon we returned to the city.

The extremely rich Yusupov family acquired its fortune from a wide range of industrial enterprises. With its luxurious interior and extensive collection of art, their palace rivalled that of the Tsar. Most of their art collection is now in the Hermitage, the Soviets having nationalized their estates and holdings.

Our tour took us to the cellar and a room that portrayed the events of the night of 16 December 1916. What we now call World War I had been raging for two and a half years, with heavy casualties sustained by the Russians. The mysterious Rasputin, a self-proclaimed holy man, had won favour with the Tsarina by seeming to prolong the life of the Tsar's hemophiliac heir. The city's nobles, among them Prince Felix Yusupov, saw his influence as a threat to their power and conspired to kill him.

The guide recited the grisly details of Rasputin's murder, or at least the most popular version. These included aspects of the ineffective poisoning, the shooting, and the dumping of the still-breathing body over a bridge into the river. Although Prince Felix admitted to firing four shots into Rasputin's back, doubt remains about his version of the murder. Recent speculation in Britain has the British secret service involved, the motivation being fear that Rasputin might persuade the Tsar to withdraw from the war. Facing a mandatory sentence of death for murder, Prince Felix escaped with a lenient decree of exile.

St. Petersburg ashore
Saying farewell to our newfound friends, we departed the ship at 10 a.m., encountering the infamous St. Petersburg traffic on our way to our hotel midway between the Hermitage and the Mariinsky Theatre. At the latter, home of the Kirov Ballet, we had excellent seats for an evening performance of the opera Madame Butterfly, front row centre with a wide aisle behind a block of three rows reserved for opera patrons.

I was somewhat disappointed with the building, a new addition to the original Mariinsky. Designed by the Canadian architect Diamond Schmitt after a botched first attempt, it sits across a narrow canal from the old Mariinsky. Some locals have dubbed it Mariinsky Mall, considering the glass facade out of keeping with the city's elegant 19th-century buildings.

The backlit translucent onyx wall in the lobby, forming the exterior façade of the auditorium, is very impressive. The interior of the auditorium is urban-modern, faced with light wood panels that likely contribute to the reputedly excellent acoustics. The backstage facilities are reported outstanding for cast and crew. But the pitch of the stalls leaves something to be desired for the audience. The first three rows are completely flat and the rise for the 12 rows behind us was about two centimetres per row, less than at Vancouver's appalling Queen Elizabeth Theatre. Although the seats are staggered, heads would obscure the view from these seats. The many seats vacant when the curtain rose were filled during the interval before the second act. Our erstwhile neighbours had been delayed by traffic, while we had but a 15-minute walk from our hotel. Location, location!

Performance and music were outstanding. The sets were minimal. Much use was made of a huge backlit screen, notably during the first act when a blue and white wavy motion accompanied the love duet. The ladies were clothed in shapeless gowns, that of Madame Butterfly having long draping sleeves used to much dramatic effect. Yet to my simple eye, Madame Butterfly without kimonos is akin to Swan Lake without tutus!

Next day, while Dany rested, I walked five minutes to the Central Navy Museum. The exhibits of paintings, models, documents, photos, and weapons were excellent, but unfortunately all the text was in Russian and in Cyrillic script. Disappointingly, the gallery exhibiting the days of sail was closed, probably as a result of the museum's recent relocation from across the Neva. A small theatre screened videos of the heavy aircraft carrier Admiral Kuznetsov launching Sukhoi Su-30 fighters from its ski-jump deck, with air manoeuvres including the legendary tail slide, and tailhook landings on the angled flight deck. Vintage movies showed the now-retired carrier Kiev launching the Yakovlev Yak-38, the Russian version of the British Harrier vertical-takeoff jet.

I then headed for the Aurora, the historic cruiser whose service ran from the Tsar's navy in the Russo-Japanese war of 1904-05 through to the Soviet navy in World War II. The Aurora is an active commissioned ship with serving seamen keeping her shipshape as a museum, like the USS Constitution in Boston and HMS Victory in Portsmouth.

Large-calibre guns line the sides and the fore and aft decks. Below deck were excellent exhibits, artwork, documents and photos, but again most of the text was in Russian, as was the guide's commentary. Unlike most of the Russian Pacific fleet, sunk by the Japanese at the Battle of Tsushima in 1905, the Aurora sustained only light damage. She escaped to shelter at the U.S. base in the Philippines for the remainder of the war.

The Aurora patrolled the Baltic during World War I, until it returned to Petrograd (as St. Petersburg was renamed in 1914) in need of replenishment and repair. When the captain refused to release three propagandist seaman, the crew killed him. They then set up a workers' committee, and fired the blank round that triggered the storming of the Winter Palace and the Bolshevik revolution.

The large guns were offloaded during World War II and positioned to counter German artillery during the 890-day siege of Leningrad. Damaged by German artillery, the Aurora sank in shallow water, later to be refloated as a museum.

And what of the weather on our cruise? Historical data suggested that the chance of a blue sky in May was rather slight, with an average temperature of 18 C in a range from 5 to 24 C. Yet save for a brief thunderstorm crossing Lake Onega, we had an unbroken series of blue-sky days, with temperatures of 24 to 32 C in St. Petersburg.

Following a delicious dinner at the nearby Stroganoff, we joined the restaurant's Champagne and Strawberries celebration of the opening of the patio season. A fitting end to a fine Russian vacation. Despite political rhetoric and military actions in the Ukraine, we found the Russians most friendly and hospitable. Next day Dany flew to Paris and I home via Frankfurt.

St. Basil's Cathedral - Red Square

The Tsar's Cannon

Kizhi Pogost

The Aurora

Chapter 31

Grouse Mountain F-86 crash

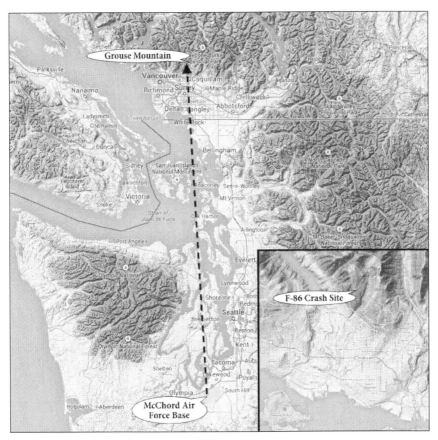

Canada – 1954 -2014

The crash site

Chapter 25 mentions the crash of an F-86 Sabre jet fighter near Vancouver and the visit of the pilot's family to the crash site. The chain of circumstances that led to that visit was extraordinary.

In April 2007, with the iconic Grouse Grind trail closed for the season, I climbed Grouse Mountain along the line of the old, derelict chairlift. I found my route blocked by a huge fallen tree, brought down by the same winter storm that felled countless trees in Stanley Park the previous December. I was obliged to divert to a path through the forest. The marked path followed the switchback turns of an old logging skid road. I normally do not do zigzags, and would never have diverged had the direct route not been obstructed.

A short way along, I came across the core of a jet turbine, which as a former F-86 fighter pilot I immediately recognized. An Internet search revealed that the turbine was from a U.S. Air Force F-86D that crashed on 12 February 1954. Lt. Lamar Barlow of 465 Squadron of McChord Air Force Base near Tacoma, Washington died in the crash.

Since many hikers pass this artifact without knowing its story, Jet Johnson and I decided to erect a plaque dedicated to the memory of Lt. Barlow. In September of the same year, at the Battle of Britain Ceremony, I met a representative of the U.S. consulate, Barry Lucero, and told him of this U.S. Air Force crash site. In August 2008 Barry attended the unveiling of the plaque, and subsequently took it upon himself to trace Lt. Barlow's family. Since Barlow is a very common name in Utah, it was only through a chance meeting with a distant cousin of Barlow that he found the family.

Family visit

I then corresponded with Susan Horne, Barlow's daughter, born three months after his death. Is there a pilot gene? Susan had a career as an airline pilot; as did her husband Tom following his military service. At her request, I arranged for a family visit on 13 June 2009, on what would have been Lt. Barlow's 81st birthday.

Two weeks before the planned visit, I was somewhat apprehensive about the date. The spring had been cold and there was still snow along the upper trail. Fortunately, a spell of hot weather melted the snow, and on the day we had a blue sky.

The management of Grouse Mountain Resorts was extremely helpful, providing the family with passes for the gondola lift and a vehicle to take them to the bottom of a ski run called The Cut, leaving only a gentle 15-minute hike to the crash site. The 12 family members at the site included Lt. Barlow's widow Gloria, their daughter Susan, and seven of his direct descendants.

From Susan I had received the now-declassified accident report, which I used to describe the events that led to the crash. After Barlow climbed through cloud, his radio compass failed, leading to a Mayday call. Unlike aircraft of today with their profusion of navigation avionics: VOR, TACAN, GPS, Barlow's F-86 had as its sole navigation device a radio compass with a needle that pointed in the direction of a radio beacon. Radar at McChord showed him about 20 miles north of McChord. The radar controller directed him on a "penetration" procedure, descending southeast then turning north. Sadly, the primitive radar of that era was subject to ghost imaging. He was 140 miles north of the position indicated on the ground radar.

I unveiled the plaque for the second time:

J-47 Jet Turbine Engine

F-86D Sabre, United States Air Force

Lieutenant Lamar J. Barlow, 25,

of 465 Squadron, Tacoma, WA

died when his aircraft crashed here

12 February, 1954

Erected by Richard Dunn & Jet Johnson

Air Force Officers' Association

Logbook

I deposited a "Logbook" at the site. Comments left by the family, and later by hikers, are transcribed in Appendix A.

Other crash debris

Contemporary newspaper reports stated that USAF personnel would remove all debris that could be carted off, and bury that which could not. The latter category obviously included the very heavy turbine.

The Vancouver Sun reported on Saturday 13 February, the day after the crash:

> The wreckage will be kept under strict security guard until detonating teams have exploded or defused the cannon-type rockets which the plane carried.
>
> [USAF Maj. Craig Fairburn, head of the investigating team] said, "We will try to remove the entire wreckage to our base, and what we can't move, we will bury."

And in Monday's follow-up story:

> A maintenance team arrived here today to begin picking up and crating the wreckage for shipment to McChord for study.

After consulting the accident report and perusing air photos from 1960, I could see the line of the crash. Adjusting my compass for the 8 degrees of magnetic variation change since 1954, I followed the crash line down the mountain. About 200 linear metres below the engine I found a large debris field that included the engine shroud, analogous to the cowl on a piston aircraft, and a piece of a wing.

On another occasion, Eric Lund, a member of the Vancouver chapter of the Canadian Aviation Historical Society, led me to a site to the west of the chairlift. He showed me two large pieces of wreckage, a landing gear strut and the afterburner.

When I considered their location, about 200 metres west of the line of crash, I was faced with a mystery. The line of the crash is almost parallel to that of the chairlift; i.e. almost due north, and there is no way those pieces could have "flown" there. I speculated that they might have dropped off a vehicle during the removal of the crash debris.

On rereading the USAF accident report, I noticed the following statements:

"Main strut found originally buried approximately 300 feet beyond initial impact with ground."

"Afterburner, approximately 700 feet from initial impact point."

"Engine approximately 1000 feet from initial impact point with ground."

"Parts of the turbine wheel and compressor indicated that the engine was operating at the time of impact. None of the wreckage was removed from the scene."

"We have a written agreement with the owner of the land to bury the remains of the aircraft. Due to heavy snow this has not been completed and there are still eleven (11) rocket heads missing. The Royal Canadian Mounted Police have this information and will notify us as soon as weather conditions permit our crews to return and complete the disposal of the aircraft. and to continue search for the missing rockets."

So it would appear that the lads took the easy way out, and just dropped the major components over the steep slope to the west of the chairlift. That would be understandable, given a recent two-foot snowfall and harsh conditions and given that these components could contribute nothing to determination of the cause of the accident. It is likely that many of the airmen came from the southern U.S. and this winter wonderland was not wonderful to them. "Let's get out of here!"

I have been removing the logbook every November to prevent water damage from snow melt. When I returned the logbook on May 1st, 2014, I decided to forgo the marked trail and struck out straight down the fall line through the forest. At 640 metres elevation, I came across another significant piece of wreckage, the horizontal stabilizer. This undoubtedly marks the impact point as the tail would be the first to strike the trees, especially if the pilot glimpsed the trees and pulled back on the control stick. This location is well below the impact point assumed in the accident report. Quite possibly the missing warheads are nearby.

The aircraft was armed with 24 Mighty Mouse 2.75-inch rockets. Eleven were missing at the time of the board of inquiry, although airmen might have found some later. Since ancient ordnance can be very unstable, it is best to leave sleeping dogs lie. I'll eschew any attempt to locate them.

The comments in the Logbook are most expressive and supportive. I found it most rewarding to have been able to contribute to the positive transformation of Gloria, and to the family's sense of closure.

Plaque unveiling 2008

Jet Turbine

2nd Unveiling 2009

Appendix A
Logbook (Abridged)

U.S. AIR FORCE

LT. LAMAR BARLOW

LOGBOOK

13 June 2009

Today all descendants of the pilot killed here on this mountain visited the site for the 1st time. To us it is sacred ground. To those who stumble upon it, please respect it as such.

Susan Horne–SLC, UT, USA

I am Lamar Barlow's Grandson. I have dedicated this ground to his memory and the place where the remains will rest (most of his ashes are still here). This place can be enjoyed by all, but since it is hallowed ground, I ask you to treat this place respectfully. Feel free to touch the engine, but please don't litter or deface the site.

13 June 2009

This is a special place to both me and my family. Once it must have been a sad and lonely place, but thanks to the efforts and sacrifice of these kind people it has become a place of peace and happiness dedicated to the life and memory of a brave pilot. Someday my children and grandchildren will visit the site and be able to partake of his legacy. I am so grateful for this special day to remember my husband. It brought to mind many memories. Sad memories but also good memories. It brought a kind of closure for me to see the actual crash site. My thanks to all those who made this possible. My heart is full. Thank you. Thank you.

Gloria Barlow Sontag

13 June 2009

Lamar is a father-in-law that I never knew. As a fellow pilot and son-in-law, today was very special. I hope you enjoy this special place.

Thomas B. Horne

13 June 2009

To all of Lt. Barlow's family. As a fellow Utahan, it was my honor to attend the first dedication of Lamar's Memorial last year. It was a very touching and heartfelt moment representing the United States government. At such an important event,

I took it upon myself to try to contact the family members to tell them the story of Dick and Jet's efforts in telling visitors to Grouse Mountain the story of how a portion of a jet engine ended up on the mountainside. I thought it appropriate to try to tell the story and was fortunate to have been able to contact Sue and her cousin Rusty in Idaho. I am glad that we were all able finally to meet and put all the pieces of the story together for Lamar's family.

Barry Lucero, Vancouver, BC

13 June 2009

Gloria & Susan

Last year while hiking up Grouse Mountain to attend Lamar's ceremony, I realized that he and I were the same age! This brought back a flood of memories of my Sabre days in Germany during the Cold War days of the '50s. During my 3 years in Germany the RCAF Squadrons there lost 60 pilots. I'm sure that all of us wondered whether we would all make it through our Squadron tour. So Lamar's death brought back memories of all our Sabre losses and aircrews to keep our countries free.

Thus having Gloria & Susan with us on the mountain today was a special occasion for all of us, and we are so thankful that they could come so far to attend with their family.

Bud & Lee White, Vancouver, BC

21 June 2009

On the morning of Saturday, 13 February 1954 while skiing on Grouse Mountain a pal and I observed from our seats on the chairlift several uniformed Air Force personnel investigating the wreckage of a jet fighter that had crashed the previous day. Fast forward to 2008.

54 years later—a good friend and a fellow former F-86 Sabre pilot, Richard Dunn told me that he was curious about a jet engine he had seen while hiking the skyline trail. I told him I remembered the event and my recollections helped him fill

in the blanks. We both felt the site should be marked by a commemorative plaque, which was done. Later a friend at the US Consulate was able to trace the descendants of Lt. Lamar Barlow. The rest is history! Kindly respect this memorial and let Lt. Lamar Barlow rest in Peace.
'PER ARDUA AD ASTRA'

'Jet' Johnson

1 July 2009

I have seen this many times hiking but was never sure who or when. It's so nice to see that some things & people are never forgotten. My heart goes to out to your family.

1 July 2009

I first saw the site in 1968. Back then most of the wings, fuselage and cockpit were still intact, however they gradually disappeared over the years. Good to see the memorial here, I hope it will withstand the harsh winters up here.

Ted O, Van, BC

1 July 2009

Much respect. A North Shore classic bike ride. I always wanted to know the history here. Happy Canada Day. As a tradition we always tap our foot on the engine for good luck.

Andy T., North Van.

10 July 2009

I have been biking past here for over 20 years as my brother mentioned we always tapped the engine with our front mountain bike tires! Thank you for sharing! Take care!

15 July 2009

I too have hiked by this site many times and just knew someone had left the earth we being here. Such a nice memorial to your father, Susan! You have done well. He would be very proud of you if he knew you now. Rest in peace, Lamar! Canada also salutes you!

Vive D., North Vancouver

15 August 2009
Hiked up to find the engine and pleasantly surprised to find
the Memorial. Had read about family visiting in paper.
Deepest respects to the pilot and his family.
P.S. Someone needs to get a better box for logbook. Won't
last the winter.

John M., North Van

1 September 2009
Have hiked here several times & was always touched & moved
by the tragedy. It always reminded me of what is important:
cherish your loved ones & enjoy each day.
Rest in peace Lamar.

Helen & Alex

11 September 2009
My fourth attempt and at last I've found you! I know your
story so well by now, I feel I knew you. My great-grandfather
was a pioneer aviator and died in a bi-plane crash, not long
before he was due to retire from flying to design his own
plane. My father was also a pilot. I'm so happy to have made
it here to meet you on this date.

Sx.

11 September 2009
I have hiked these trails and skied on Grouse Mountain since
1966. I never knew where this plane engine had come from.
It is a beautiful spot to be laid to rest. We live in N. Vancouver
and will do our best to help maintain this special place. Long
may Lt. Lamar Barlow's spirit live on!

Matt W.

A fitting day (September 11) to discover this memorial.
Thanks for sharing. I too am amazed constantly by the
beauty of this part, and will bring friends to see this sacred
spot hidden in the trees.

J. W.

12 September 2009
> Lest we forget. I'm at this site as part of my 50th birthday celebration. Some of my fellow aviators didn't make it, and I remember them at this place and time.
>> Alaine B. Captain (Ret'd) CAF

11 November 2009
> Remembrance Day. What an honour to visit this memorial on this day. My thoughts are with his family.
>> Wendy W., Frank R., NorthVan

6 June 2010
> Wrote this whilst bears watching my every move beyond the brush. Anyways, what a find. Personally, never knew the man or the family but you must pay your deepest respect to Barlow. A man, he was. A man who did what he did best, even if the consequences caught up to him. He stood up for what he believed in. I respect that. R.I.P. Barlow.
>> Ryan H.

8 July 2010
> As a fellow aviator, I've seen too many young men pay the ultimate price, doing what they love. He died doing what he loved. How many of us can be so fortunate.
> PER ARDUA AD ASTRA
>> F-18 CAF (Rtd.) B 777 Captain

24 July 2010
> Just hiking around and stumbled across the engine Memorial. I heard about this thing for a while but had never found it until now. Pretty neat!
>> Michael H., local resident

6 September 2010
> My first time here on this trail, and this memorial makes the walk mean that much more, especially for those whose parents flew in the war.
>> Bruce M. with Tina & Louise

16 September 2010

I'm so thankful to be here again in this beautiful forest. I'm sure my father would appreciate all who have taken the time to write in this Log Book. I know I do–lest we forget all the sacrifices made during the Cold War. Many other pilots were also lost defending our shores. May this memorial remind us of them.

Susan Barlow Horne

16 September 2010

A tragically beautiful place. The second time I have visited the crash site of a father-in-law I never knew. As a fellow pilot, I can relate in some way to the happenings of that day.

Tom Horne

25 September 2010

An ethereal residing site for your engine. A fabulous place to soar with new wings.

Kathleen Q.

17 October 2010

May you have the life you want and love the life you live.

Jill B, N. Van,, Karen G, East Van

10 November 2010

Dropped by for an early Remembrance Day to pay my respects. Great to read the story and life of the pilot.

Ian J., John McG.

11 November 2010

Remembrance Day–great hike; airplanes overhead, fly past & cannon shots across the inlet to signify the sacrifices of those who served for the cause of freedom.

Doug S., Karman, Fraser C., grandson of Brian R, Des F.

6 Dec 2010

Pat Hurlbert & Mike Higgins with Dick Dunn. Snow for the last half. A great hike with a very interesting and inspiring destination! Thanks.

Mike

4 August 2011
Where is the propeller? Is there any more evidence?

5 August 2011
Thank you for sharing your story with with us.
Margaret and Dennis, Burnaby, Barbara, New Zealand

13 August 2011
Alan & Damien hike this trail often. We always called it the
"jet engine run." Rest in peace.
Alan

17 August 2011
Quite moving seeing the site & plaque again and pleased I
could be of help.
Jerry Nel

31 August 2011
Sorry to hear of your loss. Thank you for keeping this place. I
come up here often and always look forward to taking others
here to show them the history of your family. Thanks
Star, North Van

1 October 2011
Our fresh air life woman's hiking group–often hikes to this
memorial. This area of the forest is very spiritual. We think
of your family every time we come to this area.
J. Hewlett

29 October 2011
I have been looking for this trail all summer and stumbled
upon it today. I remember reading the story in the paper,
however, I never knew it was so close to my home. Thanks for
sharing Lt. Barlow's story with us. It is truly a special place,
more so now that I had the privilege to read all the details. R.I.P.
D. Manay

10 November 2011

Hiking with my friend the day before remembrance Day – we will hold this close tomorrow at the Remembrance Service. Very touching story & place.

M. Barraclough

10 November 2011

Fitting we should find this a day before Remembrance Day. Thank you for sharing the story and place with us.

P. Cross–Bishop

27 May 2012

We are happy to see the memorial intact now that the snow has melted. We hope to pass by many more times this summer. R.I.P.

Dianne and Dennis Keluck

29 May 2012

We have hiked on Grouse for many years but this is the first time we have stumbled across this memorial. Hopefully it will be here for many years to come.

Wayne & Steve

3 June 2012

Had a nice hike up with uncle Dick and looked at some additional debris as well. We had just the right tools to put up the new plaque as the tree was very hard wood to drill. It was great to see the memorial again since the installation 2 1/2 years ago and share in the experience.

Dorlyn Evancic

9 July 2012

I have hiked this trail hundreds of times and have always felt this was a sacred spot but I didn't know the story of what happened until now. We are happy that Lamar Barlow's family has come and made this such a special place. Thank you for sharing this with us.

9 July 2012
> We are glad that this has transposed from a place of sadness to a place of peace and solace for family, friends and unmet friends. We are touched & grateful to be part of this.
> Tim Olmstead & Gwen

18 July 2012
> REPOSE EN PAIX
> Que l'énergie de cette montagne te donne des ailes.
> (May the mountain energy give you wings.)
> Gabriel Allard et Ctherineberube.com Montréal, QC

28 July 2012
> 2nd time up here and I am humbled again. Respect and honour to our shared Armed Forces. God bless our countries.
> Stewart Mohr

31 July 2012
> After years exploring Grouse on foot my buddy and I happened across this site today. For years we've heard about this site and had concluded it to be Urban (or Mountain) Myth. Nice memorial –our hearts go out to Mr Barlow's family. Life is fleeting and precious.
> Cheers, Marty, Mary

12 August 2012
> Too bad dogs are not allowed on the gondola, because this is such a good dog as well as hiking trail. I think Lt. Lamar would like to meet my dogs.
> Senior Nado, Dasley and Coco, Maria, Audry

29 September 2012
> We were going to hike Baden Powell trail.and met some lovely people to show us this place and up to the top. Love a nice hike.
> Cheers from Germany -Stefan & Mosen

11 November 2012
> Sunday 11 AM 2012 Remembrance Day
> Group of 11 paying their respects at this memorable site.
>> Doug Soo, Maryon T., Kamren I., Andrea S, Philip W.

29 May 2013
> R.I.P Lamar. I'll remember you as I work for Boeing.

30 June 2013
> Another great hike up with our Polish gang. You are our favourite spot for a break!
>> Pete, Maria & Andy

11 September 2013
> Rest in peace Lt. Barlow and all others who have passed away fighting and defending their countries.
>> J.S. & C.L.

13 September 2013
> As a fellow pilot I share your loss here at 2,483 feet ASL. I have said a prayer for you and your family. Forever soaring.

15 September 2013
> Life is a dream! Some of us are likely to dream a long time!
>> Martin Kafes

15 September 2013
> Found this memorial from GPS coordinates–memorial is dignified and simple. R.I.P.. In memory of my father who was in the Royal Air Force.
>> D. & C. Taylor

14 October 2013
> Stumbled upon the turbine. Always wanted to know where this is. R.I.P. Lt Barlow.
>> Jacob Ruether, North Van

11 November 2013
> Remembrance Day. Once again a worthwhile trek to give our thanks for those who gave their lives for freedom.

16 July 2014
> To Lt. Barlow: It would be hard to find a more peaceful resting place. All the best to your family.
>
> Mike and Max Upton

17 August 2014
> Thanks for providing such a wonderful resting place.I think of you each time I come up, which is quite often. I'm sorry you lived such a short life. I hope it was a wonderful one in spite.

25 August 2014
> All that remains are memories of the ones who have been lost. Keep the memories alive.
>
> K.K.

14 September 2014
> I am doing this trail for the 1st time. Was taken here by my host. I am very sorry for your loss! May he rest in peace.
>
> Paul from Germany

28 September 2014
> Found the engine on the way to the Skyride. Sorry for your loss! Have peace!
>
> Sincerely, Andy

10 October 2014
> Was exploring the forest with my group of 6 dogs. This is one of the most interesting thing we have stumbled upon up here. May the pilot R.I.P.
>
> Sam Dunbrack

11 November 2014
> Remembrance Day. Rest in peace brother.
>
> Mat P.

14 November 2014
> LOGBOOK REMOVED - to prevent snowmelt damage

Glossary

Adit	A horizontal passage leading into a mine for the purposes of access or drainage
Air Marshall	Royal Air Force three-star rank equivalent to a vice-admiral or a lieutenant-general
ATV	All Terrain Vehicle
Bf-109	WWII German fighter- Messerschmitt 109
Bolshevik	Majority faction of the Russian Social Democratic Party, re-named the Communist Party after seizing power in the October Revolution of 1917.
DEET	N,N-diethyl-meta-toluamide - the most common active ingredient in insect repellents.
F-86 Sabre	United States's first swept wing fighter,- the Korean War and later
Fw-190	WWII German fighter- Focke-Wulf 190
GPS	Global Positioning System -space-based satellite navigation system
GUM	From Russian "main universal store" known as the State Department Store

Harrier	British Vertical Takeoff Fighter
HMS	Her/His Majesty's Ship
Humvee	High Mobility Multipurpose Wheeled Vehicle (HMMWV) a four-wheel drive military automobile
Ilyushin	Russian designed Il-76 four-engine air cargo aircraft
Kalashnikovs	A series of automatic rifles based on the original design of Russian Mikhail Kalashnikov
Klondiker	Those who took part in the 19th-century gold rush to the Klondike river of the Yukon
Loop	Hand lenses for identifying gems, crystals, rocks
Mach	The ratio of the speed of a body to the speed of sound in the surrounding medium.
Messerschmitt	German aircraft manufacturer of WWII
MiG-15	Mikoyan-Gurevich - Russian jet fighter aircraft of the Korean War
MiG-19	Mikoyan-Gurevich - Soviet second-generation, single-seat, twin jet engined fighter aircraft
Neolithic	The later part of the Stone Age, when ground or polished stone weapons and implements prevailed. New Stone Age
Panamax	Term for the maximum size limit for ships traveling through the Panama Canal.
Pelton Wheel	An impulse type water turbine
Port	Left side of aircraft or ship
Pisco	A colorless grape distillation with high alcoholic content

RAF	British Royal Air Force
RCAF	Royal Canadian Air Force
Refugio	Spanish for a mountain hut
RN	British Royal Navy
Sea-doo	Personal water craft, also called water scooter
Shingle	A mass of small rounded pebbles, esp. on a seashore.
Su-30	Sukhoi Su-30, a Russian twin-engine, two-seat supermaneuverable fighter aircraft
Siam	Thailand's designation by early Westerners
Siq	Arabic for Shaft - a narrow pass through rock
Starboard	Right side of aircraft or ship
Stuka	Junkers Ju 87 - German dive bomber of WWII
Stupa	Literally meaning "heap." A mound-like or hemispherical structure containing Buddhist relics
Swordfish	A torpedo bomber biplane designed by the Fairey Aviation Company, used by the Fleet Air Arm of the Royal Navy during the Second World War.
SUV	Sports Utility Vehicle
TACAN	TACtical Air Navigation system
Tar	A common term originally used to refer to seamen of the Merchant or Royal Navy,
Thule	A country described by the ancient Greek explorer Pytheas (c. 310 BC) as being six days' sail north of Britain. It was regarded by the ancients as the northernmost part of the world.

Thus:

The Thule people or proto-Inuit were the ancestors of all modern Inuit. They developed in coastal Alaska by AD 1000 and expanded eastwards across Canada, reaching Greenland by the 13th century.

Tender	A boat used to ferry people and supplies to and from a ship
UNESCO	United Nations Organization for Education, Science and Culture
Unimog	A range of multi-purpose four-wheel drive medium trucks produced by Mercedes-Benz
USAF	United States Air Force
USS	United States Ship
VOR	Very High Frequency Omni Directional Radio Range A Journal of Journeys

Made in the USA
San Bernardino, CA
28 November 2014